...CE
LAW
ENFORCEMENT

POLICE
and LAW
ENFORCEMENT

GENERAL EDITOR
William J. Chambliss
George Washington University

KEY ISSUES IN *Crime* AND PUNISHMENT

Los Angeles | London | New Delhi
Singapore | Washington DC

Los Angeles | London | New Delhi
Singapore | Washington DC

FOR INFORMATION:

SAGE Publications, Inc.
2455 Teller Road
Thousand Oaks, California 91320
E-mail: order@sagepub.com

SAGE Publications India Pvt. Ltd.
B 1/I 1 Mohan Cooperative Industrial Area
Mathura Road, New Delhi 110 044
India

SAGE Publications Ltd.
1 Oliver's Yard
55 City Road
London EC1Y 1SP
United Kingdom

SAGE Publications Asia-Pacific Pte. Ltd.
33 Pekin Street #02-01
Far East Square
Singapore 048763

Vice President and Publisher: Rolf A. Janke
Senior Editor: Jim Brace-Thompson
Project Editor: Tracy Buyan
Cover Designer: Candice Harman
Editorial Assistant: Michele Thompson
Reference Systems Manager: Leticia Gutierrez
Reference Systems Coordinator: Laura Notton

Golson Media
President and Editor: J. Geoffrey Golson
Author Manager: Lisbeth Rogers
Layout and Copy Editor: Stephanie Larson
Proofreader: Mary Le Rouge
Indexer: J S Editorial

Printed in the United States of America.

Library of Congress Cataloging-in-Publication Data

Key issues in crime and punishment / William Chambliss, general editor.

v. cm.

Contents: v. 1. Crime and criminal behavior — v. 2. Police and law enforcement — v. 3. Courts, law, and justice — v. 4. Corrections — 5. Juvenile crime and justice.

Includes bibliographical references and index.

ISBN 978-1-4129-7855-2 (v. 1 : cloth) — ISBN 978-1-4129-7859-0 (v. 2 : cloth) — ISBN 978-1-4129-7857-6 (v. 3 : cloth) — ISBN 978-1-4129-7856-9 (v. 4 : cloth) — ISBN 978-1-4129-7858-3 (v. 5 : cloth)

1. Crime. 2. Law enforcement. 3. Criminal justice, Administration of. 4. Corrections. 5. Juvenile delinquency. I. Chambliss, William J.

HV6025.K38 2011

364—dc22   2010054579

11 12 13 14 15 10 9 8 7 6 5 4 3 2 1

Contents

Introduction

Police and Law Enforcement

Policing as we know it in the United States today is a relatively new phenomenon. Initially, police were established in England as what was known as a *constabulary*. Their job was to settle disputes on the spot, not to make arrests. "Keeping the peace" was of paramount importance, not enforcing the law. With urbanization and growing discrepancies between the rich and the poor, police were increasingly asked to punish people who did not comply with rules set down by those in power to make laws. The contradiction between imposing rules on people whose lives were not in sync with the rules laid down from above, and the traditional behavior of the less powerful, created dilemmas and conflicts witnessed in everyday practices of the police, as well as controversies over the proper role of the police in a free democratic society.

For many, the police represent an essential law enforcement entity that makes public safety and security the highest of its priorities. However, the stories creep into popular culture: the actions of unscrupulous officers confiscating drugs to later sell themselves, statistics showing unfair racial profiling in a municipality, or an officer using unnecessary force to subdue an offender. Stories like these create images of policing and law enforcement that are far less than ideal. In this volume, authors explore many debates concerning the ways in which police and law enforcement agencies operate.

In order to effectively assess police and law enforcement, it is crucial to examine many aspects of policing in society. The chapters in this volume largely focus on the discussions surrounding common duties that police must practice (i.e., arrests and interrogations), the legal regulations on those duties; problematic policing techniques; and law enforcement alternatives to traditional policing.

Essential to the duties of police officers are the duties of arresting suspects of crime and interrogating the suspects to help determine if they have, in fact, committed that crime. Arrest is described as restraining a subject and stopping him or her from continuing to engage in his or her normal activities. This process is surrounded by a great deal of controversy, because detaining subjects is a sensitive issue. Broadly, this common practice of law enforcement is commended for upholding the peace and safety of the community, because it is often shared with the public through the media. Additionally, arrests provide information for crime statistics, which inform funding decisions for local police departments. Arrests also serve as deterrence for others in the community. Those who criticize arrests focus on the collateral consequences of this policing practice. On occasion, mistakes are made, and police officers arrest individuals who are later found not guilty for the crimes of which they were accused. This strains the bond between the community and the police, a topic discussed by many authors in this volume.

There are many other aspects of the arrest that have garnered discussion in this volume. As a result of the 1966 U.S. Supreme Court case of *Ernesto Miranda v. Arizona*, officers are required to inform a suspect that he or she has certain constitutional rights before the law enforcement agency proceeds to interrogate the individual. In Butler's *Miranda Warnings*, advocates for the use of Miranda warnings believe that the warnings help protect the suspect's right against self-incrimination, limit false confessions, and promote professionalism in the police force. Critics of Miranda warnings believe that these warnings discourage confessions due to a suspect's right to remain silent. Suspects will feel, according to critics, that police are working against them and will continue to remain silent. Miranda warnings have also been criticized as being more of a formality than anything, which significantly diminishes their intended effectiveness.

The ability for police to use force is also a highly controversial topic. Boggess's *Police Brutality* and Sun's *Deadly Force* show that there are rare occasions where law enforcement may act too swiftly and intensely, leading to a suspect's death or injury. Those who downplay the prevalence of the use of deadly force by police officers focus their discussion on the lack of a clear definition of police brutality. They also believe that data on police brutality is extremely hard to capture because of the code of silence that accompanies police work, and that there is a lack of reporting of these infractions. Those who feel that law enforcement sometimes warrants the use of deadly force believe that deadly force is the ultimate symbol of the state's power over its members, and represents an import means of social control. In addition, advocates also believe that deadly force can help protect other citizens' lives and property. However, these controversial topics carry with them a great deal of criticism. These acts have a distinctly adverse effect on the public perceptions of police and law enforcement because they typically garner a great deal of negative media attention. The chapter on police brutality focuses on rotten apple theory, which posits that the few "rotten apples" in police departments should be to blame for these negative actions.

Police and law enforcement follow certain protocols that are also surrounded by a great deal of debate. In this volume, authors discuss these debates in Ingram's *Entrapment,* Oleson's *Plain View Doctrine,* Ratansi's *Warrants,* and Gizzi's *Vehicle Searches.* While the legal meaning of entrapment is still a subject of debate, it can be generally understood as a process by which law enforcement officials coax subjects into committing crimes they would not have otherwise committed. Those in favor of entrapment techniques believe that law enforcement officers should take whatever steps necessary to apprehend criminals. They also feel that victims of certain crimes, like white-collar crimes, are unaware of their victimization, and entrapment must be used to uncover these criminals. The extraordinary means the government may use, according to critics, may further strengthen the distrust of citizens toward law enforcement. Advocates for vehicle searches, the plain view doctrine, and warrants believe that these regulations protect citizens' constitutional rights, protect officers from liability issues, and increase the effectiveness of police investigations.

Some actions and police customs, like the code of silence that exists among the police, further strain the relationship between law enforcement and the citizenry. Bulen's *Police Strikes and Blue Flu,* Martinez's *Zero-Tolerance Policing,* and Rabe-Hemp's *Police Corruption and the Code Of Silence* discuss the issues behind these often-criticized practices of law enforcement agencies, despite some benefits they may provide. Police strikes help to uphold officers' First Amendment rights and serve as a powerful tool for officers, as workers, to get their labor concerns addressed. Due to its universality, advocates for zero-tolerance policing policies believe that their "popularity and relative success is the sheer simplicity of its main proposition: make arrests." While advocates for the police code of silence argue that it helps garner solidarity with the police force and helps protect police work, the potential for corruption that it creates may be detrimental to the public opinion of law enforcement.

Alternatives to law enforcement are typical in most communities, and Perry's *Police Privatization,* Geis's *Bounty Hunters and Rewards,* and Hawley's *Vigilantes* evaluate these issues. Police privatization is seen as a means to save money and increase efficiency. Conversely, law enforcement as a private entity could increase motivations for profit maximization while decreasing their intended functions of serving and protecting the citizens of the community.

Police and law enforcement is a topic that stirs a great deal of commotion because of the unique relationship these organizations have with the public. While many see officers as protectors of peace in society, others have the aforementioned reasons to be skeptical. This volume is intended to present these debates and offer solutions to potential and perceived problems.

William J. Chambliss
General Editor

1

Accountability

Martha L. Shockey-Eckles
Saint Louis University

Accountability refers to the mechanisms by which both law enforcement officers and the agencies they serve are held responsible for promoting social order, reducing crime, and treating each individual fairly and within the limits of the law. Accountability lies at the heart of citizen concerns regarding police discretion, use of force, and the internal hiring practices of those in law enforcement. It both defines and protects citizens' rights while also promoting a collective sense of faith in the larger criminal justice system. In short, accountability serves as the public's first line of defense against acts of misconduct that can, and often do, violate the rights of those whom law enforcement agents have sworn to serve and protect. Yet few among the general public are aware of the behavioral standards set for law enforcement personnel, or how accountability is promoted and maintained. Fewer still even care about these issues until the most egregious acts of police misconduct become front-page news.

Police accountability, especially as it relates to discretion and use of force, was largely a taboo subject until well into the 20th century, when a study conducted by the American Bar Foundation brought the issue to the forefront of the legal arena. Central to their findings was the distinction between the use and misuse of discretion by law enforcement. Discretion itself is not problematic, but its abuse is. This simple statement ushered in a new era of accountability, largely fueled by highly publicized, late-20th-century events.

Early History of U.S. Policing and Accountability

Both the organizational structure and public perceptions of contemporary law enforcement have their underpinnings in the cultural and historical factors that have shaped the United States. The country's history and cultural heritage have also shaped the way in which those in law enforcement are held accountable for their actions—to the public they serve and under the law.

In reality, those in law enforcement are held accountable for their actions as set forth by law in the Fourth, Fifth, and Sixth Amendments to the U.S. Constitution. These amendments—now constraining police discretion in contemporary society—were originally written to apply to the U.S. military, as it embodied the only official agency of social control in the newly founded democracy. As the nation expanded and the need for more localized social control became evident, these same amendments were intended to guide and constrain the activities of all in law enforcement. Now referred to as the *rules of due process*, the constitutional guidelines were set in place to protect the people from unfettered discretionary power, especially with regard to arrest, use of force, search and seizure, and interrogation of suspects. Unfortunately, as the shift was made from a militaristic form of social control to the establishment of both local and federal law enforcement agencies, the rules of due process were slow to follow. Seldom, if ever, were the newly sworn officers required to adhere to the mandates originally set forth in the U.S. Constitution. Simply put, accountability was virtually nonexistent in the early years of law enforcement.

The United States, established and created by British descendants, modeled its early law enforcement agencies after those in Great Britain. In 1829, following legislative approval from the British Parliament, Sir Robert Peel created the nation's first police department in London. Paramilitary in nature, the specialized units within the department were hierarchically structured, uniformed officers were clearly distinguishable, and the badge became a symbol of authority—an image that remains important to this day. Founded upon the dictates set forth in nine guiding principles, the London Police Department required professionalism from its officers; respect for authority; and perhaps most importantly, the ever-present recognition that the police are the public just as the public are the police. Hence, the groundwork was laid for crime control through police-public cooperation and mutual respect. Concomitantly, the first seeds of police accountability were sown.

In the 1800s, with its own culture in its formative stages and the ways of it citizenry still strongly entrenched in their British heritage, the first organized police departments appeared in the United States. Boston paved the way with the establishment of the nation's first police department in 1838; New York followed suit in 1845, and Philadelphia modified its town watch system to a more modernized and official police department in 1850. The London Police Department was to serve as the model for the fledgling departments—from utilizing the same organizational structure to mandating the same professionalism from officers as that demanded by Peel. Success, however, was not achieved. Few specialized units were found within the departments, officer corruption was rampant, and those in law enforcement neither deserved nor received respect from the general citizenry. Hence, the police-public cooperation and collaboration diligently sought by Peel was nonexistent in early American law enforcement. Equally nonexistent was police accountability.

Both the advent of new technology and leadership brought change to the American landscape as law enforcement began to embrace change through the 19th and 20th centuries. Much of this change is attributed to the introduction of the automobile, the telephone, and the invention of the two-way radio. However, little change could occur—even in light of this groundbreaking technology—in the absence of strong leadership. Beginning in the 1920s, August Vollmer and his protégé, O.W. Wilson, provided that leadership.

Vollmer's Framework of Leadership

As chief of police in Berkeley, California, Vollmer placed the adoption of new technology and heightened professionalism at the top of his priorities. Emphasizing the need for both officer and departmental accountability, he introduced the use of innovative hiring techniques that included psychological testing and rigorous training before one could work the streets as a member of the Berkeley Police Department. As change transpired with the introduction of a more centralized departmental structure, change also occurred among the rank-and-file officers and the manner in which they performed their duties. In a concerted effort not just to reduce corruption by holding individual officers accountable after the fact, Vollmer attempted to prevent wrongdoing by pairing new technology with an innovative policing style. Thus, the patrol car and the two-way radio were introduced to police work and the American public. Passionate about his career and determined to establish the Berkeley Police Department as a model of police professionalism, Vollmer introduced the car patrol as a means of separating the officers from the public they served. Personal relationships that often lie at the heart of corruption and bribery could not be established. At the same time, the use of the patrol car served as a deterrent to crime now referred to as *conspicuous presence.*

The efforts put forth by August Vollmer were later carried out in both Wichita, Kansas, and Chicago through the work of Wilson. In addition to the modifications introduced by Vollmer, Wilson increased officer salaries, placed street officers on rotating assignments to further prevent relationship-building between the police and the public, and established a nonpartisan board to aid in departmental governance and oversight. Prior to the American Bar Foundation's study, this represented the first serious attempt to address the issue of police accountability through means other than self-regulation. However, some problems had yet to be solved with the issue of policing the police.

Twentieth-Century Impacts on Accountability

From the 1960s into the early 21st century, both cultural changes and historical events transformed police work, public perceptions of the police, and intermittent calls by some for increased accountability for law enforcement activities. The United States was a country in turmoil from the 1960s to the mid-1970s. Although its citizens began to witness the waning of the cold war, the United States experienced unprecedented upheaval as the result of social inequality, the Vietnam War, the rise of the hippie generation, and innumerable injustices at the hands of those in law enforcement. As riots raged in the most populated cities across the nation, college and university campuses were rife with protests, sit-ins, and bombings that resulted in the destruction of property and the loss of life. One of the most notorious of these occurred at Kent State University, where the National Guard fired into a crowd of protestors, killing four students and injuring nine others. As a result of what became known as the Kent State Massacre, numerous riots and protests erupted on campuses nationwide, compelling President Richard Nixon to establish the President's Commission on Campus Unrest (also known of as the Scranton Commission). After its investigation, the commission issued its 1970 findings, concluding that the danger confronting the National Guard did not represent a lethal threat. Thus, deadly force should not have been used against the student protestors. However, following the grand jury indictment of eight guardsmen, the criminal justice system accepted the argument that the National Guard had acted in self-defense. All charges were summarily dismissed. This action had a chilling effect on many in the American public, as none of those responsible for the students' deaths were held accountable for their actions.

The passage of the Civil Rights Act of 1964, the end of the Vietnam War, and the resignation of President Nixon ushered in an era of calm after the storm. By the 1990s, the cold war had officially ended, and a renewed emphasis was placed on protecting U.S. citizens from the internal threat associated with crime. President Bill Clinton signed the 1995 Crime Bill, placing 100,000 new officers on city streets across the country and making new sources of police funding readily accessible.

Yet, while these events encouraged a renewed sense of national calm, the end of the 20th century was rife with highly publicized accounts of police misconduct that garnered the attention of the general public. Events surrounding the Rodney King beating; the death of Timothy Thomas, an unarmed African American teen killed at the hands of Cincinnati police officers; and the abhorrent victimization of Abner Louima by New York City police officers fostered citizen concerns about police brutality on a nationwide level. The publicity surrounding these events evoked a sense of national outrage and concern that extended to city leaders, chiefs of police, scholars, and citizens alike. In conjunction with the national outrage came calls for increased accountability from law enforcement as well as scholarly studies aimed at providing insight into police misconduct. Seminal among the scholarly works emanating from this era is the research conducted by Jerome Skolnick, which examines the "police personality" and its effect on the actions of those in law enforcement. Skolnick's work not only contributed to an increased understanding of the individuals who serve as law enforcement officers, it also shed light on the internal and external factors that contribute to police misconduct.

External Sources of Police Misconduct

Issues of discretionary misconduct have remained the focus when considering the need for mechanisms by which law enforcement are held accountable for their actions. The arrest decision, use of force, search and seizure, and interrogation of suspects represent the external sources of police misconduct. Each is guided and limited by the rules of due process, first elucidated in the Fourth, Fifth, and Sixth Amendments to the U.S. Constitution, and later reinforced through pivotal court cases. Of special import are the judicial decisions that reinforced the limitations placed on law enforcement when engaged in evidence gathering (i.e., search and seizure) and the interrogation of suspects.

Although the rules of gathering evidence were clearly specified in constitutional amendments, these mandates were largely ignored by police until their actions were challenged in *Weeks v. U.S.* (1914). The U.S. Supreme Court unanimously decided in favor of the plaintiff, issuing a decision that held the police accountable for the unlawful seizure of evidence pertaining to a fraudulent lottery scheme conducted by Weeks. From this decision came what is now referred to as the *exclusionary rule*, a restatement of the Fourth Amendment that holds those in law enforcement accountable for obtaining a clear and specific warrant prior to searching one's person or property and/or seizing evidence related to the commission of a crime. Although this decision has not prevented all acts of misconduct with regard to search and seizure, it has gone a long way in protecting individual rights by stating that all evidence seized in the absence of a warrant shall be deemed inadmissible in a court of law.

The Miranda Warning

A similar challenge to law enforcement authority resulted in what is now referred to as the *Miranda warning,* aimed at reinforcing the individual's right to protect himself or herself from self-incrimination as first outlined in the Fifth Amendment. Following the arrest and conviction of Ernest Miranda on rape charges, *Miranda v. Arizona* (1966) was heard by the Supreme Court. Based upon evidence indicating that Miranda had not been advised of his right to have an attorney present prior to or during his interrogation, the conviction was overturned, and he was scheduled for release from prison. Although his release did not transpire, due to evidence provided by his former girlfriend indicating he had discussed the rape with her, the case resulted in the mandate that all in law enforcement must issue the Miranda warning prior to interrogating a custodial suspect. Hence, one more line of defense was given to the American public as a result of one court's attempt to hold law enforcement accountable for their actions.

Most who enter law enforcement are trained in their respective academies to utilize the force continuum when making the frequently split decision to use deadly force against an individual. Problematic due to its definitional vagueness and subjectivity, the force continuum states that any member of law enforcement may respond to the confrontation of force with one degree of greater force. Even in light of officers' academy training, claims of police brutality and deadly use of force continue to make national news. The *Tennessee v. Garner* (1985) ruling attempted to clarify and remove the subjectivity associated with the force continuum by stating that deadly force may be used when the officer in question has probable cause to believe a suspect poses a clear and specific threat to said officer or members of the general public. While *Tennessee v. Garner* represents a laudable effort to increase specificity with regard to the conditions that justify the use of force, in reality, it fell short of achieving its goal.

Citizen Review Boards and Guilds

Judicial efforts throughout the 20th century have clearly reinforced the rules of due process and added specificity to the laws already in place to guide the external practices of those in law enforcement. Yet injustices, allegations of police misconduct, and well-documented individual rights violations have continued well into the 21st century. As a result of these events, many cities throughout the country have witnessed calls for the creation and implementation of citizen review boards as yet another line of defense against police misconduct.

In 1999, the National Police Accountability Project (NPAP) was founded by the National Lawyers Guild, the first racially integrated association of attorneys practicing in the United States. Although originally a national organization, local chapters soon began forming in cities across the country. The goal of the NPAP is to end police misconduct by educating and training lawyers and citizens, aiding nonprofit organizations that help victims of police abuse, and providing a venue through which local organizations and individuals can strategize for innovative ways to end police misconduct.

The National Lawyers Guild is not alone in its efforts to bring citizens into the forefront of efforts to hold law enforcement accountable for the actions of its individual officers and the agencies they serve. Dr. Samuel Walker, a professor of criminal justice at the University of Nebraska at Omaha, has been influential in promoting the use of citizen oversight agencies through his research and subsequent findings. In contrast to the conclusions of the U.S. Civil Rights Commission's 2000 report claiming that civilian review boards tend to be ineffective, Walker's 2000 project, *Police Accountability: The Role of Citizen Oversight,* found these same agencies to be highly effective in combating and controlling police misconduct. Hence, renewed calls for the use of citizen review boards are now being heard in cities nationwide.

Internal Sources of Police Misconduct

Whereas the actions of law enforcement officers tend to be easily observed and reported to the general public, the same cannot be said for the hiring practices of individual agencies. Both Vollmer and Wilson introduced rigorous psychological testing, the use of polygraph testing, and extensive training of recruits into the hiring practices of the departments they served. Their innovations continue to be used in contemporary law enforcement, but have failed to weed out some of the most egregious offenders who engage in misconduct in one jurisdiction, but find employment in another. All too often, it is business as usual for these officers once they procure employment in a new department. Referring to the problem as the *officer shuffle*, Roger Goldman and Steven Puro of Saint Louis University in St. Louis, Missouri, have extensively studied the phenomenon and its ability to perpetuate and sustain police misconduct. Thus, the hiring practices of individual agencies represent an internal source of potential misconduct through their placement of already identified rogue cops back on the streets. Yet, precisely because the general public tends to be highly uninformed about the hiring practices of most departments and the existence of the officer shuffle, together they comprise an area of law enforcement encompassing perhaps the greatest need for accountability.

Only recently has the work of Goldman and Puro introduced an empirical analysis of the existence of the officer shuffle into the discussions of officer misconduct. They have also been pioneers in offering concrete policy suggestions aimed at controlling the movements of the "gypsy cop" whose continued misconduct causes even the most law-abiding citizens to lose trust in the peacekeepers of society.

Forty-three states currently utilize decertification, also referred to as *revocation* or *cancellation*, of an officer's state license as a means of dealing with police misconduct. To date, this approach has done little to curb the movements of the gypsy cop as he or she merely finds employment elsewhere. In many cases of misconduct, the offending officer is allowed to resign from his or her position in order to spare the employing agency public attention. Prospective employers are thus left in the dark, so to speak, when investigating the employment history of the applicant. Even when fired for acts of misconduct, many officers find employment in neighboring municipalities with lower hiring standards and community budgets that do not attract the most qualified applicants. These officers move freely within the state of their original employment. In cases where the most egregious acts result in revocation of the state-issued license, the sanction is recorded in, and applies only to, that state. Thus, it is not uncommon for an officer who has been decertified in one jurisdiction to merely procure employment in another state.

Finally, no standardized criteria exist across jurisdictions for revocation, thus introducing a grave disparity in the quality of officers allowed to practice and/or seek employment in different states. In response to these issues, Goldman advocates for revocation to be adopted in those states where it is not already in use, standardization of decertification criteria across jurisdictions, and the development of a national database that provides hiring agencies access to the names and employment histories of all who have been stripped of their rights to serve as peacekeepers in any jurisdiction.

Pro: Arguments in Favor of External Oversight

Two sources of misconduct—internal and external—are important to any discussions of officer misconduct and the need for accountability from those in law enforcement. The Fourth, Fifth, and Sixth Amendments to the Constitution were written to protect the rights of the citizenry from its own agents of social control. Yet, history is rife with accounts indicating these initial legal mandates have been largely ineffective in containing officer misconduct and promoting accountability among law enforcement.

Those who advocate the elimination of misconduct emanating from external sources—arrest, use of force, search and seizure, and interrogation—strongly support the creation and implementation of citizen review boards to oversee the workings of local law enforcement. According to Samuel Walker, the most imperative function of citizen oversight is to actively work to change local police departments. Among his premises, which are intended to promote effectiveness from these oversight boards, are the creation of outreach programs designed to publicize and inform citizens about the complaint process, citizen review of individual complaints registered, changes in departmental policies and training, and the development of a codified and standardized procedure for auditing the quality of complaint investigations as well as their outcomes.

Simply put, Walker advocates increasing transparency among law enforcement by promoting citizen involvement in both oversight and evaluation of local officers and the agencies they serve. This increased transparency may, in and of itself, promote a heightened sense of professionalism among officers and reduce corruption and misconduct. For those undeterred by being held accountable to the citizens they serve, mechanisms designed to involve the general public in assisting individuals in filing complaints, evaluating them, and assessing the outcomes remove the cloak of secrecy that comes with the self-regulating nature of contemporary police work. Thus, citizen review boards bring contemporary law enforcement full circle through a return to Peel's original premise that officers should operate from the basic vision of the police as the public, and the public as the police.

The Officer Shuffle

Hiring practices that allow for the perpetuation of the officer shuffle represent the single most important internal source of officer misconduct that begs for change through legislative action. Individual rights violations at the hands of gypsy cops have been well documented nationwide. Departments that allow an already-identified rogue cop to leave their position in such a way as to enable future employment in another agency and/or jurisdiction must be held accountable for their actions. Departments that willfully hire the officer with a documented history of misconduct must recognize the risks posed to the people they serve and, ultimately, assume responsibility for the role they play in perpetuating the officer shuffle. Only full accountability will end the phenomena of the officer shuffle, an outcome that requires legislative change at both the federal and state levels.

According to Goldman and Puro, the general public must first be made aware of the existence of the officer shuffle, the threat it poses, and the need to impose more stringent hiring regulations on law enforcement in general. Through public pressure and calls for change, legislators will turn their attention to task of ending the officer shuffle by passing codified laws holding all departments and agencies to the same hiring practices; similarly, all will be held accountable for adhering to standardized criteria for decertifying the officer who engages in acts of corruption or other identified forms of misconduct.

Officer Misconduct Database

Along with standardized hiring and firing practices, Goldman and Puro also call for the development of a national database that would contain the names of all officers who have been decertified for misconduct. Thus, the potential hiring agency will have access to a streamlined method for conducting background checks that are vital to the pre-employment process. Standardization of hiring, firing, and decertification criteria enhance the likelihood that all within law enforcement, regardless of jurisdiction, will be held accountable to the same regulations and behavioral expectations. The creation of such a national database would streamline the hiring process, while also making it more difficult for the rogue officer to merely move to another state or jurisdiction and procure employment with another department. Hence, *decertification* would mean what the term implies. Once an officer engages in acts egregious enough to result in decertification, that individual will never again serve in law enforcement, thus ending the officer shuffle.

Con: Arguments Against External Oversight

Many people, especially practitioners, remain adamantly opposed to the creation and use of citizen review boards as a means of promoting accountability from law enforcement, citing reasons that strongly resonate with the positions already assumed by both the American Medical Society and the American Bar Association. Those in law enforcement argue the general public is ill equipped to assess the situations officers encounter and/or the split-second decisions often made in the line of duty. The concern is also raised that politics and paybacks will determine the appointment of individuals to the oversight boards, thus returning the country to a time when nepotism reigned supreme. This same nepotism raises concern that the appointment process itself is rife with risks of increased corruption as appointees serve their supporters first and the needs of the community and its law enforcement second. In short, the potential for politicization of the appointment process, the lack of firsthand knowledge of law enforcement among lay persons, and the risk of introducing new venues for corruption represent the primary concerns voiced by those opposed to the creation of citizen oversight boards as a mechanism for promoting and maintaining police accountability.

Legislative Changes

When considering the best way to address the perpetuation of corruption and misconduct associated with the officer shuffle, Goldman and Puro recommend dramatic legislative changes that would affect all within the law enforcement community. Just as cultural factors helped shape law enforcement from its early beginnings to its contemporary organizational structure, so too has America's evolving culture influenced opposition to the suggestions offered by Goldman and Puro. Americans tend to hold to many of the same beliefs that led the nation's founders to fight for independence. Central to these beliefs is the value placed on a decentralized form of government, states rights, and a political process designed to uphold the will of the people. American law enforcement is dedicated to serving the people, but is just as ardently committed to self-regulation. Often based upon the belief that regional differences dictate the manner in which individual departments and agencies operate, criticism is leveled at suggestions to implement jurisdictional standardization of hiring and firing regulations.

In a similar vein, many states are resistant to calls that all must implement decertification, and that standardized criteria be used for revocation of the right to serve in law enforcement. While few oppose the creation of a national database for warehousing pertinent information about officer misconduct, revocation, and/or decertification, this represents the limit to which they value federal intervention in local and state practices. Of added concern to many in law enforcement is the cost associated with implementing new regulations and creating the suggested national database. At a time when many local and state departments are financially strapped and experiencing difficulty in meeting their requirements of both personnel and technology, the cost associated with database proposals are met with disdain. Until local departments can claim to have enough boots on the ground, the issues associated with cost will remain a major obstacle in achieving the goals set forth by Goldman and Puro. Concomitantly, until state and local agencies no longer feel threatened by outside intervention, particularly federal intervention, calls for jurisdictional standardization with regard to internal accountability will continue to be met with strict opposition.

See Also: 2. Arrest Practices; 4. Entrapment; 5. Internal Review Practices; 7. Miranda Warnings; 9. Police Brutality; 10. Police Corruption and Code of Silence; 15. Use of Deadly Force; 18. Vigilantes.

Further Readings

American Civil Liberties Union of Eastern Missouri. "Citizen Oversight Agencies Effective in Fighting Police Misconduct." Press Release. http:// www.aclu-em.org/pressroom/2000pressreleases/civilianoversightof police.htm (November 14, 2000).

American Civil Liberties Union of Northern California, Sonoma County Chapter. "Police Accountability." http://www.aclusonoma.org/police Accountability.html (Accessed January 2010).

Caputo, Phillip. *13 Seconds: A Look Back at the Kent State Shootings.* New York: Chamberlain Bros., 2005.

Goldman, Roger L. "State Revocation of Law Enforcement Officers' Licenses and Federal Criminal Prosecution: An Opportunity for Cooperative Federalism." *Saint Louis University Public Law Review,* v.21/1 (2003).

Goldman, Roger L., and Steven Puro. "Decertification of Police: An Alternative to Traditional Remedies for Police Misconduct." *Hastings Constitutional Law Quarterly,* v.15 (Fall 1987).

Goldman, Roger L., and Steven Puro. "Revocation of Police Officer Certification." *Saint Louis University Law Journal,* v.45/2 (2003).

Harki, Gary A. "Still in Uniform: W. Va. Police Rarely Lose Certification." *The Charleston Gazette* (December 26, 2009).

National Police Accountability Project. "About NPAP: History." http://www.nlg-npap.org/html/history.htm (Accessed January 2010).

Reiss, Albert J, Jr. "Police Organization in the Twentieth Century." *Crime and Justice,* v.15 (1992).

Richmond, Paul. "A Brief History of Police Accountability." *Eat the State,* v.11/23 (July 26, 2007).

Walker, Samuel. *The New World of Police Accountability.* Thousand Oaks, CA: Sage Publications, 2005.

Walker, Samuel. "Police Accountability: Current Issues and Research Needs." Washington, DC: Paper Presented at the National Institute of Justice Police Planning Research Workshop. (November 2006).

2

Arrest Practices

Michael D. Lyman
Columbia College

Of the many duties performed by police officers, the arrest of suspects remains at the core. The word *arrest* is a derivative of the French word *arreter,* which means "to stop or stay" and signifies the restraint of a person. In a literal sense, the word *arrest* means the apprehension or restraint of a person, or the deprivation of one's personal liberty. The question of whether or not a person is under arrest depends not on the legality of the arrest, but on whether the subject of the arrest has been deprived of his or her personal liberty to leave.

Typically, arrests are associated with taking someone into custody by a government official empowered by law to do so, for the purpose of holding or detaining him to answer a criminal charge, or to prevent the commission of a criminal offense. An arrest is the action by which a person is stopped from their normal activities by virtue of a legal authority or sanction, either by detaining them or stopping their ability to leave. For all intents and purposes, when a person is under arrest, they are deprived of their freedom.

The Probable Cause Requirement

An arrest represents a seizure by law enforcement of a person; as such, probable cause must first exist to justify the arrest. This is a legal distinction, but one made in the field by police and law enforcement officers every day.

Probable cause can be a difficult principle to establish. There are several general factors that should be taken into account when establishing probable cause.

Observations Made by the Officer

One of the most straightforward applications of probable cause is when the arresting officer personally observes actions, behaviors, or evidence that would cause the officer to believe that a crime has been or is being committed. Factors that create probable cause include the following:

- Information or evidence obtained during an investigation detention or Terry stop (based on the 1968 Supreme Court decision, a police officer may stop a person for questioning if there is reasonable suspicion); or during consensual contact with a citizen
- A specific complaint by a member of the public
- Information provided by a police informant of proven reliability
- Information provided by other law enforcement sources

Anonymous Sources With Unknown Reliability

Police sometimes receive information from sources that are anonymous, but they must be cautions with their response to that information. This is because probable cause does not apply when information is received from an anonymous source, or if it is based on mere suspicion alone. For example, in 2000, the U.S. Supreme Court ruled in *Florida v. J.L.* that an anonymous tip that a person is carrying a gun, without more information, does not justify a police officer's stop-and-frisk of that person. The Court cautioned that if a police officer is relying on a tip to conduct a Terry stop, then that tip must be considered reliable to provide the officer with reasonable suspicion to make the stop. Normally, an anonymous tip does not constitute a reliable source of information.

Reliable Anonymous Sources

On the other hand, an anonymous tip that is supported through accurate information may be considered reliable enough to provide the officer with a reasonable suspicion to initiate a Terry stop. The Supreme Court cited two instances where this could be the case: (1) If the police officer knew, either by his or her own observations, experience, or prior knowledge of the suspect or area; or (2) If the anonymous tip showed that the informant had predicted accurately the suspect's movements or had prior knowledge of any concealed criminal activity. A tip that merely identifies a specific person would not be considered reliable enough to show knowledge of concealed criminal activity.

Arrest Warrants

Arrest warrants are another way in which a police officer may make an arrest of a person. Generally, when an arrest warrant exists for a specific person, any law enforcement officer can arrest that person based on the existence of that warrant.

An arrest warrant should clearly identify the person to be arrested, the criminal violation, and other information as required by law. Once an arrest warrant has been issued, the officer who is responsible for its execution should inspect it to make certain that it is properly prepared, that all information required by law is provided, and that the warrant is valid on its face. The arresting officer should also be aware of any restrictions that may be placed upon the arrest by the warrant as well as restrictions issued by departmental regulation, state or local legislation, or applicable court decisions. Police have a legal obligation to ensure that arrest warrants are served in a timely fashion or risk that the warrant will become stale or otherwise invalid.

It is also important for police to know that if an arrest is to be made on private property belonging to third parties, they may not enter the premises to search for the suspect unless the officer is in possession of a separate legal basis for doing so. For example, this can include a search warrant, consent of a person empowered by law to give such consent, or exigent (emergency) circumstances. An arrest warrant is not sufficient to protect the Fourth Amendment interests of third parties who are unnamed on the warrant.

Making an Arrest

Once law enforcement positively identify the person to be arrested, the arresting officer(s) should identify themselves as police officers, inform the person of his or her arrest, and inform the person of the charges for which the arrest is being made. Officers not in uniform should display their badges and credentials when making the arrest to ensure proper identification.

If deemed necessary while conducting the arrest, the officer(s) may display their weapons to the extent necessary to ensure the safety of the arresting officers and the successful accomplishment of the arrest. This is generally done in the case of an arrest for a felony violation or under circumstances under which the law enforcement officer feels a threat against him or someone else might reasonably exist. Officers should not point their weapon at the suspect unless there is reason to believe that deadly force may be necessary.

Officers should use only a degree of force that is reasonably necessary to bring the situation under control and to ensure the safety of the officers involved. Officers are to determine the degree of force to be used in accordance with departmental policy and the circumstances of the individual case (i.e., a force continuum). As a rule, a suspect's degree of resistance/threat will determine the force response by officers. Officers must be careful that their force response is reasonable under the circumstances. In the most extreme circumstances, deadly force may be utilized only in accordance with the department's use-of-force policy.

Law enforcement officers are authorized to use deadly force to protect the officer or others from what is reasonably believed to be a threat of death or serious bodily harm, and/or to prevent the escape of a fleeing violent felon whom the officer has probable cause to believe will pose a significant threat of death or serious physical injury to the officer or others. Where practicable, prior to discharge of the firearm, officers shall identify themselves as law enforcement officers and state their intent to shoot.

Miranda Warnings

A Miranda warning is given by police in the United States to criminal suspects in police custody, or in a custodial situation, before they are interrogated or otherwise questioned. A custodial situation is one in which the suspect's freedom of movement is restrained (judged by the "free to leave" test), even if he is not under arrest. An elicited incriminating statement by a suspect will not constitute admissible evidence unless the suspect was informed of his/her Miranda rights and made a knowing, intelligent, and voluntary waiver of those rights. However, a 2004 Supreme Court ruling upheld state stop-and-identify laws, allowing police in those jurisdictions to require biographical information such as name, date of birth, and address without arresting suspects or providing them Miranda warnings.

The Miranda warnings were mandated by the 1966 Supreme Court decision in the case of *Miranda v. Arizona* as a means of protecting a criminal suspect's Fifth Amendment right to avoid coercive self-incrimination. The reading of the Miranda warning might be omitted during arrest, such as if the evidence is already sufficient to indict, or if the suspect is talkative and volunteers information without being asked. The admissibility of conversations, as evidence, is judged on a case-by-case basis and is subject to appeal.

Every U.S. jurisdiction has its own regulations regarding precisely what must be said to a person arrested or placed in a custodial situation. The typical warning states: "You have the right to remain silent. Anything you say can and will be used against you in a court of law. You have the right to an attorney. If you cannot afford an attorney, one will be appointed to you. Do you understand these rights as they have been read to you?"

The courts have since ruled that the warning must be "meaningful," so it is usually required that the suspect be asked if they understand their rights. Sometimes, firm answers of "yes" are required. Some departments and jurisdictions require that an officer ask, "do you understand?" after every sentence in the warning. An arrestee's silence does constitute a waiver. Evidence has in some cases been ruled inadmissible because of an arrestee's poor knowledge of English and the failure of arresting officers to provide the warning in the arrestee's language.

Because of various education levels of suspects, officers must make sure the suspect understands what the officer is saying. It may be necessary to translate to the suspect's level of understanding. Courts around the nation have ruled this admissible as long as the original waiver is said and the translation is recorded, either on paper or on tape.

Some jurisdictions provide the right of a juvenile to remain silent if their parent or guardian is not present. Some departments in New Jersey, Nevada, and Oklahoma have modified the providing-an-attorney clause as follows: "We have no way of giving you a lawyer, but one will be appointed for you, if you wish, if and when you go to court." Even though this sentence may seem somewhat ambiguous to the layperson, the Supreme Court has approved of it as an accurate description of the procedure in those states.

In international border states, including Texas, New Mexico, Arizona, and California, suspects who are not U.S. citizens are given an additional warning: "If you are not a United States citizen, you may contact your country's consulate prior to any questioning."

Oral waivers are often sufficient, but written waivers, particularly in the case of felony charges, are preferred and should be obtained whenever possible on the appropriate agency form. If the arrestee has not waived his or her Miranda rights, no questioning can be conducted beyond that necessary to accomplish the booking procedure (name, address, etc.). If the arrestee declines to waive his or her Miranda rights to counsel, or if the arrestee, after waiving that right, elects to reassert them, questioning must cease immediately and no further questioning may be conducted unless an attorney representing the arrestee is present or the arrestee voluntarily initiates another interview. Should the arrestee not waive his or her Miranda rights, even though the arrestee is not being questioned directly, officers should refrain from engaging in conversation between themselves in the presence of the arrestee that is calculated to elicit admissions.

Investigative Detention and Arrest

Police officers should also be aware of the distinction between an investigative detention and a full-blown arrest. Sometimes, it is necessary to stop and question a person who is not under arrest. Officers may conduct an investigative detention based upon reasonable suspicion that the person detained has committed, is committing, or is about to commit a crime.

Officers should not prolong the investigative detention beyond the period necessary to accomplish the purpose of the detention. Officers must be aware that prolonging an investigative detention unnecessarily may cause a court to view the detention as an actual arrest. Officers should take precautionary measures for their own safety during an investigative detention, including display of firearms or handcuffing the detainee. However, the prolonged display of firearms, handcuffing, and other activity during the investigative detention may also cause a court to view the detention as an actual arrest.

If there is a reasonable belief that a person under investigative detention may pose a threat to the officer's safety, a frisk or pat-down of the detainee may be conducted in order to search for weapons. Any further search of the detainee is prohibited unless it appears that there is probable cause for the arrest of the detainee. During the investigative detention, if it becomes apparent there is probable cause that the detainee has committed a criminal offense, the detainee should be placed under arrest, followed by a search incident to the arrest as well as all appropriate booking procedures as instructed by departmental policy.

The Terry Stop Case

In 1968, the Supreme Court declared in the case of *Terry v. Ohio* that a police officer may stop a person for questioning if the officer reasonably suspects that the person has committed, is committing, or is about to commit a crime. It is not necessary for the officer to have probable cause to arrest the individual at the time that the stop is made. All that is required is that the officer has a reasonable suspicion that the individual is involved in criminal activity. However, to be reasonable, this suspicion must be based upon articulable facts that would lead a reasonable person to suspect that the individual is involved in criminal activity. The Court further declared in *Terry v. Ohio* that an officer who has stopped a suspect may ."... search for weapons for the protection of the police officer, where he has reason to believe that he is dealing with an armed and dangerous individual."

This case is the landmark legal decision that grants officers the authority to conduct the field interviews (also called *investigative detentions* or *Terry stops*) and pat-down searches (often referred to as *frisks*). Numerous federal and state court decisions have interpreted and applied the principles of a Terry stop. In addition, many states have enacted statutes dealing with field interviews and pat-down searches.

Field Interviews Versus Consensual Encounters

An officer who lacks reasonable suspicion may still approach a suspect and ask questions designed to produce evidence of criminal activity as long as the encounter is voluntary, or consensual.

The distinction is a critical one: Field interviews are "seizures" of the person within the meaning of the Fourth Amendment, and the discovery of any physical evidence during such an interview is valid provided Fourth Amendment requirements are observed.

By contrast, consensual encounters are not seizures of the person. Should the officer discover evidence during the consensual encounter, it will normally be admissible in a trial, even though there was no basis for reasonable suspicion at the time the officer initiated the encounter. As such, it will often be desirable for the officer to approach a suspect in a manner that will make the initial contact a consensual encounter rather than a field interview.

Factors Defining a Field Interview

The Supreme Court has held that a police-citizen encounter is consensual (does not amount to a seizure of the person) as long as the circumstances of the encounter are such that the reasonable person would feel that he or she was "free to leave," that is, to terminate the encounter and depart at any time. The following factors, among others, may be considered by a court in determining whether the contact was a consensual encounter or a field interview (investigative stop):

1. Interference with the suspect's freedom of movement. If officers position themselves or their vehicles in such a manner as to block the suspect's path, this indicates that the suspect is not free to leave and may render the encounter an investigative stop.

2. Number of officers and their behavior. Confrontation of the suspect by more than one officer may create an atmosphere of intimidation that will cause the courts to consider the contact an investigative stop. Excessive display of weapons, such as drawn or pointed firearms, will have the same effect. Even the prolonged or repeated display of badges or other police identification may be considered intimidating. A threatening or bullying manner may lead to the same result.

3. Physical contact with the suspect. Any physical contact with the suspect for purposes of stopping or holding the individual or to search for weapons or evidence will almost certainly cause the contact to be considered a nonconsensual investigative stop or even a full-fledged arrest.

4. Retaining personal property of the suspect. If the officer wishes the contact to be regarded as consensual, any personal property taken from the suspect, such as a driver's license or other identification, should be returned promptly to the suspect. Prolonged retention by the officer of such items may lead a court to conclude that the suspect was not free to leave.

One method of emphasizing the consensual nature of the encounter is for the officer to advise the suspect that he or she has the right to refuse to answer questions, the right to refuse to consent to a search, and so on. Such warnings may not be legally required under the existing circumstances, but if given, will often persuade a court that any continuation of the encounter beyond that point was still voluntary on the part of the suspect.

Even if the contact is not consensual, it is still lawful if conducted in accordance with the principles applicable to investigative stops.

Initiation and Conduct of Field Interviews

Initiation of a field interview is justified only when the officer has a reasonable suspicion that the suspect is engaged in criminal activity. This suspicion must be based on specific facts known to or observed by the officer that the officer can later articulate in detail to a court. Such facts may include the demeanor of a person (furtive behavior); the time of day or night; the area in which the encounter occurred; the inappropriateness of the suspect's presence in that area at that time; the fact that the suspect was carrying suspicious objects; objective evidence that the suspect was armed (bulge in the clothing); and knowledge of the officer that a crime had recently been committed in that area, especially if the suspect matched the description of the perpetrator of that crime.

In addition, on January 12, 2000, the Supreme Court decided the case of *Illinois v. Wardlow*, which provides officers with an additional criterion for establishing reasonable suspicion to initiate a field interview. Wardlow deals with the common scenario in which a person notices police approaching and runs away to avoid them. In the past, it has generally been held by the courts that the act of fleeing from police does not, in and of itself, justify officer pursuit and stopping of the individual concerned. The Wardlow decision does not alter that basic fact, but it does permit officers to include fleeing as one more element that police may consider in determining whether reasonable suspicion exists sufficient to justify a Terry stop.

Officers must conduct the field interview in such a manner that the courts will not consider it an unlawful arrest. In the view of the courts, an arrest may occur even though the actual words "you're under arrest" have not been uttered by the officer. Therefore, unless the stop produces probable cause to arrest the suspect, the officer should still conduct the field interview in a manner that will not convey the impression that the suspect is under arrest. For this reason, the officer should exercise reasonable courtesy and avoid intimidating or threatening behavior, minimize physical contact that may induce a court to treat the encounter as an arrest, and avoid detaining the suspect any longer than is reasonably necessary.

One of the more common bases for judicial rulings that a stop has become an arrest is detention of the suspect for an excessive period of time. In addition, any movement of the suspect from the point of initial contact, such as to an area where there is more light, should be limited to that which is reasonably necessary for officer safety and the determination of criminal involvement. However, notwithstanding cautions regarding the legal requirements for a field interview, officer safety is understood as the paramount consideration, and therefore, is usually emphasized in any departmental policy.

Arrest and Prone Restraint

It is not uncommon for law enforcement officers to place an arrestee face down on the ground until handcuffs can be placed on him, but officers are cautioned that doing so can also be a dangerous undertaking. Depending on the circumstances, the person being arrested may be physically unable to breathe during the handcuffing process.

The arrestee should be restrained by use of handcuffs or other authorized devices after being taken into custody, except as otherwise provided by departmental policy. Other lawful forms of restraint should be used in order to ensure the safety of the arresting officer(s). Police trainers caution that arrestee(s) should not be restrained face down, especially in the four-point restraint (with hands and feet bound behind their back). Doing so is inherently hazardous unless the person being arrested is violently resisting and is placed on his or her side to facilitate breathing.

Numerous deaths have occurred among suspects who, while in custody of the police, have been restrained in the four-point restraint or what has been referred to as *hog-tie* position. Studies have shown that when a suspect is face down on his or her stomach, respiration is impaired, and the result may be positional asphyxia—the suspect essentially dies of suffocation. This outcome is increased in situations where the suspect is overweight, has exerted substantial energy in resisting arrest or in other ways prior to being restrained, and when the suspect has ingested alcohol and/or drugs prior to the event.

Arrests by Off-Duty Officers

Occasionally, officers who are off duty are faced with situations involving criminal conduct that they are neither equipped nor prepared to handle in the same manner as if they were on duty. This may lead to unnecessary injuries to off-duty officers and confusion for those on-duty officers arriving at the scene trying to correctly assess the facts.

As a rule, law enforcement is considered a 24-hour responsibility. Law enforcement officers, whether on or off duty, are expected to respond when necessary and permissible to potential or actual violations of the law and to provide assistance, as necessary, to citizens under emergency conditions. In most cases while off duty, police officers are therefore responsible for reporting any suspected or observed criminal activities to on-duty authorities. Generally, off-duty police officers need not enforce minor violations such as harassment, disorderly conduct, or other nuisance offenses or minor traffic infractions.

To protect the officer and the department, an off-duty police officer should make an arrest only when:

1. The arresting officer is not personally involved in the incident underlying the arrest. This requirement is geared primarily toward ascertaining whether, for liability purposes, the officer was acting within the scope of his employment. An example of this would be an off-duty officer who is drinking in a bar with a friend and the friend becomes involved in a dispute with another person, all of whom have been drinking. A fight results, and the off-duty officer arrests the person who punched his friend. The officer can possibly be sued at a later time for false arrest. In situations like this, off-duty officers who are personally involved in a situation should summon on-duty personnel.

2. There is an immediate need to prevent a crime or apprehend a suspect. In all instances of true emergency, where a crime is being committed or lives or property are endangered, immediate action by an off-duty officer may be justified.

3. The crime would require a full custodial arrest. For example, an off-duty officer sees someone breaking into a neighbor's house and the suspect flees immediately. The officer chases the suspect and apprehends him. This would be a permissible arrest, as the officer acted properly to prevent the immediate escape of a fleeing suspect of a serious crime.

4. The arresting officer possesses appropriate police identification and equipment. Before making a permitted off-duty arrest, an officer should have complete police identification such as a badge and police photo identification, and should be armed. This will greatly reduce the possibility that the officer will be mistaken as a perpetrator when on-duty officers arrive at the scene. Actual police identification will also forestall situations where the off-duty officer intervenes in an altercation or other situation and is mistaken as another assailant.

Arresting Juveniles

Arrest, transportation, and booking of juveniles are subject to special legal requirements. When dealing with juveniles, police officers are given reasonable discretion on deciding appropriate enforcement options. Based on the seriousness of and circumstances surrounding the offense, the background and demeanor of the juvenile, and other relevant factors, an officer may release a juvenile to his parents, guardian, or other responsible adult.

Juveniles who are arrested for criminal offenses should be subject to the same security requirements as adults, and may be handcuffed or otherwise restrained as necessary during transport and processing. Juveniles who are placed under arrest should be securely detained for a period of time and in a manner that is prescribed by state law to allow for identification, investigation, processing, and then release to the juvenile's parents or a responsible adult, or transfer to a juvenile facility or court.

Pro: Positive Aspects of the Arrest Function

It is widely accepted that a police arrest is one of the primary and expected functions of the police. Police recruits are intensely trained in arrest procedures and situational scenarios designed to prepare them for encounters with suspects on the street. The arrest function also presents law enforcement with the potential for a unique public relations tool. When an arrest takes place, news of the arrest will often be shared with the general public, typically through local media. These include local television stations, radio stations, and newspapers.

Chief executive officers of law enforcement agencies are often provided the opportunity to speak with the local media regarding crime statistics, crime rates, and use of department resources. When a police chief or sheriff, for example, is able to articulate the number and type of arrests their agency is making, doing so effectively lays the groundwork for future financial appropriations. In other words, more arrests tell the public that the police department is working hard to keep the streets safe and any additional money spent would be worthwhile.

When newspapers report stories about the arrest of citizens, they also typically report names of those persons along with the crimes for which they are charged. Doing so not only provides the police department a public relations tool, but also presents a potentially effective deterrent for others in the community who might otherwise be subject to an arrest under similar circumstances.

Con: Limitations of the Arrest Function

Knowing when and how to conduct an arrest is crucial to police officers, and the exercise of discretion is essential. Officers require a clear understanding of their powers, duties, and responsibilities under the laws of arrest. However, states may impose more restrictive limitations on arrests than those required under federal court rulings, and officers should be aware of those departures where appropriate in individual jurisdictions.

In most states, police officers are required to arrest an individual who is thought to have committed a felony. On the other hand, when a misdemeanor violation has been observed, officers generally have the discretion to arrest or handle the situation through other means, such as a verbal warning, written warning, or citation. In a practical sense, if the person who has committed the misdemeanor is not arrested, then police, jail, and administrative personnel are not burdened with the processing and handling of that person. As such, the expenses normally incurred in the physical arrest of a person are lessened. Conversely, when an officer physically places a misdemeanor violator under arrest, that officer is now temporarily suspended from his or her duties while involved with the arrestee and unable to conduct other police duties addressing public safety.

Effects on the Suspect

While an arrest will not necessarily lead to a criminal conviction, it may nonetheless have serious ramifications for the suspect such as absence from work; social stigma; and in some cases, the legal obligation to disclose an incidence of arrest when applying for a job, loan, or professional license. These collateral consequences can be severe. In many cases, a person who was not found guilty after an arrest can remove his arrest record through an expungment or a petition for a finding of factual innocence, which is first made to the law enforcement agency having jurisdiction over the offense. In some cases, legal action is sometimes filed against the police for wrongful arrest.

The wrongful arrest of a citizen or one for which there was excessive force can result in legal action being taken against the police officer responsible for the arrest and the department in which he or she is employed. If a lawsuit results in a judgment against the department, it can result in literally millions of dollars of fees and expenses. Moreover, a police lawsuit can severely damage a department's public image and can result in the termination of the officers and all of those who provided supervision or were otherwise associated with the incident.

See Also: 6. Interrogation Practices; 7. Miranda Warnings; 9. Police Brutality; 19. Warrants.

Further Readings

"Arrest-Probable Cause-Observation of Street Transaction-Police Officer's Experience." *Criminal Law Reporter*, v.86/17 (February 3, 2010).

Florida v. J.L., 120 S. Ct., 1379 (2000).

Hechinger, John, and Simmi Aujla. "Police Arrest Black Scholar in Dispute." *The Wall Street Journal* (July 21, 2009).

Heppl, Bob. "The Right to Privacy and Crime Detection." *The Cambridge Law Journal*, v.68/2 (July 2009).

"Juveniles-Interrogation-Officer's Knowledge of Arrestee's Juvenile Status." *Criminal Law Reporter*, v.85/18 (August 5, 2009).

Lyman, Michael. *The Police: An Introduction*. Upper Saddle River, NJ: Prentice Hall, 2010.

"Premature Miranda Warning." *Criminal Law Reporter*, v.86/15 (January 20, 2010).

Rutledge, Devallis. "The Stupid Factor." *Police*, v.33/12 (December 2009).

Smith, Dave. "Reasonable Suspicion." *Police*, v.33/12 (December 2009).

Steagald v. United States, 451 U.S. 204, 101 S. Ct. 1642 (1981).

Stevens, D. *American Policing*. Sudbury, MA: Jones and Bartlett, 2009.

Walker, S., and C. Katz. *The Police in America*. New York: McGraw Hill, 2011.

"Whether Cops Must Identify Themselves When Making Arrest in Public Isn't Clear." *Arrest Law Bulletin*, v.33/10 (October 2009).

3

Bounty Hunters and Rewards

Gilbert Geis
University of California, Irvine

Rewards for information leading to the capture of a wanted person have figured prominently in some of the most memorable events in human history and legend. Particularly notorious is the biblical account of the bounty given to Judas Iscariot for identifying Jesus to the authorities, an act that led to Jesus's capture and crucifixion. Judas's treachery exemplifies the view that accepting money for informing on another human being is an immoral act. Nonetheless, rewards have proven useful for gaining important information that otherwise may not have been forthcoming. In contemporary times, millions of dollars in reward money have been offered—and sometimes earned—in the war against terror.

In earlier times, the prospect of financial rewards fueled the formation of groups that set out to capture outlaws. The practice was particularly common in the frontier era in the United States. Such groups, commonly known as *vigilantes*, often took the law into their own hands, bringing into question the desirability of bounty incentives.

Current disputes about bounty center not only on the moral implications of rewards for information, but also on pragmatic concerns: Does the tactic produce unreliable information? Is it cost effective or merely symbolic? Is too much or not enough money offered? Are those who benefit from a reward often no more than accomplices of the individual they turn in, or are they likely to be admirable persons working for the greater good?

The Judas Jigsaw

For thousands of years, the story of Judas Iscariot has been regarded as a cautionary recital about an evil man engaged in betrayal in order to collect a reward. Such behavior has been roundly condemned based on the details supplied in the New Testament. The irony is that the story of Judas Iscariot is something of an anomaly, because in virtually every instance in which a bounty is in play, the person being sought is considered a villain—often a kidnapper, rapist, murderer, or terrorist—and those offering the reward are heroes. Besides, the story of Judas Iscariot has taken an unusual twist in recent times.

In the biblical account, the Iscariot drama unfolds during the Passover celebration on the evening before Christ is apprehended. Identified as a betrayer, Judas abruptly leaves the gathering, later meeting with the temple priests and collecting his reward, the blood money of 30 pieces of silver (about $25 today). The next day in the Garden of Gethsemane in Jerusalem, Judas identifies Christ for the arresting solders of the high priest by a kiss of betrayal. Christ is turned over to the Romans under Pontius Pilate and, after a trial, is executed. The subsequent fate of Judas Iscariot has been variously reported. The best-known biblical version records him being struck with remorse, hanging himself after the priests in the temple refuse his attempt to later return the money.

Sometime around 1978, however, an ancient codex, commonly known as the Gospel of Judas, was discovered. It was written by Gnostics, followers of Jesus, and portrays Judas as a favorite of Jesus who had carried out Jesus's request to betray him in order to carry out the end of his existence on Earth. The villain in this rendering becomes the hero. Nonetheless, Judas is commonly regarded as the leading illustration of the trumping of righteousness by greed and the arguable morality of bounty hunting.

Good Samaritans

A biblical source also figures prominently in contemporary reward programs that provide funds for persons who intervene to aid a person in distress, often as a result of a criminal event. The parable of the good Samaritan tells of a man on his way from Jerusalem to Jericho who comes upon a person lying beside the road. He had been waylaid by robbers who stripped him, beat him, and went off leaving him to die. Both a priest and a Levite subsequently come upon the senseless victim, and ignore his plight. But the Samaritan bathes the man's wounds with oil, places him on a donkey, and carries him to an inn, leaving money with the innkeeper to care for the stranger. The parable has been employed to justify good Samaritan laws that seek to encourage altruistic aid by compensating persons who suffer losses sustained in actions to help prevent a crime, apprehend an offender, or aid the police in their effort to deal with a crime. The statutes typically exempt from coverage individuals acting in self-defense or protecting members of their own families.

A study of interveners who qualified for awards found that overwhelmingly, they were male. The only female among the 32 persons interviewed was an older woman who heard her neighbor scream and hastened to the rescue. She was knifed about a dozen times, but was spared from death by the steel stays on her old-fashioned corset. A major distinction between the interveners and a matched population sample was that the Samaritans had training, such as in karate and lifesaving, that led them to believe they could pull off the rescue successfully. They also tended to be physically stronger than the criminals they dealt with. Interestingly, none were aware of the statute that allowed them to be rewarded for any deprivations they suffered because of their good deeds; they said they did not see any other option but to help, and after all, they hoped that if they in a dire situation, someone would come to their aid.

Good Samaritan rewards also can be made on an ad-hoc basis rather than as part of an ongoing program. In 2009, for instance, two men in Delray Beach, Florida, rescued an 80-year-old woman from a burning car engulfed in black smoke while bystanders yelled warnings that the vehicle might explode. It was so hot that the glasses of one rescuer melted. The explanation of one of the rescuers for his action was simply expressed: "I just had to do something." The Palm Beach County Commissioners and the Delray Beach City Commissioners together gave the two men monetary rewards or their heroic act.

Frontier Vigilantes

Old-fashioned Wild West movies often show posted signs with large letters spelling out WANTED below a picture of a mustachioed culprit. The poster also indicates the amount of the reward for the apprehension of the person, "dead or alive."

The same pattern prevailed in the offer by the governor of Missouri in 1881 of a $5,000 reward for the arrest of the bandit Jesse James and his brother, Frank. A member of the James gang shot Jesse to death, but there is no record regarding whether or not he collected the bounty. In comparison, $20,000 was the price on the head of bank robber John Dillinger, who was fatally shot by the FBI in July 1934 as he emerged into an alley from a Chicago movie house that had been showing a gangster film. Dillinger was accompanied by two women. One of the two, Romanian-born Anna Sage, a former prostitute who ran a brothel in East Chicago, Indiana, had informed on Dillinger in the hopes of receiving the reward and avoiding deportation. She nonetheless was declared an "alien of low moral character" and was sent back to her home country two years later, after the courts ruled that the implied promise of immunity made to her by the lead FBI agent was not binding on the Department of Labor that dealt with deportations.

Bail and Bounties

Apprehending persons who fail to appear in court after a surety company has posted their bail has spurred a coterie of individuals who specialize in tracing such fugitives in order to claim a bounty. About 20 percent of people who post bail become fugitives from justice after failing to appear at a scheduled court hearing.

Only the United States and the Philippines permit bounty hunters, who typically receive from 10 to 20 percent of the bail money that otherwise would have been forfeited if the accused did not appear in court. It is estimated that bounty hunters apprehend about 90 percent of the fugitives whom they pursue. Many states have examinations before a person may receive a license as a bounty hunter. In California, for instance, the test includes knowledge of sections of the penal code. If qualified, bounty hunters are accorded special privileges; in some states, for instance, they have the right to enter private property without a warrant. At the same time, the work can be alternately boring and dangerous. The head of the National Enforcement Agency, a networking group for bounty hunters, notes that the excitement of the chase compensates for the tedium of the downside, which is hours of legwork.

Police and Community Rewards

Today, rewards for information that will lead to the apprehension of a criminal are a regular feature of the enforcement apparatus. Police have funds to pay off informants, although such undercover arrangements tend to be kept from the public eye because of the controversy that surrounds them. Quite often, the informant is spared arrest and prosecution and given a reward if their revelations are more valuable than carrying out charges against them. The temptation for police informants to exaggerate or even to create stories is a common problem, however.

A not uncommon trajectory of cases involving rewards is that of Helen Stewart, who was strangled to death in 1979 in her home in Hanover Township, Ohio, and her naked body was then moved into the back seat of an abandoned car. The county Crime Stoppers program offered $1,000, and the family added $10,00 to that amount for information to help solve the case. Nothing has developed during the years, and recently, the family doubled its offer to $20,000.

More successful was an offer of $36,500 raised by the community as payment for information regarding the 1964 lynching of three political activists who were seeking to register African American voters in Neshoba County, Mississippi. Two members of the Ku Klux Klan turned in their fellows to collect the bounty. The FBI agent handling the case said the information was purchased cheaply, expressing the willingness of their department to pay much more if necessary. Seventeen people were convicted in October 1967 and received sentences ranging between three and 10 years in prison; nine of them remained in prison for at least six years.

How Do the Police Feel About Rewards?

A survey, published in 1991, was conducted on police chiefs in 250 of the largest national police departments to determine the law enforcement view on rewards. Each police chief was presented with the following vignette: While working overtime, a 31-year-old secretary was raped and beaten in her employer's parking lot in a small town. There were no witnesses, and she had only fragments of a description about her assailant. She was not hospitalized, but missed several days of work. After the well-reported incident, the company installed improved lighting and a security station in the parking lot. The victim expressed no intention to sue the company.

Somewhat more than half of the police chiefs believed that the company would offer a reward for help in solving this case. Four out of five believed that the company should offer such a reward, and a majority believed that the reward would be helpful in identifying the offender. There was considerable agreement that the reward amount should be somewhere between

$1,000 and $10,000. Oddly, a slightly greater number of chiefs believed it was more likely that a company would offer a reward in this rape case than in a murder.

The same vignette elicited a somewhat different pattern of responses from a random sample of business firms, the results of which were published the following year. A slightly higher percentage of company executives than the police chiefs believed that a reward would and should be offered. The average amount of the reward specified by the business firms was lower than the amount suggested by the police chiefs (more responses were in the $1,000 to $5,000 range), but four times as many of the company respondents went above $10,000 as a the preferred reward. The company respondents were even less inclined than the police to favor rewards for a murder case than were the police.

Notable Reward Cases

Significant rewards for suspects reach far back in history. Five thousand dollars was offered for information leading to the arrest of Francisco "Pancho" Villa, the infamous Mexican insurgent general who in 1916 crossed the border into Columbus, New Mexico, with 500 men and killed 18 people, including 10 soldiers and eight civilians. Villa led a quiet life until 1923, when political opponents assassinated him, an aide, and four of his bodyguards. One of the assassins tried, unsuccessfully, to collect a $5,000 reward that had been offered by the authorities in Columbus. In 2008, the grandchildren of one of the men who killed Villa sought to obtain $50,000 in reward money, calling it a matter of honor. The U.S. Embassy in Mexico City claimed no such amount had ever been offered, although a bill specifying that sum had been introduced in Congress.

In more recent years, particularly prominent cases involving rewards include the Panama dictator Manuel Noriega, who had a $1 million reward on his head for federal drug charges in 1988. He was apprehended without outside help by American agents during the 1989 U.S. invasion of Panama, and taken into custody in 1990 after sequestering himself in the Vatican Embassy in Panama City. No reward money was paid out. In 1992, Noriega was convicted of eight counts of drug trafficking, racketeering, and money laundering.

The bombing of the Alfred P. Murrah Federal Building in downtown Oklahoma City on April 19, 1995, resulted in 168 deaths and more than 780 injuries. Timothy McVeigh, the perpetrator, was tracked down in a local jail, where he had been placed for driving without a license and unlawfully carrying weapons. McVeigh was later executed by lethal injection, and Terry Nicolas, an accomplice, received a life sentence. A reward of $2 million remains outstanding for apprehension of the person or persons believed to have been in the truck that drove McVeigh and Nichols to the bombing site.

There was a $1 million reward for information on the location of Eric Rudolph, who planted a bomb during the 1996 summer Olympics in Atlanta that killed two and injured 120. Rudolph also had bombed an abortion clinic and a lesbian bar in Atlanta. He hid in the Appalachian mountains, supported by allies, but finally was apprehended by a policeman while Rudolph was foraging in the garbage in a North Carolina town. Rudolph pled guilty, avoiding a possible death penalty, and received a life sentence.

Theodore Kaczynski, known as the Unabomber for the lethal packages he sent to various persons, was turned in by his brother, David, who identified him in 1999 on the basis of a 35,000-word diatribe that Kaczynski submitted to the *Washington Post*. The brother used part of the reward money, which he was initially unaware was being offered, to pay taxes and legal fees. He distributed the remainder among the bombing victims and their survivors.

In July 1994, former football star O.J. Simpson offered $500,000 for the "real killer or killers" of his wife Nicole and her friend Ronald Goldman, who were found slain a month earlier. Simpson's defense team later upped the amount by another $1.5 million. The fact that no evidence was found that would qualify for this reward has been regarded by students of the Simpson case as further evidence that Simpson himself, who was acquitted of the charge of murder after a sensational trial, nonetheless was in fact the guilty party.

In foreign jurisdictions, a particularly well-publicized reward case arose when numerous Muslim religious leaders and Iranian business and government leaders, including Iran's Ayatollah Ruhollah Khomeini, raised bounties totaling $5.2 million on the head of the Anglo-Indian novelist Salman Rushdie on the grounds that Rushdie had defamed Islam in his 1989 book, *Satanic Verses*. Almost immediately, outraged Muslims began offering bounties, including Iranian officials; an Iranian businessman, who offered $3 million; and an Iranian religious foundation, which offered $1 million, a number that was later nearly tripled. Ayatollah Ruhollah Khomeini himself called for a *fatwah*. Among other alleged blasphemies in the book, Rushdie wrote about prostitutes in a brothel taking the names of Mohammed's 11 wives. Heavily protected by the British, and knighted by Queen Elizabeth II in 2007, Rushdie remained alive more than two decades after the reward was first decreed.

Crime Stoppers and Tax Whistleblowers

The Crime Stoppers program, founded in Albuquerque, New Mexico, in 1976, strongly suggests that rewards for information can be a valuable law enforcement tool. Funded privately and administered by local police, Crime Stoppers has local chapters throughout the United States and in many other countries. It pays up to $2,000 for information leading to the arrest of criminals. Law enforcers, the crime victims, and perpetrators are not eligible for rewards. From 1981 through 2008, the program's efforts led to 1,272 arrests.

One of the most prominent government programs involving rewards was inaugurated in 1899. It pays persons who provide useful information to the Internal Revenue Service (IRS) about tax evaders. The IRS estimates an underreporting of taxes due to cheating—the so-called *tax gap*—in the range of $200–$300 billion annually.

The taxpayer whistleblower program was upgraded by Congress in December 2006, when the award for reporting on evaders, typically businesses, that had cheated the government out of a minimum of $2 million was raised from a mandatory minimum of 15 percent to a possible maximum of 30 percent of the recovered amount. In the fiscal year ending September 30, 2009, the IRS reported that the number of apparently useful tips had quadrupled from the previous year.

About 100,000 persons volunteer such information each year. The motive is sometimes a grudge: disaffected employees, disgruntled ex-wives, and displeased neighbors are common IRS informants. In a typical year, the federal government collects $100 million on the basis of tips and pays out between $2–$4 million, although only about 10 percent of the tips result in rewards. The IRS has a policy of carefully auditing the returns of the rewarded informers to make certain that the bounty is reported as income.

Targeting Terrorists

When the U.S. government became deeply involved in the reward business during its campaign against terrorists, the amounts offered escalated dramatically.

The rewards offered by the State Department during the war in Iraq—often advertised on matchbooks—promised not only money, but also possible permission for the informant to reside in the United States. Sometimes, the rewards were successful lures, sometimes not. One unsuccessful effort involved Imad Mughniyeh, a notorious member of Hezbollah. He was regarded as the instigator of numerous acts of terrorism against American targets in the 1980s, and was believed to have killed more Americans than any other militant before the attacks on September 11, 2001. Mughniyeh was number one on America's most wanted terrorist list until Osama bin Laden took that position, and there was a long-standing $5 million reward for information that led to his capture. However, Mughniyeh was killed on February 12, 2008, in Damascus, Syria, by a bomb planted in his automobile. Hezbollah claimed that the assassination was the work of the Israeli security forces; Israel denied it.

The price on the head of Osama bin Laden has now risen to $25 million. An additional $2 million was added to the bounty by the Airline Pilots Association and the Air Transport Association, making it the largest reward ever offered by the United States. The Defense Department has sought to prompt interest in the reward by dropping leaflets throughout Afghanistan and announcing the bounty on regional radio. For Afghans, whose average monthly wage is about $4, the reward money spent at that rate by one individual would last 500,000 years. The reward authorization also established a committee that would decide on the amount to be paid out on the basis of the relevance of the information supplied, the risk involved to the informer, and the cooperation accorded by the informer in terms of the arrest and trial of the person apprehended.

The antiterrorist Rewards for Justice Program had its most prominent success in 2003 when military authorities questioned about a dozen members of the extended family of Saddam Hussein, the deposed Iraqi leader. One pinpointed Hussein's whereabouts, explaining that he was hiding in a tiny bunker on a farm 10 miles south of Tikrit, his home town. The informant reportedly collected a reward, and he and his family are said to have been relocated to an unspecified site.

The largest prior antiterrorist award was given to an unidentified man in 1995. He had fingered Ramzi Ahmed Yousef, the leader in the 1993 attack on the World Trade Center. Yousef and four accomplices drove a rented van into the basement of Tower One and set off bombs that killed six and injured more than 1,042 others. He escaped to Manila and then to Pakistan after an associate was arrested in their Manila apartment after a misfire from a bomb they were manufacturing. The informant against Yousef, a Muslim from South Africa, notified the American Embassy in Islamabad as to the location of Yousef, and collected the $2 million bounty. Yousef, described by the sentencing judge in New York as an "apostle of evil," is serving a life term without the possibility of parole in the Supermax prison in Florence, Colorado.

Pro: Arguments in Support of Bounties and Rewards

The strongest argument favoring the use of monetary rewards to procure information leading to the resolution of a crime is the success of their use. However, it is not possible to precisely quantify how often this occurs, and there are numerous elements that operate against attempts to quantify their success—the nature of the event, the setting, the amount of the reward, the characteristics of the perpetrators, and the desire and ability of someone to collect the bounty, among others.

Rewards usually are not established until the authorities have been stymied in their more routine efforts to resolve the situation; therefore, they are implemented in the most difficult cases and often only as a last resort, a major reason why all reports indicate that the percentage of cases resolved by rewards are low—approximately 10 percent or fewer. In one report, the Los Angeles Police Department indicated that for a recent five-year period, it had offered nearly $8 million in reward money for assistance in resolving 337 crimes. The department paid out only $535,000 in rewards in 21 cases, almost all of them murders. Those arguing for rewards point out that 21 resolutions are better than none, and that the reward program is therefore deserving of endorsement.

An illustration of the last-resort pattern potentially taken by the reward process came in the aftermath of the Oklahoma City bombing case. Kenneth Trentadue, whom the FBI implicated in the bombing, died while being held in a federal transfer center in the city for a parole violation. He had earlier been convicted of a bank robbery and released on parole after serving his sentence. The authorities ruled that his death was by suicide, but his brother, an attorney, sued for wrongful death damages and received $1 million on the basis of what the judge declared to be a mishandling of the case. Twelve years later, frustrated by his failure to obtain information from the authorities and driven by the belief that the FBI had killed Trentadue, his brother offered a $250,000 reward for information that led to evidence of what he believed was a murder.

Con: Arguments Against Rewards and Bounties

A common argument against the use of rewards for resolving crime is that they encourage immoral behavior. The offer by American authorities of very large sums of money for information about terrorists is lambasted by many Muslims as further evidence that the United States is a heathen and materialistic society, operated by the principle that money can buy anything, including treachery.

More pragmatically, rewards, especially high amounts, often produce an overwhelming response, much of it from crank callers who tie up police resources and lead to frustrating, blind alleys. In the month following the Oklahoma City bombing, a toll-free hot line fielded one call offering information every 55 seconds, or a total of 40,000 calls. Following these leads may often inconvenience and embarrass innocent persons who have been reported to law enforcement by people who simply wish to harass them. There is also a tendency toward racial profiling in reports of suspected perpetrators. There is the danger of targeted persons being treated brutally in order to obtain information, accurate or otherwise, that could justify a reward claim.

That appeals to higher values might be more effective than financial reward was indicated in a California case, in which an Arizona couple supplied essential information to the authorities regarding the murder of Denise Huber. The 23-year-old woman had been kidnapped in 1991 on her way home from a rock concert, handcuffed, beaten, and placed in a country club freezer by John Famalaro, her abductor. The couple reporting Famalaro turned down the $10,000 reward that had been offered by her family.

Another major objection to bounties and rewards is that they can encourage irresponsible tactics that are employed for greedy purposes. A prime example is the Fugitive Slave Act of 1850 that provided bounties for persons capturing an alleged runaway slave. The act allowed hunters to call upon bystanders for assistance in their work, and provided fines and terms of incarcerations for those who failed to offer such help. The captive was not allowed a trial or an appeal. The rising price of slaves in the south at the time led bounty hunters to apprehend both fugitive slaves and free blacks.

See Also: 2. Arrest Practices; 11. Police Privatization; 18. Vigilantes.

Further Readings

Acocella, Joan. "Betrayal: Should We Hate Judas Iscariot?" *The New Yorker* (August 3, 2007).

Armstrong, Joshua, and Anthony Bruno. *The Seekers: A Bounty Hunter's Story.* New York: HarperCollins, 2000.

Campbell, Stanley W. *The Spy Catchers: Enforcement of the Fugitive Slaw Law, 1860–1860.* Chapel Hill, NC: University of North Carolina Press, 1970.

Geis, Gilbert, and Ted L. Huston. "Bystander Intervention into Crimes: Public Policy Considerations." *Policy Studies Journal,* v.11 (1983).

Geis, Gilbert, Ted L. Huston, and Joseph T. Wells. "Rewards by Businesses for Crime Information: The Views of Law Enforcement." *American Journal of Police,* v.10 (1991).

Geis, Gilbert, Ted L. Huston, and Joseph T. Wells. "Scrutiny on the Bounty: Business Rewards for Crime Tips." *Business Horizons,* v.35 (November–December 1992).

Giradin, G. Russell, and William J. Helmer. *Dillinger: The Untold Story.* Bloomington: Indiana University Press, 2009.

Gorn, Elliot J. *Dillinger's Wild Ride: The Years that Made America's Public Enemy Number One.* New York: Oxford University Press, 2009.

Gubar, Susan. *Judas: A Biography.* New York: W.W. Norton, 2009.

Jones, Stephen, and Peter Israel. *Others Unknown: The Oklahoma City Bombing Case and Conspiracy.* New York: Public Affairs, 1998.

Kaser, Rodolphe, Marvin Meyer, Gregor Worst, and Francois Gaudard. *The Gospel of Judas.* Washington, DC: National Geographic Society, 2008.

Katz, Friedrich. *The Life and Times of Pancho Villa.* Stanford, CA: Stanford University Press, 1998.

Klassen, William. *Judas: Betrayer or Friend of Jesus?* Minneapolis, MN: Fortress Press.

Lasseter, Don. *Cold Storage.* New York: Kensington, 1998.

Pagels, Elaine, and Karen L. King. *Reading Judas: The Gospel of Judas and the Shaping of Christianity.* New York: Viking, 2007.

Pope, Jacqueline. *Bounty Hunters, Marshals, and Sheriffs: Forward to the Past.* Westport, CT: Praeger, 1998.

Reeve, Simon. *The New Jackals: Ramzi Yousef, Osama bin Laden, and the Future of Terrorism.* Boston: Northeastern University Press, 2002.

Rosenbaum, Dennis P., Arthur Lurigio, and Paul J. Lavrakas. *Crime Stoppers: A National Evaluation of Program Operations and Effects.* Washington, DC: National Institute of Justice, 1987.

Schuster, Henry, and Charles Stone. *Hunting Eric Rudolph.* New York: Berkley Books, 2005.

Weatherby, William J. *Salman Rushdie: Sentenced to Death.* New York: Carroll and Graf, 1990.

4

Entrapment

Scott Ingram
Indiana University

E ntrapment is a legal defense to alleged criminal conduct that claims law enforcement lured the suspect into committing a crime. Its precise legal meaning is subject to debate. It first appeared as a defense in the 19th century with the rise of professional policing. Over the last 150 years, the defense of entrapment has changed both in its meaning and its application. Courts have differed regarding how to determine if entrapment has occurred. With changes in criminal law and criminal justice administration, entrapment has been applied to a growing range of situations. The lack of definitional precision and the growing use of undercover operations by law enforcement have made entrapment a controversial topic.

In its present form, entrapment is an affirmative defense to criminal conduct. This means that the person who asserts the defense admits the criminal conduct, but claims that the offense would not have occurred if law enforcement had not induced the person to commit the crime. The critical question is how to determine whether or not the person would have engaged in the conduct if the government had not intervened. Legal precedent has decided that the determination can be made one of two ways: either subjectively or objectively. The subjective test evaluates the charged individual's conduct, while the objective test evaluates the government's conduct during the course of the investigation. Each jurisdiction can choose which test to apply.

Historical Origins

The origin of entrapment coincides with the beginning of professional law enforcement. Early cases dealing with entrapment involved the scrutiny of law enforcement tactics. Defendants argued that the police, should they learn of a potential crime, should not wait for it to occur and then arrest the perpetrator. Instead, they should take steps to prevent the commission of the crime. Many of these cases involved thefts or burglaries. Likewise, law enforcement took steps to apprehend those who might be seduced into violating a statutory prohibition. For example, several early cases involved the illegal sale of alcohol to slaves. Slaves, with the consent of their owners, would be sent into various establishments and would attempt to purchase alcohol. If they were successful with their purchase, the seller would be arrested. The offenses in these cases, as the examples show, were more regulatory in nature.

From the outset, courts differed in their approach to entrapment allegations. They took one of three approaches. One approach was to look at the person accused of the crime. Did the person's character indicate they were a criminal? If so, the court concluded the person was not entrapped into committing the offense. The remaining two approaches focused on police conduct. The approach taken depended upon the judge's feelings about law enforcement's purpose. Those who thought police should apprehend criminals found the police officer's conduct appropriate. Those who thought the police should prevent crime found the police conduct inappropriate.

For the most part, these first cases originated in state courts. As a result, there was wide variation regarding how entrapment allegations were handled. By the late 19th century, however, the federal courts began examining police conduct as Congress began creating more federal crimes. This led to more federal law enforcement. Most of the new federal crimes were regulatory in nature, meaning that the knowing performance of an act was sufficient for criminal liability. During this time, fraud also became an interest of federal law enforcement, which began investigating organized criminal activity. As the government agents began making cases, the defendants challenged the manner in which law enforcement gathered evidence.

Legal Development in the Supreme Court

Eventually, these challenges reached the U.S. Supreme Court. In the 1895 case of *Grimm v. United States*, the Supreme Court reviewed the conviction of a man accused of sending obscene material through the mail at the written request a person interested in such material, who was in fact a postal inspector posing as a decoy. The defendant argued that he mailed the material at the government's request and therefore could not be held criminally responsible. The Supreme Court dismissed this claim, stating that the mere fact that the decoy letter writer used a false name and that he was a government detective did not establish a defense to mailing obscene material. Implicitly, the Court found nothing wrong with the government's conduct in the case, and viewed the defendant as one who engaged in the business of selling obscene material through the mail.

Early entrapment cases like *Grimm* began against the backdrop of increased prosecution of vice offenses. During this time, private agencies began investigating prostitution houses, gambling establishments, and other businesses the agencies believed were undermining societal values. In order to gather evidence of criminal activity against these businesses, agents had to enter the businesses and partake of the services. This was especially true of gambling establishments. With the proof of violation easily established, the defense was left with challenging the means of evidence collection. This led to the defense of entrapment.

The U.S. Supreme Court first recognized the defense in *United States v. Sorrells* (1932), which occurred against the backdrop of prohibition—perhaps most significantly, while prohibition was coming to an end. Sorrells, who lived in North Carolina, was introduced to another man by a friend. The man claimed to have been a veteran of World War I, like Sorrels, and they talked together for some time. After a while, the man asked Sorrells if he could provide some liquor. Sorrells said he could not, but after some more conversation, the man repeated the request. This time Sorrells agreed, and returned half an hour later with half a gallon of whiskey, for which the man paid Sorrells $5. Soon after the sale, the man identified himself as a prohibition agent, and Sorrells faced indictment for the illegal sale of alcohol. At trial, Sorrells asked for a jury instruction that the government induced him to commit the offense, which the trial court denied. After an appeal to the U.S. Supreme Court, the Court stated the evidence was clearly sufficient to justify such an instruction. To justify its position, the Court drew upon both strands of prior decisions indicating that courts had to evaluate the defendant's willingness to commit the offense and the methods used by law enforcement. The Court made no effort to distinguish *Grimm* or provide any guidance to future courts when evaluating whether an entrapment defense exists.

The Supreme Court would return to the entrapment issue 26 years later when it decided *United States v. Sherman*. In August 1951, Sherman was a drug addict undergoing treatment. During the course of his treatment, he met another reforming addict at a pharmacy and struck up a conversation. They met off and on over a period of time, and the person began asking Sherman if he could provide him with narcotics. Sherman initially refused, but later agreed to provide the narcotics. After several sales transpired, the man informed the government that he could provide evidence against a drug dealer. The government observed the man and Sherman making three more transactions before indicting Sherman for the illegal sale of narcotics. At trial, Sherman argued that he was induced to commit the offense by the man and was otherwise unwilling to engage in the criminal conduct. The government responded that the defendant was predisposed to commit the offense based on his prior convictions for drug use, and that Sherman's initial reluctance was the product of his hesitancy to sell drugs to someone he did not yet trust. The trial court instructed the jury on entrapment and, following his conviction, Sherman appealed, claiming he was entrapped as a matter of law.

In 1958, the Supreme Court agreed with Sherman, stating that the informant induced Sherman to make the transactions. Sherman's prior convictions were not relevant because it was apparent that he was attempting to reform himself. The Court also indicated that the government presented no other evidence that Sherman had sold to people other than the informant. As a result, the Court found the government had entrapped Sherman.

Subjective and Objective Approaches

From these two Supreme Court cases, state and federal courts took different paths. Because the Supreme Court did not base its rulings on a provision of the U.S. Constitution, the state courts were free to determine their own definitions of entrapment. Courts took one of two approaches. The first approach focused upon the person accused of crime, also called the *subjective approach*. Courts using this approach sought to determine if the defendant was predisposed to commit the particular crime, and did not examine the conduct of law enforcement. The federal courts adopted this test. A second approach was termed the *objective approach*, which examined the conduct of the law enforcement officers to determine whether their conduct improperly lured the person into committing the offense. States split between the subjective and objective approach used in the federal courts.

The Supreme Court was asked in the 1970s to reconsider its approach to entrapment in the case of *United States v. Russell*. Russell was convicted of producing methamphetamine after undercover narcotics agents had supplied him with necessary ingredients. According to the evidence presented at trial, Russell and two others had been making methamphetamine prior to meeting the undercover agent. The chemical the agent provided was difficult, but not impossible to obtain. At various points during the investigation, Russell and his partners provided the agent with quantities of methamphetamine and showed the agent their lab. Eventually, the agent obtained a search warrant and law enforcement officers seized the lab. The U.S. District Court for the Western District of Washington instructed the jury on entrapment, but he was found guilty. Acknowledging he had the predisposition to commit the offense, Russell argued to the U.S. Court of Appeals for the Ninth Circuit that the government's conduct in supplying him the necessary chemical was so inappropriate, the court should grant a directed verdict in his favor. The Court of Appeals agreed, and the government sought review by the Supreme Court. After reviewing the two approaches, the Court declined to change its approach, thus reversing the Court of Appeals. The Court also declined to base the entrapment defense in the Due Process Clause of the Fifth Amendment. In doing so, the Court determined that to base entrapment on the Due Process Clause would unnecessarily grant the courts veto power of law enforcement methods.

The Groundbreaking Case of Jacobson v. United States

The most recent significant Supreme Court case dealing with entrapment was the 1992 case of *Jacobson v. United States*. Jacobson was a war veteran and a farmer in Nebraska. At a time when federal law permitted such conduct, he received, through the mail, nude photographs of boys. The year after the Child Protection Act of 1984 banned such material from the mail, government investigators came across his name on the mailing list of the company that supplied the material. Over the next two and a half years, the government, posing as companies in the business of selling child pornography, sent Jacobson several mailings inquiring first about his willingness to purchase such material, and then asking if he would like to purchase specific items. When he agreed to purchase some pictures, the government made a controlled delivery and arrested him once he had received the mailing. A subsequent search of the residence revealed no other similar pictures. He was convicted and the decision was affirmed on appeal. In 1992, the Supreme Court disagreed and reversed Jacobson's conviction. The Court stated that the government, through its repeated mailings, had failed to demonstrate how Jacobson was predisposed to purchase the material, stating that if the government had made only a single offer and Jacobson had agreed, then the situation would have been different.

The *Jacobson* case has caused confusion among the federal circuit courts. *Jacobson*'s reasoning indicates that some type of analysis of the law enforcement's conduct is necessary to determine if the defendant is predisposed to commit the crime. At least one circuit court has begun to analyze whether law enforcement enabled the particular activity. In *United States v. Hollingsworth* (1994), the defendant was accused of money laundering after law enforcement agents instructed him on how to launder the money. The defendant argued he would never have laundered the money but for the law enforcement's instruction. The U.S. Court of Appeals for the Seventh Circuit considered law enforcement's conduct in the case similar to law enforcement's conduct in *Jacobson*. It reasoned that Jacobson would not have committed the offense if law enforcement agents had not sold him the child pornography, much like the accused money launderer would not have laundered the money if law enforcement agents had not taught him how. Not all circuit courts of appeal have adopted this perspective, however, and the subject awaits a resolution from the U.S. Supreme Court.

Entrapment Applied: Abscam

To illustrate the difference between the subjective and objective approaches and to see how entrapment relates to law enforcement activity, the Abscam investigation and prosecutions from the early 1980s are useful. Following five years of congressional investigations into the executive branch, the Federal Bureau of Investigation (FBI) began an undercover investigation known as Abscam. The code name resulted from a combination of a fictitious entity, Abdul Enterprises, and the word *scam*. The FBI created Abdul Enterprises as a means to test whether certain public officials would accept bribes.

To conduct their operation, the FBI employed several agents to pose as wealthy Arab sheiks who wanted to immigrate to the United States and invest in real estate and business ventures. As part of their operation, the FBI hoped to obtain government contracts, meeting with various government officials ranging from senators to local city councilmen. At these meetings, the undercover agents proposed their plan and provided suitcases filled with cash. Several officials took the money immediately; others did not. Those who did not immediately accept the money became subject to other inducements, which included cruises on the Potomac River and invitations to lavish parties. Eventually, the undercover operation led to 25 indictments in three federal judicial districts.

All of the charged defendants employed an entrapment defense to some degree. Most argued from an objective standard, claiming that the government's conduct was so outrageous, the defendants should be acquitted. They argued that the government lacked any suspicion to believe that any of the individual defendants would accept a bribe, and that the inducements provided were excessive. A few defendants, generally those who had refused at first, defended themselves using the subjective test, claiming that they lacked any predisposition to commit the offense. Arguing similarly to those who used an objective measure, the defendants claimed that the inducements were excessive and that the repeated attempts to bribe the public officials demonstrated that the government created the crime rather than the defendant's predisposition to commit the offense. Before juries, neither defense had any success.

The judges who presided over the cases took varying views of the defenses. Some took the view that the government's conduct was justified by the great harm public corruption could cause, and that it was not the judiciary's role to second-guess how the executive conducted criminal investigations. These judges declined to consider the merits of the objective entrapment standard because Supreme Court precedent dictated the subjective approach.

Other judges did not comment on the advisability of the government's conduct. Instead, they focused on the subjective test, finding that the defendants lacked a predisposition to commit the offense. They also focused on the lavish inducements provided by the government and stated that those who initially refused—but later succumbed to the inducements—were entrapped. Judges who ruled in this manner found their decisions overturned on appeal when the appellate courts ruled that the jury findings of guilt were not unreasonable.

A third view adopted an objective standard. These judges decided that restraint in government investigatory tactics was necessary, and that the government should have some reasonable suspicion before approaching targets in an undercover investigation. They also stated that government agents should not be permitted to make repeated attempts to induce those who initially decline an offer. These judges also had their rulings reversed on appeal because they had applied the wrong test to determine entrapment.

The outcome of the Abscam cases led to much debate regarding the propriety of government undercover operations. Legal scholars and others proposed statutory definitions of entrapment to limit future Abscam-type investigations. Others proposed solutions merging the subjective and objective tests so that courts could examine both the person charged and the government's conduct. Another faction argued that limits needed to be placed on government undercover investigations through various statutory and administrative processes. Ultimately, no conclusions were reached. As a result, the debate over entrapment and undercover investigations continues.

Pro: Support of Government Undercover Investigations

While few would claim they are in favor of the government luring innocent people into committing criminal activity, people do advocate for minimal restrictions on government undercover investigations. Supporters of this view take the position that these investigations are necessary in order to protect society from certain crimes, and may be the only method available to law enforcement in such situations. Such investigations are also necessary to properly protect society against terrorism. Finally, proponents of the subjective test argue that if the concern is to ensure that only the guilty are convicted and not those who were merely lured into committing criminal conduct by the government, then the proper focus of the inquiry is the person charged and not the government conduct.

As one function of law enforcement is to apprehend criminals, some argue that law enforcement must take whatever steps are necessary, consistent with the Constitution, to apprehend criminals of all types. As the early entrapment cases illustrate, one way to catch criminals and secure a conviction is to observe their behavior. Different approaches exist to conduct this observation, some of which are more intrusive than others. The courts have taken the approach that, in most cases, the executive has the discretion to determine which methods are best suited for each type of crime.

Some types of crime require the use of undercover investigations through the use of law enforcement officers or the use of informants, such as in the case of Abscam. Generally, those who give bribes and those who receive them do not report their conduct to law enforcement because both are aware that their acts are illegal. Without any victims to come forward to testify, law enforcement must act in an undercover capacity to unearth the criminal activity. Sometimes the necessary undercover activity is simple to perform, such as an agent approaching a legislator and explicitly offering money in return for a favor. However, this type of approach is most likely be rejected, even by a corrupt legislator, because of its obvious nature. Instead, law enforcement agents must devise more elaborate schemes, such as

Abscam, to gain the target's trust. To guard against discovery by the target, law enforcement must have wide discretion when conducting these investigations.

Law enforcement also exists to protect society from dangerous activity. The current concern about terrorism provides an example. Following the September 11, 2001, attacks, the government tasked law enforcement with the mission of preventing future terrorist attacks. One means to this end is to prosecute those who commit precursor crimes to prepare for an act of violence. Another means is to infiltrate suspected terrorist organizations. This latter strategy requires undercover activity, usually in the form of confidential informants, which are part of the suspected terrorist organization. In some instances, law enforcement may provide these organizations with materials in order to gain evidence of the organization's intent to carry out terrorist acts. In cases such as these, those who are prosecuted can advance an entrapment defense. Those who advocate a strong preemptive response to terrorism argue that an entrapment defense that limits law enforcement's ability to conduct these types of operations will endanger national security.

Those who support the law enforcement goals of apprehension and protection likely advocate for the subjective approach to entrapment because it fulfills the stated purpose of the defense. Pointing to the Supreme Court's decisions in *Sorrells* and *Sherman*, advocates of the subjective test assert that the courts need only separate those who are unwary criminals from those who are unwary innocents in regard to the undercover operation. This requires an examination of the individual defendant, rather than law enforcement's actions. Unwary innocents in the context of a terrorism investigation might accept fake explosives, for example, but will not take any steps to use them. Conversely, unwary criminals would accept decoy explosives and begin carrying out a plot to deploy them. While the determination may be more difficult in other types of criminal investigations, the necessity of criminal apprehension and public safety justify the difficulty.

Con: Opposition of Broad Law Enforcement Discretion

Arguments against a great deal of law enforcement discretion and a focus on the individual defendant focus upon an analysis of the government's conduct in the undercover investigation in question. These arguments stem from the need to protect unwary innocents from criminal prosecution, limit law enforcement discretion, and ensure integrity in law enforcement. Those supporting the objective test argue that it better protects people from government sting operations because it is consistent with the presumption of innocence by requiring the government to justify its conduct and assume the suspect would not have committed the crime without the government's actions. Limits on discretion are also necessary, they argue, because as Abscam demonstrates, the government might take extraordinary means to apprehend those who are most susceptible to inducement. Finally, any undercover operation necessitates police deception. By permitting the police to lie, trust in law enforcement may diminish.

Failure of the Subjective Test for Government Conduct

According to those who favor a test focusing on government conduct, the subjective test for entrapment fails to accomplish its purpose. First, through its focus on a subject's propensity to commit the crime charged, the subjective test requires an analysis of something that does not exist. Turning to research on the causes of crime, advocates of this position argue that there is no such thing as the propensity to commit a crime, and that everyone will commit a criminal act when the inducement is sufficient. In making this argument, proponents point to self-defense where the law permits the use of force, something that would be unlawful otherwise. Self-defense exists because the inducement to use violence when attacked is overwhelmingly strong. Through this logic, the application of a similar inducement in a public corruption case should permit a similar defense. By limiting the types or amounts of inducement the government may employ, the legal rationale for defenses remains consistent.

Unjustifiable Governmental Tactics

Second, through its focus on the person charged rather than on government conduct, the subjective test permits the prosecution and conviction of those subject to extraordinary government inducements or unjustifiable governmental tactics. Abscam and terrorism cases provide examples for this argument. In the Abscam case, the government hosted lavish parties and provided a great deal of cash in order to induce legislators to assist the undercover agents to obtain government contracts. Some legislators took more inducing than others. The objective test creates a bright line for law enforcement. After a certain amount of inducement, the undercover operation must cease. In terrorism cases, the opportunity not only exists to create terrorists through inducement, but the investigations also run the risk of punishing protected speech. For example, a person who expresses dissatisfaction with the government may talk carelessly about blowing up a federal building. An undercover FBI agent might supply that person with a fake bomb in order to carry out the plot. Although the person may never take any other steps, other than taking the bomb, the person could face arrest and prosecution. By placing restrictions on law enforcement actions or by requiring evidence independent of the government's inducements, those who might otherwise never act are shielded from criminal liability.

A similar argument exists for repeated government solicitations to engage in criminal activity or when the government solicits a person to commit a crime that they otherwise would not have committed. Advocates point to the *Sherman* and *Jacobson* cases as examples of this activity. In both instances, the charged defendants initially refused the advances of the government or its informant. Instead, in order to secure the defendant's participation in the criminal activity, the agent or informant made several offers. Eventually, the person succumbed to the inducements and participated in the criminal activity. In both instances, the government presented no other evidence that the defendants participated in the illegal activity with any other people. While the subjective standard led to a reversal of the convictions, an objective test focusing on law enforcement would have spared the defendants a trial and permitted them to raise the defense as a matter of law for the judge, as opposed to a question of fact for the jury.

Those who advocate replacing the subjective test for entrapment also advocate limits on law enforcement discretionary decisions. By imposing statutory or constitutional constraints on the methods of criminal investigation, law enforcement is restrained from engaging in unacceptable undercover investigations. Such restraint is necessary because law enforcement cannot be entrusted to respect the rights of the subjects of their investigation. Instead, in an effort to demonstrate the effectiveness of such investigations, law enforcement lures people into committing criminal acts. By imposing some form of sanction, such as a bar to prosecution, the government will be discouraged from using questionable investigation techniques. While some argue that court-imposed sanctions gives the judiciary veto power over criminal investigation methods used by the executive, advocates of limiting police discretion point to Fourth Amendment law. When the government violates the Fourth Amendment, courts rectify the unconstitutional searches and seizures by excluding the evidence from trial. Those who advocate for the objective test for entrapment argue a similar rule would best protect unwary innocents from law enforcement.

The Ethics of Deception

Finally, the use of undercover investigations raises ethical questions. Any undercover operation necessitates false statements on the part of law enforcement. Undercover agents and informants must earn the trust of their targets, and must devise cover stories that survive scrutiny. This necessitates, at minimum, lying to the suspect and, in many cases, lying to innocent parties such as other government offices or private individuals. Resorting to these false statements undermines trust in society as a whole and in law enforcement specifically. It also creates a double standard, whereby the government approves of criminal conduct on behalf of law enforcement in order to apprehend others who violate the same criminal prohibition. While this may protect society from immediate criminal activity, in the long run, it undermines the public's confidence in their government.

Conclusion

The entrapment defense originated with the advent of professional law enforcement and evolved as law enforcement undercover operations became more sophisticated. Those who support the subjective approach point to the need for flexibility in government investigations so that criminals may be apprehended and society is protected from harm. Those who support the objective standard point to the fact that everyone is susceptible to criminal activity, and that the subjective test harms those with low tolerance for inducement. They also assert an objective test better protects society from questionable law enforcement tactics and from the distrust that results from the agents of the government lying to its citizens.

See Also: 1. Accountability; 8. Plain View Doctrine.

Further Readings

Allen, Ronald J., Melissa Luttrell, and Anne Kreeger. "Clarifying Entrapment." *Journal of Criminal Law and Criminology,* v.89 (1999).
Gershman, Bennett L. "Abscam, the Judiciary and the Ethics of Entrapment." *Yale Law Journal,* v.91 (1982).

Goldwasser, Katherine. "After Abscam: An Examination of Congressional Proposals to Limit Targeting Discretion in Federal Undercover Investigations." *Emory Law Journal*, v.36 (1987).

Grimm v. United States, 156 U.S. 604 (1895).

Hampton v. United States, 425 U.S. 484 (1976).

Jacobson v. United States, 503 U.S. 540 (1992).

Sherman, Jon. "A Person Otherwise Innocent: Policing Entrapment in Preventative, Undercover Counterterrorism Investigations." *University of Pennsylvania Journal of Constitutional Law*, v.11 (2009).

Sherman v. United States, 356 U.S. 369 (1958).

Sorrels v. United States, 287 U.S. 435 (1932).

United States v. Hollingsworth, 27 F.3d 1196 (7th Cir. 1994).

United States v. Russell, 411 U.S. 423 (1973).

5

Internal Review Practices

Jeffery Shantz
Kwantlen Polytechnic University

Juvenal posed the question during Roman times: "Who will watch the watchmen?" This has been a persistent question for civil society in regard to police, particularly as concerns of civil liberties and individual rights have grown in liberal democracies over the course of the 20th and 21st centuries. Police are central players within the administration of criminal justice and the primary point of interaction between the criminal justice system and the public. The issue of internal review, and public perceptions of the veracity of such review practices, is one that most impacts citizens and their understanding of police and issues of police legitimacy.

Police have access to a range of resources that can be used for addressing problems. Yet these resources are unique to the role and not shared with others in society—particularly the legitimized capacity to use force. Police have powers of enforcement that are not available to other citizens. These extraordinary powers are accompanied by a profound responsibility to engage them properly. Beyond this, the criminal justice system provides police greater access to practices of law enforcement in terms of what they can do, beyond their legal powers, and in terms of organizational access to other components of the system.

Attempts have typically been made to balance the unique powers of police with individual civil liberties and due process, both for officers and for citizens with whom they interact, and possibly conflict. Where complaints have been made against officers, efforts have focused on internal procedures, investigations, and hearings. Debates have tended to revolve around the most effective and appropriate means to facilitate and defend personal liberty while not unduly or overly restraining police through regulations. The police in many jurisdictions in North America are self-regulating, with internal oversights and discipline the only primary control. The involvement of external actors in internal review practices can spur police officer resistance, particularly from police associations or unions.

An effective system is necessary to deter and punish abuse or misconduct. The demands for accountability are among the most pressing for law enforcement agencies. Currently, most academic researchers and commentators have argued for the need to change police internal discipline systems that allow the police themselves to be judge and jury in their own cause for cases in which a citizen files a complaint against an officer. These published voices include former police officers, such as Alan Grant (1992), Juan Antonio Juarez (2004), and Norm Stamper (2006). Kelly suggests that ineffective or inadequate responses can have negative impacts on community-police relations that can last a generation or more, so the stakes are high.

Overview of Police Internal Review Practices

Police have experienced substantial increases in their powers, reach, and resources since even the middle of the 20th century. In the early days of modern policing in the 19th century, police forces were loosely organized and numerically small with limited powers and resources. Their limited powers were further discouraged from expansion through restricted budgets. This was partly a reflection of suspicion of newly emergent police forces and their potential as powerholders. At the same time, citizenship rights were also circumscribed.

Under such circumstances, a regular, independent oversight apparatus organized to receive and investigate complaints made by citizens against the police was not viewed as a necessity, much less a priority, at least as far as governments and police themselves were concerned. The limited granting of powers to police by government was believed to mitigate the need for a regulatory or oversight body. This is a system that, borrowing economic language, has been described as *laissez faire*.

By the 1970s, the legal restraints upon police and the mechanisms deployed for addressing complaints by citizens against police were little different than those devised in the 19th century. The emphasis remained on self-regulation and internal investigation. This, despite the rapid growth in numbers, technological advances, and proportion of government budgets devoted to policing. This also, in spite of the fact that police have taken up many of the civic functions and duties vacated by standing armies in countries such as Canada.

In the United States, the internal affairs division of law enforcement agencies typically investigates complaints or accusations of wrongdoing or misconduct involving police officers or other members of the force. In other jurisdictions, such functions may be carried out by a Special Investigations Unit (Ontario) or Office of Police Integrity (Australia).

The internal disciplinary rules of the force remain primary controls for the actions of police officers. Sanction against police does not typically involve criminal prosecution or lawsuit, but disciplinary hearings and the penalties that arise from those hearings, which often include counseling or ameliorative, rather than punitive, measures. Different procedures are used when police investigate police compared to investigations of non-police. The investigator often plays the central role and possesses a great deal of (perhaps inappropriate) discretion with regard to the file. Officers suggest that internal review by officers allows for restorative approaches that focus on learning and reorientation of behavior within the department, thus contributing to a successful amelioration of behavior as opposed to an imposed or punitive system of punishment from outside.

Research suggests that the substantiated complaint rates in internal reviews are very low—often below 10 percent. Furthermore, a very low percentage of substantiated complaints that result in investigations involve formal disciplinary procedures, including charges and/or trials. Where a complaint is initiated by a police officer against another officer, the laying of charges and resulting disciplinary hearing occur with greater frequency.

Public Complaints and Access

In some jurisdictions, there is no requirement for public complaints to even be recorded, let alone investigated. For most of their histories, the Metropolitan Toronto Police, Ontario Provincial Police, and Royal Canadian Mounted Police (RCMP) did not make available information about the number or nature of complaints against their officers. Neither did they provide information about the response to complaints. Reformers note the importance of outside oversight in the recording of complaints and decisions about investigations. Public complaints should not only be recorded by the police, but also by an independent organization, which would then decide whether or not an investigation should be launched.

Police agencies have long denied public access to records regarding internal affairs investigations, typically citing concerns of privacy. This has made it difficult for members of the public to assess the fairness or credibility of the process. A recent case in Springfield, Illinois, could have an impact on longstanding practices of secrecy in internal police investigations. In July 2009, the Fourth District Court of Appeals ruled that internal affairs files are of public record, regardless of the outcome of the probe. The decision could have implications for how longstanding complaints over police brutality in Chicago are addressed. In Chicago, the police superintendent has long refused to provide to citizens or journalists a list of officers accused of excessive force. The initial complaint involved a dentist who accused a sheriff's deputy of physical abuse during a traffic stop. The sheriff's Division of Professional Standards ruled the complaint unfounded, prompting the complainant to request to see the records of the internal investigations. That request was denied, leading to the court challenge. The judges' unanimous decision noted that complainants have a right to know if their claims, identified as unfounded, really are unfounded. The new ruling could make all files public, in which internal investigations clear officers of wrongdoing.

In the United States, numerous police agencies have been brought under civilian review of complaints, largely as a result of community concerns that internal reviews are protective of police officers or biased against complainants. In San Francisco, an Office of Citizen Complaints was formed by voter initiative in 1983. Complaints are investigated by civilians who have never been members of the department.

Maintaining Legitimacy

The independence and integrity of investigations are essential in establishing the legitimacy of the process. Critics maintain that investigators must be insulated from institutional or peer group pressures to favor the party under investigation. This is particularly relevant given the awareness of police subcultures and tendencies for officers to cover for each other. Critics suggest that investigations can be thwarted by the so-called "blue wall of silence." All of these are believed to work against internal investigations of police departments by police themselves.

There is a public misperception that police departments have dedicated teams whose work consists of policing the police, a situation that holds only for some larger departments. Most departments in the United States are rather small, however. As Kelly notes, about 87 percent of police departments in the United States are composed of fewer than 25 sworn officers.

In many U.S. departments, officers involved in internal affairs report directly to the chief or a board of civilian commissioners. Agencies do not necessarily have an officer or officers dedicated solely to carrying out internal affairs matters. In some smaller departments, such arrangements may not be appropriate, given the closeness of officers to one another. In many agencies, particularly those that are smaller, responsibility may rest with an uninvolved superior officer reporting to the chief. A range of issues, including personal bias, friendships, grudges, or animosity may impact the judgment of even the most disciplined and well-meaning investigator. In most small agencies, the task falls to an uninvolved superior officer or detective who, ultimately, reports to the chief. Larger agencies may have a separate unit or institution to deal with such issues.

In the United States, departments that are accredited through the Commission on Accreditation for Law Enforcement Agencies (CALEA) develop certain practices relating to internal affairs. These include the disciplinary system; the internal affairs function; the mission, ethics, and values of the department; and investigative processes of a complaint. In California, there is a Police Officers Bill of Rights.

Internal affairs investigations attempt to make a variety of determinations based on available evidence. Primarily, they try to determine if an officer has violated any laws or departmental policies. Often, they find that while an officer has acted within the constraints of policy, the policy itself may be in need of change. Typically, in cases that involve investigation of a violation of law, the investigator measures an officer's conduct against a clearly defined statute, judicial review, or ordinance. However, this may not be the case with departmental policy violations.

Commentators, both inside and outside police departments, suggest that the integrity of the agency and the process requires that all complaints be treated seriously and fully investigated. The acceptance of all complaints sends the message to the community that citizen views are important, and that the agency is responsive to constructive criticism and committed to quality service. It makes clear the dedication to ongoing review and improvement. Upon receipt of a complaint, the department should confirm receipt directly to the complainant, who should be notified that an investigator has been assigned. Likewise, once an agency receives a complaint, it should also ensure the integrity of the complaint by sending a letter of receipt to any identifiable complainant. Agencies should inform complainants that they have assigned an investigator and that complainants should contact this person if any member of the department has contacted them in an effort to get them to retract the complaint, or worse, if anyone has threatened them in any way. Complainants should be informed throughout the process about the investigation's progress. They should feel that their concerns were met and that officers were held properly accountable.

Once an agency receives a complaint, it must decide the nature of the alleged violation. Does it constitute a crime or a policy infraction? Where a complaint involves a serious breach of conduct, such as excessive force, an alleged crime, discrimination, or a gross ethics violation, a command-level officer with proper training to conduct such a sensitive investigation should be responsible for the investigation. In departments of all sizes, the emotional or psychological toll of a serious and difficult investigation can be immense. Especially in a small department, the closeness and familiarity of members may make investigation of a serious complaint extremely difficult or even impossible. In fact, it may not be possible to find an appropriate investigator within the department, so it may be necessary to turn an outside agency, such as a nearby department, the state police, or district attorney's office to carry out the inquiry. In all cases, investigators must have proper training and undertake appropriate investigative practices. They must also be given adequate time to carry out the investigation and build the case.

Four Possible Conclusions

As an investigation may show that some of the allegations within one complaint may have different conclusions, the investigator must render a finding for each individual allegation, not for the complaint as a whole. Kelly suggests that at the conclusion of an internal investigation, investigators will be left with one of four findings: not sustained, exonerated, unfounded, and sustained. Complaints are not sustained when there is insufficient evidence to prove or disprove the complaint. Exoneration results when an event in question has occurred, but the officer's actions are found to be justified, proper, and lawful. The complaint is unfounded when the charges are found to be false or do not involve the officer identified. A complaint is sustained when evidence is sufficient to conclude that the officer in question did commit an alleged act.

The process must include notification of the officer in question and the complainant with regard to the findings. Where a complaint against the officer is sustained, disciplinary action will result. Where a complaint is not sustained or unfounded, there should be no legal action taken against the complainant. It is understood that such action would send a questionable message to the public and serve to discourage future complaints or open interactions.

Police are entrusted with extraordinary powers. These include powers of detention, interrogation, and even the power to take a life. The institution of policing, particularly given its unique and powerful status, fundamentally relies on a positive and cooperative relationship with the public for its continuance and proper functioning. Reformers have long noted that the most effective means for maintaining a cooperative relationship with the public is through the establishment and maintenance of a system of review and discipline that is understood to be fair by both citizens and police. It is also true that the perceptions and standards of the given community may not coincide in important ways with those of the police.

Pro: Arguments in Favor of Internal Review Systems

Proponents of internal review systems have long argued that any procedure of external review and oversight over police practices, including dealing with complaints, will be opposed, perhaps strenuously, by police officers. They argue that internal reviews by officers are more likely to get beyond the "blue wall of silence."

Those who have opposed external review have included representatives of police associations or police unions, and chiefs of police alike. For police association representatives, the argument has been made that outsiders do not properly or adequately understand the unique issues, work conditions, and threats faced by police officers. Associations also raise concerns about possible violations of the individual rights of officers who may face investigation by hostile or critical bodies. There is also a concern that pressures for institutional reform will be carried out through the undue targeting of individual officers who may have acted according to existing policy. In the United States, there has been a history of Patrolman's Associations taking an activist role in seeking court injunctions to prevent the civilian review of internal police disciplinary procedures. For the unions, reviews are matters of workplace rights and working conditions, and should take place within the context of collective agreements and collectively bargained practices. On the other side, chiefs of police have expressed concerns about the weakening of their own capacities to discipline their own members.

Concerns have also been raised about issues of defensiveness, openness, and engagement when officers are confronted with external reviewers. Proponents argue that information-gathering and honest discussion about departmental practices, discussions that might lead to reform, are more likely to be facilitated within the context of internal rather than external reviews. The negative impacts of police perception of intrusion by outside actors on internal reviews is evidenced in a recent case in New Mexico. On November 8, 2010, members of the Santa Fe police officers union voted no confidence in the city manager and a deputy city attorney. Citing complaints about favoritism at City Hall, and perceived interference with the department's internal affairs procedures, officers voted 90 to four in support of a no-confidence motion.

Proponents of internal review by police also argue that such procedures allow for more restorative or ameliorative approaches to dealing with problems than do external reviews that might emphasize punishment. Restorative approaches are more suited to problem-solving, training, counseling, and measures that facilitate reform in less disruptive ways.

Proponents argue that an effective internal review process can improve policing. It can alert executives to pressing or emerging problems that can allow for changes to be made before problems become serious or more serious. It can also help to improve practices and establish better procedures, all of which might help to prevent future crises while restoring the public's confidence.

Disciplinary systems must be enacted in a way that is perceived to be fair and equitable for all involved. Kelly suggests that regular evaluations with effective feedback can contribute to a sense of fairness as departmental expectations are regularly reinforced rather than drawn out in an ad-hoc fashion after the fact.

Con: Arguments Against Internal Review Systems

Even officers who are involved in conducting internal review systems have raised concerns about internal versus external processes. On the one hand, there is a substantial amount of labor and time invested in carrying out an investigation of another officer. Interviews, the gathering of information, assessments, hearings, the deliberations on findings, and report writing all draw a heavy burden on labor and organizational resources, including often intense face-to-face practices. This is time taken away from other important work that needs to be done by those officers.

In addition, there is the potentially tricky situation of colleagues investigating colleagues. Investigating officers cannot forget that the person they are investigating is also an officer. Numerous studies suggest this is a tense and unsettling process for those involved; one that can potentially strain or damage relations in the future. Even more, investigating other officers has not provided the foundation for building a career. Clearly, evidence supports the notion that complaints against an officer are not investigated in the same manner as investigations of general citizens. Much evidence suggests that internal review systems are too lenient or sympathetic in dealing with police officers against whom complaints have been leveled.

Critics make the expected claim that internal investigations are subject to the potential for leaks that alert the subject of an investigation to information that could allow for obfuscation or the improper sharing of information with the accused. Even the possibility of an officer being made aware of the nature of an investigation before it begins can be problematic. Lower-level problems can be protected or obscured by group practices, or as part of police subcultural activities or the phenomenon of covering for each other.

Much research shows that public suspicions of internal reviews are well founded, even in more dramatic cases. Records show that in-house investigations in which officers of the same force investigate a colleague often produce minimal outcomes. This reinforces public perceptions of inappropriateness, veracity, or "cover up." To back this up, few complaints made by citizens against police result in a formal disciplinary trial involving the officer, as uncovered in research by Alan Grant in 1992 and the Human Rights Watch in 1998. Many studies, including those by John Lambert (1986), Alan Grant (1992), Maurice Punch (2009), and Sankar Sen (2010) suggest that most complaints are decided to be unsubstantiated or unfounded. Those that are agreed to be substantiated in some way are typically addressed through internal mechanisms, including counseling or verbal reprobation rather than penalty. This includes cases involving complaints of violence, neglect of duty, or improper conduct. Few of the cases in which an investigation occurs and shows wrongdoing result in interdisciplinary hearings. Internal reviews can make it difficult for the public or researchers to uncover or determine how many substantiated complaints are subject to an internal disciplinary hearing or trial involving the officer or officers in question.

Typically, internal reviews have been more effective even when another force is brought in to carry out the investigation. In the absence of truly independent investigative bodies, some jurisdictions, such as British Columbia, attempt to achieve a level of separation by having outside police forces involved in carrying out investigations by another force. In British Columbia, complaints against Vancouver police are carried out by officers from the nearby Delta, British Columbia police, for example. Even here, public perceptions of partiality or sympathy can be strong.

Conclusion

Most efforts at reform conclude with the need for independent processes and procedures for addressing complaints against police by members of the public in a way that facilitates the transparency and perceived legitimacy of the process. In light of this, most reformers call for the establishment of some office outside of, and independent from, the police institutions themselves. For critics, these structures should be autonomous at all levels, from receipt of complaint, through oversight of investigations to the rendering of decisions, and the recommendations for action. Emphasis for reform is typically placed on addressing structural or causal factors rather than administering blame in a post-hoc manner. External procedures will rely on multiple players within a systemic structure and limit the discretionary means available for each person occupying a role in the structure.

The perils of leaving review to internal procedures alone can involve dramatic declines in public perceptions of police legitimacy and accountability. In some contexts, this has threatened the existence of policing institutions themselves. In British Columbia, Canada, during the first decade of the 21st century, provincial governments have faced growing calls for the cancellation of contracts with the Royal Canadian Mounted Police (RCMP), who are contracted as the provincial police force. These calls, echoed by notable criminologists such as Robert Gordon, have come following a series of suspicious in-custody deaths that have only been handled through internal review procedures, as is standard practice for the RCMP. In British Columbia, there are no citizen oversight bodies for review of any police forces, provincial or municipal. The result is a persistent climate of suspicion, mistrust, and delegitimization of police, particularly the RCMP.

In some jurisdictions, citizens sense that internal procedures will not result in, or are unlikely to result in, a proper investigation, let alone a trial, hearing, or disciplinary action. Therefore, citizens have begun avoiding the police review mechanisms entirely. Instead, citizens are taking their cases to trial in courts, often small-claims courts. In Toronto, for example, activists have taken to filing suit against officers and departments in small claims court, based on their perceptions of police misconduct in the policing of protests or improper arrest and charging of political organizers. In recent years, many of these suits have been highly successful, resulting in awards of thousands of dollars against police and departments found to have breached the rights of citizens.

In Toronto, as much as 25 percent of complaints against police involving violence are made directly to the courts rather than to the police themselves. This number may even be low, given evidence of reluctance on the part of judges to issue summonses against prospective defendants: police officers who are carrying out their police duties.

The conclusion drawn from all of this is that the responsibility for dealing with complaints against the police should reside in an organization that is independent from the institutional structure of the police. The rather large proportion of people who might be unwilling to take a complaint to the police, particularly where they have already experienced violence, may be willing to complain to an oversight body that is clearly independent of the police. For reformers, removing investigative functions from police departments is a necessary first step in developing processes that can be viewed as legitimate by the public. The credibility of investigations is a part of facilitating and maintaining positive relations between the community and police. Effective internal review procedures can also free up resources for other policing priorities while also helping to avoid potentially costly litigation. Agencies can find themselves defending their actions in a civil proceeding deriving from an internal affairs investigation that has not been accepted, in practice or in finding.

Another larger issue of concern to critics is that available review mechanisms have typically focused on complaints toward individual officers and dissatisfaction with specific practices, as in cases of abuse, corruption, or the use of force. Citizens have not had mechanisms available to review and lodge complaints about policies and institutional priorities or the overall operations and structures of the police as an institution.

See Also: 1. Accountability; 9. Police Brutality; 10. Police Corruption and Code of Silence; 11. Police Privatization; 14. Riot and Demonstration Responses.

Further Readings

Archbold, Carole A. *Police Accountability, Risk Management, and Legal Advising.* El Paso: LFB Scholarly, 2004.

Colaptete, Frank A. *Internal Investigations: A Practitioner's Approach.* Springfield, IL: Charles C Thomas, 2007.

Collins, Allyson. *Shielded From Justice: Police Brutality and Accountability in the United States.* New York: Human Rights Watch, 1998.

Grant, Alan. "The Control of Police Behaviour." In *Understanding Policing,* edited by Kevin R. E. McCormick and Livy A. Visano. Toronto: Canadian Scholars' Press, 1992.

Juarez, Juan Antonio. *Brotherhood of Corruption: A Cop Breaks the Silence on Police Abuse, Brutality, and Racial Profiling.* Chicago: Chicago Review Press, 2004.

Kelly, Sean F. "Internal Affairs: Issues for Small Police Departments." *FBI Law Enforcement Bulletin,* v.1/6 (2003).

Lambert, John L. *Police Powers and Accountability.* London: Routledge, 1986.

Larson, Richard C. *Police Accountability: Performance Measures and Unionism.* Lanham, MD: Lexington, 1978.

More, Harry W., and Peter Charles Unsinger. *Managerial Control of the Police: Internal Affairs and Audits.* Springfield, IL: Charles C Thomas, 1992.

Nelson, Jill. *Police Brutality: An Anthology.* New York: W.W. Norton, 2001.

Noble, Jeffrey J., and Geoffrey P. Alpert. *Managing Accountability Systems for Police Conduct: Internal Affairs and External Oversights.* Long Grove, IL: Waveland Press, 2008.

O'Hara, Patrick. *Why Law Enforcement Organizations Fail: Mapping the Organizational Faultlines in Policing.* Durham, NC: Carolina Academic Press, 2005.

Oliver, Ian. *Police, Government and Accountability.* London: Macmillan, 1997.

Prenzler, Tim. *Police Corruption: Preventing Misconduct and Maintaining Integrity.* London: CRC Press, 2009.

Punch, Maurice. *Police Corruption: Deviance, Accountability and Reform in Policing.* London: Willan, 2009.

Quinn, Michael W. *Walking With the Devil: The Police Code of Silence.* Minneapolis: Quinn and Associates, 2004.

Reiner, Robert. *The Politics of Policing.* Brighton, UK: Wheatsheaf Books, 1985.

Sen, Sankar. *Enforcing Police Accountability Through Civilian Oversight.* Thousand Oaks, CA: Sage, 2010.

Shearing, Clifford D., and Jeffrey S. Leon. "Reconsidering the Police Role: A Challenge to a Challenge of a Popular Conception." In *Understanding Policing*, edited by Kevin R. E. McCormick and Livy A. Visano. Toronto: Canadian Scholars' Press, 1992.

Simey, Margaret. *Democracy Rediscovered: A Study in Police Accountability*. London: Pluto, 1988.

Skolnick, Jerome H., and James J. Fyfe. *Above the Law: Police and the Excessive Use of Force*. Glencoe, IL: Free Press, 1994.

Stamper, Norm. *Breaking Rank: A Top Cop's Expose of the Dark Side of American Policing*. New York: Nation Books, 2006.

Walker, Samuel. *The New World of Police Accountability*. Thousand Oaks, CA: Sage, 2005.

Walker, Samuel. *Police Accountability: The Role of Citizen Oversight*. East Windsor, CT: Wadsworth, 2000.

Williams, Kristian. *Our Enemies in Blue: Police and Power in America*. Boston: South End Press, 2007.

6

Interrogation Practices

Jeffery Shantz
Kwantlen Polytechnic University

Interrogation is perhaps the most controversial area of policing practice. It is also one of the areas around which public perceptions of police procedures have been shaped most dramatically by media representations, particularly dramatic fictional accounts. Generations of television viewers and moviegoers have been presented with highly stylized and often tense portrayals of interrogations. In such renderings, interrogations usually involve high-pressure tactics, shouting, threats, and even acts of violence. Even more, suspects are typically portrayed as cunning, evilly manipulative, and shrewdly deceptive. Suspects range between being manic and cold, calculated killers. No one can forget portrayals such as those in *L.A. Confidential, Basic Instinct, The Dark Knight,* or *The Usual Suspects.* Interrogation, and both fictional and factual representations of it, have a potent place in the cultures of liberal democracies. Interrogation is portrayed, discussed, and debated on a daily basis in public and media venues. Confessional speech has become a regular form of public and popular discourse in countries like the United States.

Yet, real world interrogations tend to be much more subtle in most cases. Even high-risk cases such as those involving murder will engage a variety of interrogation practices, often calm and controlled rather than angry and heated. At the same time, regardless of specific methods deployed, interrogation by police is an issue of contention. The very fact of an officer being alone with a suspect while trying to gather evidence or a confession is a subject of intense scrutiny and questioning. Issues of coercion, respect of interviewee's rights, due process, and legitimacy of information gained is front and center.

Critics and civil libertarians go further, questioning whether or not a police interrogation can ever be a fair, just, or even a legitimate process. For critics, a process developed and deployed to manipulate a respondent to provide information desired by police (though not the interviewee) will always be coercive in character. Interrogation attempts or makes use of psychological techniques to influence someone without their consent. For some, this is simply unethical and unjustifiable.

Overview

Critics and civil rights advocates have long worked to make courts aware of the illegitimacy and inaccuracy of involuntary confessions. As a result of ongoing research, and a history of U.S. Supreme Court challenges, procedures and practices have been established to prevent illegitimate confessions and to protect the civil rights of suspects and defendants.

Contrary to popular belief, confessions secured by torture were long permitted as evidence in trials, even in liberal democracies. In English common-law trials, confessions obtained through torture were admitted to trial up to the middle of the 18th century. Through the end of the 18th century in the United States, there was no rule excluding coerced confessions as evidence at trials.

Early Judicial Decisions

As questions about the reliability of confessions, given their importance in determining the outcome of a court case, became more pressing, judges came to examine the circumstances involved in securing confessions, particularly the use of threats or rewards during interrogations. The earliest U.S. Supreme Court case to address the character of confessions was *Hopt v. Utah* in 1884. That case examined whether a suspect had made a confession voluntarily or as a result of threat or promise, and confirmed the requirement of voluntariness.

The most significant early case dealing with interrogation in the context of the Constitution was *Bram v. United States* in 1897. In the 1897 decision, the Court applied the Fifth Amendment protection against self-incrimination within the context of confessions introduced in federal courts. The ruling affirmed that any application of influence used to gain a confession would render the confession inadmissible on the basis of being involuntary.

Prior to the Court's decision in *Bram*, even confessions secured through torture were deemed admissible. Even with this ruling, the prohibition against coerced confessions was not uniformly enforced. Until the middle of the 20th century, physical force was a regular feature of police interrogations, even in liberal democracies such as the United States and Canada. This was the infamous "third degree" that has a lasting place in the popular imagination.

In 1937, a Supreme Court decision in the case *Brown v. Mississippi* ruled that confessions secured through force were not acceptable as evidence at trial. This case involved three suspects who confessed to a crime after being repeatedly hung from a tree and whipped by police officers.

It was only with the decision of *Malloy v. Hogan* in 1964 that the Court concluded that the Fifth Amendment privilege against self-incrimination maintained in *Bram* applied to state cases as well as those of federal courts. Only then were the standards applied to confessions in federal courts, and the rights of suspects extended to state courts and suspects in state cases.

Another 1964 Supreme Court decision, *Massiah v. United States,* found that the Sixth Amendment provides defendants the right to counsel in post-indictment interrogations, and where a defendant's rights are violated, confessions are inadmissible. Again in 1964, the Court's ruling in *Escobedo v. Illinois* further extended Sixth Amendment protections to pre-indictment confessions. Following this decision, right to counsel holds as soon as a police investigation takes an accusatory character.

The Changing Meaning of Voluntary Confession

Over time, the definition of voluntary confession changed, becoming more circumscribed. Confessions came to be viewed as involuntary not only if they had been secured through the use of physical force or violence. Sleep or food deprivation, unduly lengthy detention, as well as denial of bathroom access came to be viewed as conditions rendering a confession involuntary or coerced. Threats of violence or the promise of rewards for confession also came to be viewed as illegitimate practices.

A key moment in the history of police interrogations occurred with the Supreme Court decision regarding *Miranda v. Arizona* in 1966. This landmark case centered on Ernesto Miranda's confession to rape and kidnapping following two hours of interrogation. In the appeal to the Court, it was argued that Miranda was unaware of his constitutional right under the Fifth Amendment to remain silent, or of his right under the Sixth Amendment to legal counsel. The Court ruled in favor of Miranda in a decision that famously implemented Miranda rights (reading of rights), in which police are required to fully and clearly notify a suspect of their right to counsel and silence before any attempt can be made to interrogate. The Miranda rights stand as a protection against the possibility that a suspect will give an involuntary confession simply due to ignorance of their rights or the belief that they must communicate with officers and answer any question addressed to them. In the United States, a suspect can immediately end an interrogation at any point simply by invoking his or her right to silence or asking for legal counsel. Interrogators will try to prevent this from happening early on by interrupting or halting attempts by the suspect to speak.

The Christian Burial Case

Another key moment in addressing the legitimacy of interrogations appears in the Christian Burial Case, decided in 1977. The case arose from the murder in Iowa of a 10-year-old girl in 1968. The suspect, Robert Anthony Williams, a man with strong religious beliefs who was known to suffer from mental illness, was interrogated by police during a lengthy ride in which all were confined within an automobile. An officer, detective Learning, appealed to Williams's religious views, asking him to take them to the body so that the girl's family could give her a proper Christian burial. At no time did Williams waive his rights to counsel or silence. In fact, he had insisted that he did not wish to be interrogated, and the officers agreed not to question him during the ride. Williams was convicted of murder, and his case went through several appeals, all the way up to the Supreme Court. In the 1977 *Brewer v. Williams* decision, the Court concluded that his constitutional rights had been violated.

In a 1991 decision in *Arizona v. Fulminante*, the Supreme Court found that despite Miranda rights, coerced confessions could be used in court if they were deemed harmless. Thus, coerced confessions could be used where it was reasonably believed that the jury would convict even in the absence of a confession. For some critics, this calls into question the capacity of Miranda rights to protect suspects from coercion while in police custody. In 2000, the Supreme Court decision regarding *Dickerson v. United States* strenuously upheld the Miranda decision of 1966. Yet, the Court's decision in *Chavez v. Martinez* (2003) ruled that testimony could be coerced through interrogation in cases where the information gathered is not used against the suspect in their own criminal prosecutions.

Police Interrogation Tactics

As a result of citizen initiatives, including movements for civil rights and civil liberties and against police brutality, as well as judicial oversight and decisions such as *Miranda*, the application of physical force as a part of interrogation techniques has been greatly restricted. Instead, police interrogators have come to rely on a variety of psychological strategies and techniques. Police typically use a range of deceptive and manipulative practices to secure confessions. Notably, these techniques are not viewed as coercive, thus, the confessions they produce are generally allowed as evidence in court.

Police interrogators work to bring a suspect to the point that they come to believe that there is no further sense in denying their involvement in a criminal act, or they find it more agreeable to acknowledge their actions than to continue denials. Often, interrogators will pose questions that present alternatives such as asking if the act was planned in advance or if it was an immediate act. They may claim to know that the suspect was at a victim's home and ask why they were there, or whether they went there with the intention to do harm or not.

There are no legal restrictions on police interrogators to prohibit the use of lies, deceit, or the presentation of untrue information or fake evidence during an interrogation. Typically, suspects will be led to believe that there is more evidence against them than there actually is. Suspects will often be told that a witness has come forward who can identify them, or that there is a piece of physical evidence that links them to the crime. More recently, it has become common for interrogators to suggest that DNA tests are underway, which will surely connect the suspect to the crime. These statements are then followed up with the suggestion that the suspect might as well come forward with a confession. In some cases, polygraph tests are used, and the suspect is informed that they have failed, even where they have actually passed the test. In a recent high-profile interrogation in Ontario, Canada, that successfully secured a confession to two sexual assaults and murders from a colonel in the Canadian Armed Forces, the interrogator showed the suspect tire tracks in snow and led the suspect to believe that this evidence was as reliable as fingerprints. Yet unlike fingerprints, tires are not unique, and do not confirm that the suspect was at the wheel of the vehicle.

Interrogators will often play upon a suspect's value systems or concerns for family or friends. In some cases, as in the Christian Burial Case, religious perspectives can be invoked when interrogators suggest that the suspect's religion calls for a confession that would allow forgiveness. In other cases, suspects are told that a confession will make things easier on their spouse, children, family, or friends, sparing them from a lengthy investigation, including interviews and a search of homes or belongings, and avoiding a difficult trial process.

In most cases, the suspect is told that their treatment by prosecutors and the courts will be less punitive if they confess. This is a deception. It is almost certain that a prosecutor will be more punitive, and less willing to plea bargain, where there is no confession, and the case is therefore weakened. Furthermore, even if this were not the case, the police cannot make such promises. Deals worked out in an interrogation room have no bearing on prosecution or the decisions of the court.

Some suspects choose to speak with police in the mistaken belief or hope that they can convince their interrogator of their innocence. This can also contribute to a successful interrogation for police if the suspect inadvertently provides information useful to the police in carrying out their investigation.

Interrogation Environment

Among the most potent practices in interrogation is the simple act of isolating a suspect from outside contact with people other than police officers. The physical environment in which interrogations occur plays a key part. Typically, interrogations take place in small, windowless rooms designed to heighten the sense of isolation and separation. After even limited time in such spaces, the appearance of a police officer can be treated favorably by suspects otherwise deprived of human contact. Isolation effectively produces sensations of fear, insecurity, and anxiety in suspects.

Even the physical arrangement of the interrogation room is designed to contribute to successfully securing a confession. The structure of the room is organized to magnify or reinforce the power of the interrogator and the vulnerability of the suspect. Seating is arranged to disempower the suspect, with the interrogator sitting alongside or diagonally in relation to the suspect, rather than directly across from him or her. Suspects will typically be seated in an uncomfortable chair. Interrogators will strategically violate personal space, without making contact with a suspect. Control of lighting, refreshment, or bathroom visits also serve to heighten the sense of disempowerment and dependence. This serves to heighten the suspect's sense of anxiety and insecurity.

Interrogation Programs and Published Techniques

The influential manual *Criminal Interrogation and Confessions* suggests that interrogations take place in a small, soundproof room outfitted with nothing more than chairs for two detectives and the suspect and a desk. There should be nothing on the walls, and suspects should be seated so that they have no control over room lighting or temperature.

Many law enforcement agencies practice the Reid Technique for questioning suspects. The Reid Technique refers to a nine-step program for interviewing and interrogating people using a variety of behavioral guides and nonaggressive questions designed to identify nonverbal signs of guilt and draw out confessions through specific questioning practices. The Reid Technique is a trademarked practice of the firm John E. Reid and Associates, a company that offers training in the method.

The Reid Technique consists of three main aspects: factual analysis, interviewing, and interrogation. If the investigative interviewing gives interrogators reason to believe that the suspect committed the crime being investigated, they will pursue more pressing interrogation deploying the program's nine steps of interrogation. Prior to the formal nine-step interrogation, police conduct a preliminary interview to try to get a sense of the suspect's guilt or innocence. This process is largely about developing rapport with the suspect on the recognition, through behavioral analysis, that people are more likely to trust or feel comfortable conversing with others whom they perceive to be like them or to be sympathetic. Behavioral analysis also suggests that once suspects begin talking, it becomes more difficult to stop talking; and further, once honest conversation has been undertaken—even around trivial issues—it becomes more difficult for suspects to become deceptive or to lie. During this interview, police pay attention to verbal and nonverbal cues that suggest heightened stress levels in the suspect. This can include sweating, fidgeting, eye movements, and so on. If reactions generally suggest deception, the officer will move to more pressing interrogation.

The first step in the nine-step process of the Reid Technique begins with direct confrontation. In this step, the suspect is presented with the evidence against them. This may be real or fabricated. The suspect is led to believe that the conclusion of guilt from the evidence is unavoidable. There will be a first attempt to provide the suspect a chance to explain or justify their actions. The second step is theme development, in which the officer tries to offer the suspect themes that they might use to excuse or justify the crime. It might be suggested that a victim was at fault. Perhaps the suspect was experiencing undue stress at work or was feeling external pressure from someone else. If one theme is not picked up, the interrogator will shift themes, offering other alternatives.

Step three involves halting denials. The more often a suspect is allowed to deny responsibility and affirm their innocence, the more confident they become, and the less likelihood there is of a confession of guilt. Step four involves using subject objection to draw out a confession. If a suspect provides explanations about why they could not have committed the crime (personal history or values, for example), the interrogator may use this to suggest a theme that is more agreeable to the suspect or to draw out information about the case (suggesting it was a crime of passion or unplanned, for example).

The fifth step uses signs of officer sincerity or compassion, such as expressions of concern or a gentle touch to reinforce camaraderie or sympathy with the suspect. During step six, the officer looks for signs of defeat in the suspect and moves from theme presentation to the offering of alternatives by which the suspect might choose to explain why they committed the crime. The suspect crying at this point should be taken as a show of guilt. Step seven involves the presentation of alternatives, typically providing a more and a less socially acceptable alternative. Regardless of which choice is taken, the result is a confession. In step eight, witnesses are brought in to repeat their confession. Further information is gathered in support of the admission of guilt. The final, ninth step concludes with documentation, written or video, of the confession in a prepared statement. The suspect confirms that the confession was not coerced and is in fact voluntary.

Critics suggest that the Reid Technique is susceptible to false confessions from innocent suspects. There has been some concern about its use on children, and the dangers of false confessions in those cases. In some jurisdictions, including the United Kingdom, the technique is not permissible for use on youth.

Pro: Benefits of Securing a Confession

For defenders of interrogation practices, the simple fact is that nothing can contribute more forcefully to ensuring a case is taken to trial and a conviction will be secured than a confession, which also can determine a prosecutor's decision to try a case or conversely opt for a plea bargain. Much evidence suggests that a defendant has little chance of securing an acquittal where there is a confession admitted as evidence.

Some proponents argue that the key issue is obtaining reliable evidence and advancing fact finding. Where interrogation is able to do this, it is effective and should be supported.

In the years following the enactment of the *Miranda* decision, U.S. law enforcement agencies lobbied Congress to repeal the Miranda rights. Some commentators have opposed Miranda as a restriction on law enforcement and, in their view, an unreasonable constraint on policing. They have vocally opposed the upholding of Miranda in the 2000 case, and argue for the use of more forceful and aggressive interrogation practices.

Other proponents of contemporary interrogation practices hold that Miranda rights suitably ensure that the civil rights of suspects are protected, since they do not have to make comments at all during interrogation and can at any moment end the interrogation simply by requesting a lawyer. At the same time, despite some early resistance, police have come to recognize that the provision of a framework for acceptable interrogation and the recognized baseline of suspects' rights is helpful for police in carrying out their work, and offers some protection against public complaints of abuse or misconduct while reducing the likelihood of costly litigation by suspects against police.

Con: Drawbacks of Securing a Confession

Critics note that interrogation as a process presumes guilt rather than innocence; that is, it is guilt-presumptive. It begins from an assumption of guilt and proceeds in an effort to compel, in one way or another, a respondent to reveal hidden information or to confess.

Critics note the tendency toward latent coercion within interrogations. Latent coercion refers to the fact that during interrogation, officers may imply threat for noncompliance or reward for compliant behavior simply through tone, body language, or facial expression. Even more, of course, there can be suggestions or the implication that delivery of a desired response may assist the suspect in court or in sentencing. Often, there is a sense provided by an officer to a suspect that confession will contribute to a more positive result before the courts than would a conviction without a confession. Critics note that often, the characteristics assumed to suggest guilt, such as sweat, shifting bodily position, or fidgeting, are simply manifestations of nervousness or a loss of control in situations where interviewees are lacking power.

A range of human rights concerns have been raised over interrogation practices, including less forceful or invasive practices. It has been noted that police interrogation practices, particularly the "scientific" or psychological procedures are, in important ways, similar to so-called brainwashing practices. Techniques such as the invasion of personal space, presentation of confessions as a means of escape, control of respondent's capacity to speak, and use of dire alternatives have all been cited as techniques used in brainwashing to elicit fear, confusion, and/or insecurity in respondents.

The inducement of stress, and distress, typically renders people in a condition in which capacities for critical and autonomous thought are weakened or even impaired. This makes people more susceptible to suggestive conditioning or leading by interrogators. The likelihood of impairment and suggestibility increases where the respondent is a minor or mentally challenged. In such cases, the interviewee may lack defensive mechanisms that could mitigate practices designed to induce stress.

Critics note that the impacts of interrogation can be unequally and negatively felt for members of criminalized groups, particularly racialized groups, as well as people lacking citizenship status, for whom lack of rights or threats of deportation can contribute to a sense of personal peril or endangerment beyond concerns over possible conviction for the specific crime in question.

Conclusion

A pressing danger in all cases is the very real threat of false confession. It has been suggested that there are as many as 300 false confessions extracted each year in the United States alone. Among the more impactful false confessions are those of Peter Reilly, Earl Washington Jr., and the Central Park Five. Peter Reilly, who was 18 at the time of his questioning, was subjected to eight hours of interrogation by Connecticut police in relation to the killing of his mother in 1973. Based on his confession, a jury convicted him of first-degree manslaughter, resulting in his serving three years in prison. It was only after new evidence emerged, linking someone else to the killing, that Reilly was released.

Earl Washington Jr. was convicted of rape and murder and served 18 years in prison, nine of them on death row, on the basis of his confession alone. Nine days before his scheduled execution, he was pardoned by the governor of Virginia after DNA evidence showed the perpetrator to be another man. Washington had an I.Q. of 69.

Perhaps the most famous recent case involves the Central Park Five. In 1989, five teenagers, ranging in age from 14 to 16, confessed, after 20 hours of interrogation, to attacking and raping a woman who had been jogging in New York's Central Park. In 2001, another man confessed to the crime, a claim that was supported by DNA evidence. The wrongly convicted teenagers had spent between six and 12 years in prison.

Critics suggest that practices like the Reid Technique place an inaccurate sheen of scientific method or reliability on what are fundamentally unscientific, even biased, practices designed not to pursue alternatives or discover truth, but to extract a confession. Once the primary determination becomes to extract a confession in each case, all other considerations can be downplayed or ignored.

U.S. Supreme Court Chief Justice William Rehnquist has noted that simply providing the Miranda warnings can protect a confession from charges that it was coerced or involuntary. In this way, the Miranda warnings can help to give a false impression of the character of interrogations and the confessions that they extract. Confessions may still be, and usually are, the result of sophisticated psychological procedures and a range of deceptive practices.

Comprehension of a Suspect's Rights

Critics argue that suspects often fail to understand the significance or meaning of the rights read to them, particularly where they are recited in a bureaucratic or rote manner that presents them as mere formality and little more. A lengthy record of research suggests that Miranda rights have had minimal impact on either the numbers of requests for counsel or the number of actual confessions by suspects held in police custody. Even more, there are concerns that police can fabricate waivers of Miranda rights. This is particularly troubling given that there is no requirement that waivers be recorded in any way or presented to a neutral third party.

Legal commentators have criticized *Miranda* and its subsequent line of decisions, stating that criminal suspects seldom truly understand the meaning or importance of the rights recited to them. Studies have indicated that the *Miranda* decision has had little effect on the numbers of confessions and requests for lawyers made by suspects in custody. What is more, critics of *Miranda* cite concerns that the police might fabricate waivers, as a suspect's waiver of Miranda rights need not be recorded or made to a neutral party.

In Canada, suspects do not have any right to have a lawyer present during police interrogations. Instead, there is a requirement, not present in the United States, that all interrogations be videotaped. In this way, it is believed that any misconduct or inappropriate practices may be captured and used as evidence if the case in question comes to trial. Suspects do maintain the right to maintain silence and refuse to answer questions during the interrogation. This has been a key point of criticism of policing in Canada. Civil libertarians view it as a basic violation of human and civil rights, noting that even in the absence of explicit wrongdoing or abuse, not having a lawyer present can leave people vulnerable to intimidation, manipulation, or pressures to answer or act in ways that they otherwise would not if they had a supporter or advisor. In 2010, a legal challenge to the denial of counsel presence was launched. The Supreme Court of Canada ruled that police interrogations were legally justifiable as practiced, rejecting the claim of complainants who argued that the absence of legal representation during interrogation was a violation of individual rights.

The issue of videotaping interrogations is one that has been at the forefront of some reform efforts in the United States, and calls for videotaping as a requirement for interrogations have grown in the 21st century. Proponents want video recordings to be mandatory for all stages of the interrogation from beginning to end. There have been cases in the United States in which the presence of video evidence of interrogations in pretrial hearings has led judges to find confessions to be involuntary and excluded from trial.

See Also: 2. Arrest Practices; 4. Entrapment; 7. Miranda Warnings.

Further Readings

Brooks, Peter. *Troubling Confessions: Speaking Guilt in Law and Literature*. Chicago: University of Chicago Press. 2001.

Bryan, Ian. *Interrogation and Confession: A Study of Progress, Process and Practice*. Surrey, UK: Ashgate, 1997.

Gordon, Nathan J., and William L. Fleisher. *Effective Interviewing and Interrogation Techniques*. Maryland Heights, MO: Academic Press, 2006.

Gudjonsson, Gisli H. *The Psychology of Interrogations and Confessions: A Handbook*. New York: Wiley, 2003.

Guiora, Amos N. *Constitutional Limits on Coercive Interrogation*. New York: Oxford University Press, 2008.

Inabu, Fred E., John E. Reid, Joseph P. Buckley, and Bryan C. Jayne. *Criminal Interrogations and Confessions*. Sudbury, MA: Jones and Bartlett Learning, 2004.

Inabu, Fred E., John E. Reid, Joseph P. Buckley, and Bryan C. Jayne. *Essentials of the Reid Technique: Criminal Interrogations and Confessions*. Sudbury, MA: Jones and Bartlett Learning, 2004.

Kamisar, Yale. *Police Interrogation and Confessions: Essays in Law and Policy*. Ann Arbor: University of Michigan Press, 1980.

Lassiter, G. Daniel. *Interrogations, Confessions, and Entrapment*. New York: Springer, 2006.

Lassiter, G. Daniel, and Christian A. Meissner. *Police Interrogations and False Confessions: Current Research, Practice, and Policy Recommendations*. Washington, DC: APA, 2010.

Leo, Richard A. *Police Interrogation and American Justice*. Cambridge, MA: Harvard University Press, 2009.

Leo, Richard A., and George C. Thomas III, eds. *The Miranda Debate: Law, Justice, and Policing*. Boston: Northeastern University Press, 1998.

McInnis, Thomas. *The Christian Burial Case: An Introduction to Criminal and Judicial Procedure*. Santa Barbara, CA: Praeger, 2000.

Rabon, Don, and Tanya Chapman. *Interviewing and Interrogation*. Durham, NC: Carolina Academic Press, 2008.

Shantz, Jeff. *Racial Profiling and Borders: International, Interdisciplinary Perspectives*. Lake Mary, FL: Vandeplas, 2010.

Shuy, Roger W. *The Language of Confession, Interrogation, and Deception*. Thousand Oaks, CA: Sage, 1997.

Skerker, Michael. *An Ethics of Interrogation*. Chicago: University of Chicago Press, 2010.

Stuart, Gary L. *Miranda: The Story of America's Right to Remain Silent*. Tucson: University of Arizona Press, 2008.

Warden, Rob, and Steven A. Drizen, eds. *True Stories of False Confessions*. Evanston, IL: Northwestern University Press, 2009.

White, Welsh S. *Miranda's Waning Protections: Police Interrogation Practices after Dickerson*. Ann Arbor: University of Michigan Press, 2003.

7

Miranda Warnings

Frank Butler
La Salle University

The Miranda warning is as follows: "You have the right to remain silent. Anything you say can and will be used against you in a court of law. You have the right to speak to an attorney, and to have an attorney present during any questioning. If you cannot afford a lawyer, one will be provided for you at government expense."

In the case of *Ernesto Miranda v. Arizona* in 1966, the U.S. Supreme Court's decision required all federal and state law-enforcement agencies to warn suspects in custody, prior to interrogating them, that they have certain constitutional rights. Before this decision, the Court rarely became involved in cases involving confessions, and when it did, its major concern was simply whether the confession was "voluntary," as is required for due process of law. Voluntariness, however, is often a matter of degree, especially when psychological coercion by law enforcement is involved, and the Court was able to create few general rules, thereby necessitating a case-by-case approach to assessing voluntariness.

In frustration with this cumbersome approach, and with the continued use of seriously coercive tactics by the police to extract confessions, the Court used the *Miranda* decision to create a "bright-line rule" that theoretically would make it abundantly clear to the police what procedure they needed to follow any time they wished to question a suspect in custody.

The Supreme Court based its creation of the Miranda warnings on the Fifth Amendment to the U.S. Constitution, which specifies that in a criminal case no person can be compelled to be a witness against himself. If the police force confessions through coercive interrogation tactics or environments, they deny the suspect this Fifth Amendment privilege against compelled self-incrimination.

The privilege against self-incrimination dates from at least the 1600s in English common law. Most of the original 13 colonies that became the United States included a privilege against self-incrimination in their original state constitutions.

Foundations of the Miranda Warnings

By the mid-1960s, the Supreme Court grew frustrated with controlling police abuses during interrogations. In 1964, the Court ruled that in interrogations of suspects already formally charged with a crime, the suspects have the right to have counsel present (*Winston Massiah v. United States*). In the case of *Danny Escobedo v. Illinois* (1964), which was decided a few weeks later, the Court required that if the police have focused on and decide to interrogate a particular suspect who is in custody, and if that suspect has not been warned of his right to silence, the police must give the suspect an opportunity to consult with his lawyer if he requests to do so. Both of these cases were based in the Sixth Amendment's provision for a "right to counsel."

Law enforcement fears about where the Supreme Court was headed with the *Massiah* and *Escobedo* cases involved concerns that soon all interrogation would be permitted only if done in the presence of counsel, which would effectively prevent most interrogation. The Court, however, chose a much more moderate approach involving warnings and waivers. The Court's emphasis on the Sixth Amendment in *Massiah* and *Escobedo* was replaced by a Fifth Amendment analysis based in the right against self-incrimination.

In 1963, an 18-year-old woman in Arizona was kidnapped on her way home from work. The assailant forced her into a car, drove into the desert, and raped her. He also robbed her of a small amount of money she had in her purse. Based on their investigation, the police arrested Ernesto Miranda at his home and took him to the police station, where he was placed in a lineup with three other Mexican Americans. The victim was unable to clearly identify Miranda from the lineup. The police then took him to an interrogation room; he was not told about a right to counsel or a right not to be forced to incriminate himself. Within a couple of hours, the police reported that Miranda had confessed to the rape.

Miranda suffered from mental illness and had many sexual fantasies. At trial, his attorney objected to the use of the confession, but the judge overruled the objection. Based largely on his confession, Miranda was convicted of rape and kidnapping and sentenced to 20 to 30 years in prison. His appeal was one of the few eventually heard by the Supreme Court, which ultimately decided that use of the confession at trial violated Miranda's right to counsel and his right not to be compelled to incriminate himself.

The Supreme Court consolidated Ernesto Miranda's case with three other state cases and one federal case, and the entire set was considered under the rubric of *Ernesto Miranda v. Arizona,* decided in 1966. In its decision, the Court for the first time required that all government law-enforcement agents must inform a suspect in custody of the right to silence and the right to counsel, prior to interrogating the suspect. If the agents fail to abide by this rule, any resulting confession cannot be used against the suspect at trial. Similar warnings had been used by the Federal Bureau of Investigation (FBI) prior to the *Miranda* case.

The *Miranda* decision was produced from a heavily split Supreme Court: five of the nine justices joined the majority opinion in the case. Chief Justice Earl Warren, author of the decision, bore the brunt of criticism of the case. Ironically, Warren probably had a more comprehensive background in law enforcement than any Supreme Court justice to date. Warren had served for many years as a prosecutor, and he also had served as state attorney general and governor of California.

In 1967, after a second trial that used actual evidence instead of Miranda's confession, he was found guilty, and sentenced to 20-30 years in prison.

Repercussions of the Court Decision

The warnings quickly became a cultural phenomenon, incorporated into television cop shows such as *Dragnet,* where the character Sergeant Joe Friday routinely issued the warnings to arrestees in his professional monotone. Invariably, suspects in the series made incriminating statements even after being given the warnings. In this way, the mass media tended to portray the warnings largely as ritualistic and symbolic.

The *Miranda* decision also became fodder for national political interests. Though police departments generally complied with at least the letter of the law, the decision was heavily criticized by prosecutors, police, and political conservatives. Claims were made that once police gave the warnings, large numbers of suspects who otherwise would have confessed would now invoke their Miranda rights, causing police clearance rates and prosecutors' conviction rates to plummet as crime rates soared.

In 1968, Congress passed Title II of the Omnibus Crime Control and Safe Streets Act in an attempt to overrule the *Miranda* decision in federal cases. This legislation added Section 3501 to Title 18 of the U.S. Code, specifying that voluntariness (of which the Miranda warnings are only a part) is the determining issue in decisions about using confessions in federal trials. In spite of this provision, the vast majority of law enforcement implemented the Miranda warnings in accord with the *Miranda* decision.

Miranda was a major issue in the 1968 presidential campaign. Richard M. Nixon, the Republican candidate, lambasted the decision as well as the general tenor of the Warren Court's decisions granting rights to criminal suspects and defendants. The American Independent Party candidate (Alabama governor George Wallace) also ran on a "law and order" platform similar to Nixon's, though Nixon won the election.

The initial rationale of the Supreme Court for use of the Miranda warnings involved the need to dispel the compulsion that permeates in interrogation in a police-dominated atmosphere. In part as a result of Nixon's appointment of conservative justices to the Supreme Court, subsequent cases often diluted the strength of the Miranda warnings as controls on police interrogations.

In the 1970s and 1980s, the entertainment media tended to portray police as hamstrung by the rules of criminal procedure, including the Miranda warnings. Those rules were commonly portrayed as allowing criminals to go free because the police were powerless. Police who took the law into their own hands, circumventing legal procedures, were heroic. A prime example of this perspective is the movie *Dirty Harry* (1971), in which a police detective tortures information out of a depraved killer who is presented as a major threat to public safety. The detective is too machismo to be bothered with procedural regularities like the Miranda warnings, and the audience cheers him on.

Vacillations on Miranda

The Burger Court

Consistent with his platform of rolling back the criminal procedural reforms of the Warren Court, President Nixon was able to appoint conservative jurist Warren Burger as chief justice of the Supreme Court in 1969. The

Burger Court decided a variety of cases related to the Miranda warnings, and those decisions tended to enervate the impact of the warnings.

In *Vivien Harris v. New York* (1971), the Burger Court ruled that incriminating statements obtained after defective Miranda warnings can be used to impeach a defendant's credibility if he or she chooses to testify at trial. In 1974, the Court noted in its decision in *Michigan v. Thomas Tucker* that the *Miranda* decision is only a "prophylactic rule," rather than a requirement based in the Constitution: The constitutional provision against self-incrimination is violated only if a confession is "involuntary." A Miranda violation does not necessarily render a confession involuntary.

In 1975, the Court clarified that even if a defendant asserts his Miranda rights (requesting a lawyer) and the police continue to question him, his incriminating statements can be used to impeach his testimony at trial (*Oregon v. William Hass*). That same year, in *Michigan v. Richard Mosley,* the police immediately ceased interrogating a suspect when he refused to answer questions. After a couple of hours, however, they gave a fresh set of warnings and then interrogated the suspect about a different crime. The suspect's incriminating statements made in response to questioning about the second crime were not a Miranda violation, the Court ruled.

In *Oregon v. Carl Mathiason,* decided by the Court in 1977, a suspect came to a police station, at a police officer's request, to be questioned about a burglary. He was not given the Miranda warnings, and he made incriminating statements during the half-hour interview. The Court ruled that the Miranda warnings were not required, because the suspect was not in "custody." Two years later, in *North Carolina v. Willie Butler,* the Court allowed waiver of Miranda rights without any express written or oral statement of waiver (the suspect had refused to sign the waiver form).

A few *Miranda*-related decisions of the Burger Court seemed to support the original *Miranda* decision. For example, in *Rhode Island v. Thomas Innis* (1980), the Court gave a fairly broad interpretation to the meaning of "interrogation," ruling that it refers not only to "express questioning" but also to the "functional equivalent" of express questioning (i.e., words or actions of the police that they should know are reasonably likely to elicit incriminating statements). The definition, however, was of no benefit to Thomas Innis. After he was arrested and given the Miranda warnings and invoked his right to counsel, he was escorted in a police car to the police station. En route, the officers in the car discussed the shotgun involved in the robbery, noting that there was a school for disabled children nearby, where one of the students might find the weapon and get hurt. Innis interrupted and agreed to show the police the location of the gun. The Court decided that the conversation among the officers was not something that they should have known was likely to elicit an incriminating statement. Thus, it was not "interrogation."

In *Robert Edwards v. Arizona* (1981), the Court invalidated a confession obtained the day after the suspect in custody had invoked his right to counsel after being given the Miranda warnings. Though police re-warned the suspect prior to questioning him the second day, the Court ruled that such an interrogation was unlawful because the suspect had not been given access to counsel, nor was he the one who initiated further communication with the police.

The Rehnquist Court

Through the end of the 20th century, the Supreme Court continued to generally weaken the legal significance of the Miranda warnings. Chief Justice William Rehnquist, who succeeded Burger in 1986, had been a fierce opponent of the *Miranda* ruling when he worked for the Justice Department in the Nixon White House. Though the chief justice does not control the Court, a variety of decisions of the Rehnquist Court served to continue to erode the impact of *Miranda*. Thus, paradoxically, as the Miranda warnings were becoming entrenched in the public consciousness, they were also being generally weakened by the Court. By the end of the century, the warnings had become in part a procedural formality with largely symbolic significance.

Although the more conservative Supreme Court after the 1970s tended to characterize the Miranda warnings as merely "prophylactic" and not protected by the U.S. Constitution, the Court in 2000 clarified that *Miranda* is a decision that is a constitutional rule, not simply a court procedural rule (*Charles Dickerson v. United States*). In this case, the Court also declined to overrule the *Miranda* decision, maintaining that "the warnings have become part of our national culture."

Interpretation of the Warnings

Police need not use any precise formula when giving the Miranda warnings, but whatever words they use must effectively warn the suspect of their continuing right to silence and their right to counsel. The warning about the right to silence was intended to inform the suspect that their refusal to talk, at the outset or at any time after the interrogation has begun, would not subject them to penalties. The warning that "anything you say will be used against you" admonishes the suspect that this is an adversarial proceeding in which the police are not acting on the suspect's behalf. The warning about the right to counsel was intended to reassure the suspect that they could choose to have a skilled ally and legal protector with them during the interrogation. The last warning, regarding providing counsel for indigent suspects, was supposed to clarify that counsel is available not just for those with economic means.

The procedural safeguards set forth in the *Miranda* decision apply only to custodial interrogations; i.e., when law enforcement agents initiate questioning of a person who is in custody or who in any other way has been significantly deprived of their freedom. The police presumption in such cases is generally that the suspect is guilty, and the process commonly manipulates the suspect's fears and anxieties. Prior to questioning, the suspect must be warned specifically of their right to remain silent; that any statement may be used as evidence against them; and that they have the right to the presence of an attorney, either retained privately or appointed for them if they are indigent. A suspect can waive these rights at the outset or at any time during interrogation, as long as they do so voluntarily, knowingly, and intelligently (*Moran v. Brian Burbine,* 1986).

A "knowing" waiver is one where the suspect has been given adequate information; an "intelligent" waiver requires that the suspect can make an informed choice; and a "voluntary" waiver is one that is free and deliberate, that is, not the product of intimidation, deception, or coercion.

When Miranda Is and Is Not Required

The Miranda warnings are required only when a suspect is in custody and is to be interrogated by law enforcement. The warnings are not needed for routine booking questions, since those are not considered interrogation of the suspect. Police officers conversing about the case among themselves while the suspect is in their presence is likely not "interrogation" (*Rhode Island v. Thomas Innis,* 1980), so no Miranda warnings are necessary. Only "express questioning or its functional equivalent" is deemed interrogation.

A noncustodial interrogation does not require Miranda warnings before questioning (*California v. Jerry Beheler,* 1983). For example, if a suspect voluntarily goes to the police station for questioning, he or she probably is not in "custody," even if accompanied by the police on the trip.

If the police fail to give the Miranda warnings when they should, any testimonial evidence (e.g., incriminating statements or a confession) generally must be excluded from evidence used at the suspect's trial. Physical evidence obtained as a result of unwarned statements (such as a videotape of a suspect being booked for driving under the influence, when not given the Miranda warnings) does not need to be excluded (*Pennsylvania v. Inocencio Muniz,* 1990). Obtaining unwarned statements from a suspect becomes a constitutional (Fifth Amendment) violation only if the statements are used as evidence in court against the suspect.

Thus, other evidence the police obtain as a result of the suspect's "unwarned" statements can usually be used in court against the suspect (*Michigan v. Thomas Tucker,* 1974; and *United States v. Samuel Patane,* 2004). Even though the "unwarned" statements themselves cannot be used in court, other evidence that the police obtained as a result of their learning the information from the unwarned statements can be used. This is in contrast to illegally seized evidence: Generally, evidence derived from the illegally seized evidence ("fruit of the poisonous tree") must be excluded from trial along with the illegally seized evidence itself.

Likewise, if the accused testifies at trial, the unwarned statements can be used at the trial to impeach his credibility (*Vivien Harris v. New York,* 1971). This applies even if the suspect has asked for counsel and the police continued to question the suspect anyway (*Oregon v. William Hass,* 1975). The accused's unwarned statements that are contradictory to his trial testimony can be read to the jury, ostensibly to show the suspect is not truthful. Also, if the police inadvertently fail to give the Miranda warnings and obtain incriminating statements, but then give the warnings and re-obtain similar statements, the mid-stream warnings are deemed to have "cured" the initial deficiency, and the post-warning statements can be used in court.

If a suspect is in custody and there is an urgent need to ask very limited questions due to an imminent threat to the public safety, the police may do so without first giving the Miranda warnings (*New York v. Benjamin Quarles,* 1984). This so-called "public safety exception" to the *Miranda* requirements has potentially broad implications for investigations involving suspected terrorism.

A suspect may invoke his Miranda rights at any time before or during police questioning, at which point the police must cease all questioning. The suspect must be clear that he is invoking his rights; if the suspect is ambiguous or equivocal, the police may continue questioning. When a suspect invokes the Miranda right to silence, the police must "scrupulously honor" the right, but may resume questioning later. In contrast, when a suspect invokes his Miranda right to counsel, all interrogation by law enforcement (even for other, unrelated crimes) must cease until counsel is present, unless the suspect reinitiates communication with the police and clearly waives the right to counsel.

The Right to Silence Versus the Right to Counsel

Whether the suspect invokes the right to silence or the right to counsel is significant, with the latter giving much greater protection to the suspect. With invocation of the right to silence, law enforcement is free to later check whether the suspect has changed his or her mind and wishes to talk (*Michigan v. Richard Mosley*, 1975). In contrast, invocation of the right to counsel necessitates the cessation of all questioning (unless the suspect initiates conversation) about any offense until counsel is actually present during interrogation (*Robert Minnick v. Mississippi*, 1990).

The right to counsel that is part of the Miranda warnings is not the Sixth Amendment assistance of counsel that applies when a defendant is in court. The latter involves comprehensive legal help in a defendant's legal defense. At interrogation, the right to counsel is based in the Fifth Amendment right against compelled self-incrimination. Counsel's role is to help the suspect deal with the pressure of the custodial environment, and it is triggered only if the suspect invokes it.

Proper Use of Miranda and Suspect Voluntariness

If the police elicit a confession after unintentionally failing to give the Miranda warnings, and if they subsequently give the warnings and then the suspect confesses again, the second confession can be used in court against the suspect, since giving the Miranda warnings prior to the second confession "cures" any compulsion from the first interrogation (*Oregon v. Michael Elstad*, 1985). However, if the police intentionally omit the Miranda warnings and elicit a confession, and soon thereafter give the warnings and re-interrogate the suspect and again get the confession—a so-called "two-stage interrogation" employing "question first" tactics—neither confession can be used (*Missouri v. Patrice Seibert*, 2004).

Police sometimes "game" the Miranda warnings in an attempt to induce suspects to waive the Miranda rights. For example, the police might downplay the importance of the rights, implying they are just a formality, sometimes simultaneously feigning a friendly relationship in which they identify with the suspect. Another strategy is to tell the suspect that waiver of rights will enable him to have a chance to tell his side of the story.

It is important to note that even if the Miranda warnings are properly given, a suspect's statement still may be excluded from use at court if the statement was not made voluntarily. Such "voluntariness" is required by the Due Process Clause of the Fifth Amendment and the Fourteenth Amendment. Prior to the *Miranda* decision in 1966, voluntariness was the only issue a defendant could raise with regard to a confession. Courts assess voluntariness by examining a wide variety of facts (the so-called "totality of the circumstances") surrounding a confession, including factors like the suspect's age and educational level and the amount of psychological pressure used by the police.

Juvenile Suspects and Comprehension of Miranda

One particularly debated issue concerns the use of Miranda warnings with juvenile suspects, especially pre-teens and those in their early to mid teens. There is some empirical evidence that youth frequently misunderstand the warnings, even more so than adults. For example, juveniles may view lawyers as protecting only innocent persons, or they may link invocation of a right with increased likelihood of judicial punishment in the future, or they may seek to respond to authority figures in socially appropriate ways. Suspects must comprehend the interrelated words and concepts that the warnings convey, while simultaneously assessing potential present and future outcomes if the rights are invoked. This can be particularly taxing for the incompletely developed brains of adolescents, which tend to give greater weight to immediate gratification without adequately weighing long-term costs.

Juvenile suspects are commonly mentally ill and/or substance abusers. Learning disabilities are also frequent, as are histories of abuse and neglect. The right to silence has a comprehension level of under fifth grade, but the other warnings require approximately a ninth-grade reading level for full comprehension (e.g., words like appointed and waive). The array of such issues can lead youth to decide too quickly to waive rights. In spite of these factors, the Supreme Court has not required any form of special warnings for juveniles, nor does it require the presence of a parent or attorney. Parental involvement may be problematic anyway, in that the interests of the parent and child may conflict.

Adult suspects can also have difficulty comprehending the Miranda warnings, especially suspects with mental disabilities. It has been estimated that suspects who fit the borderline category for mental retardation under-stand less than half of the warnings. Suspects who do not comprehend the warnings probably cannot fairly be expected to freely waive their rights.

Pro: Arguments in Support of the Miranda Decision

The U.S. Supreme Court's major concern in the 1966 *Miranda* decision related to what it called "incommunicado interrogation in a police-domi-nated atmosphere." Since the suspect is generally isolated from all his social supports during the interrogation, and since it occurs on police turf and without impartial observers, there is a real danger of abusive manipulation of suspects. In their zeal to solve a crime, some law enforcement agents may physically or, much more commonly, psychologically abuse a suspect in order to promote a confession. In the *Miranda* decision, the Court cited a variety of police tactics that were specifically designed to weaken the confi-dence of suspects and play on their fears and insecurity in the custodial set-ting. Inquisitorial tactics—forcing confessions from suspects through actual or threatened abuse—are diametrically opposed to the American accusatory system, in which the government must produce the evidence against a sus-pect by its own work.

When counsel is not present at interrogation, the Court believed there is a major danger that any resulting confession is untrustworthy. Counsel was seen as protecting the suspect's right against compelled self-incrimination, since counsel's presence would inhibit police use of coercion and would serve to ensure that any confession was later correctly reported at trial.

The Miranda rule did not significantly impact rate of confession, and it provides clear guidelines for the police. The police have found it to be a workable rule: as long as they give the warnings and follow procedure, confessions generally are admissible.

Since the late 20th century, DNA evidence has shown that a major basis for wrongful convictions (i.e., convictions of persons who are factually in-nocent) is false confessions. Particularly among homicide defendants who are later found wrongfully convicted, the defendants commonly had con-fessed. The Miranda warnings can serve a valuable role in encouraging sus-pects to see the adversarial nature of interrogation by reminding them at the outset of their right to silence and their right to counsel.

Overturning *Miranda* might convey tacit approval of abusive police prac-tices in interrogation. The *Miranda* decision is likely the most famous deci-sion ever issued by the U.S. Supreme Court. More so than any criminal case, it enhanced the general public's awareness of constitutional rights. The decision also promoted professionalism among the police and helped to curb at least the most abusive interrogation methods.

Coercive interrogation techniques ultimately impede the solving of crimes, in that they are apt to lead to unreliable confessions and wrongful convictions. As police focus on the wrong culprits, the actual criminals remain unpunished. The *Miranda* decision, including its warnings, is an important reminder for the police that every suspect has basic legal rights that must be respected.

Con: Arguments Against the Use of Miranda

Once suspects are made aware of the rights contained in the Miranda warnings, they may be unlikely to confess to anything, since they will understand that the police are not on their side and that there is an absolute right to remain silent. Factually guilty suspects may not talk to the police, but rather may seek legal advice, thereby halting interrogation and hindering the police investigation. Thus, the ability of law enforcement to solve crimes will be seriously impeded. Also, if the police lie in court about abusing suspects to extract confessions, they can just as easily lie about giving suspects the Miranda warnings. These were the major points made by Justice John Marshall Harlan III in his dissenting opinion in the *Miranda* case.

If the police-dominated atmosphere of custodial interrogation is inherently coercive, would suspects feel free to assert their rights, such as asking for a lawyer, in such settings? Also, confessions are highly useful in gauging a suspect's guilt, and it may even be psychologically beneficial for guilty suspects to confess their crimes. Justice Byron White raised these issues in his dissenting opinion.

The definitions of *custody* and *interrogation*—the two essential triggers for the Miranda warnings—have been problematic, leading to confusion as to which situations require the warnings. For example, the Supreme Court has decided a variety of cases involving the question of custody for *Miranda* purposes, but the inquiries tend to be fact-specific, making it difficult to generalize. A suspect who is awakened by the police and questioned in his bedroom at 4 A.M. is in custody (*Reyes Orozco v. Texas,* 1969), but a parolee who is summoned to a police station to be interviewed about a burglary is not in custody (*Oregon v. Carl Mathiason,* 1977). Likewise, "interrogation" includes not just express questioning, but also its "functional equivalent" (*Rhode Island v. Thomas Innis,* 1980).

The Miranda warnings have become so famous and are administered in such a perfunctory manner that they can be seen primarily as ritual with no real consequences. Reliance on the fact that the warnings were given often militates against any real judicial inquiry into whether an interrogation was otherwise coercive. The great majority of suspects, especially those with no prior felony convictions, waive the right to silence and the right to counsel after receiving the Miranda warnings. Once the Miranda rights are waived, all the suspect's statements are generally admissible as evidence in court.

Coercive Interrogation Tactics

Since the great majority of suspects (especially those without criminal records) generally waive their Miranda rights, it may be presumed that the police have developed methods to encourage waivers. Also, as long as a suspect waives their Miranda rights, the police can use coercive psychological interrogation tactics that the warnings were intended to prevent. Thus, in spite of the Miranda warnings, custodial interrogation remains coercive.

The warnings do not prevent coercive interrogation techniques by the police. Such techniques are likely to produce false confessions and subsequent wrongful convictions. The coercive psychological techniques that the Court was so concerned with in the *Miranda* case—and which are still possible once a suspect waives the Miranda rights—can lead even an innocent person to confess. Unfortunately, jurors commonly believe that an innocent person would never confess, especially after that person has received the Miranda warnings. Approximately one-fourth of the persons who were convicted and later found factually innocent via DNA testing had confessed.

The Miranda warnings mask judicial inquiry into whether a confession was voluntary. Courts tend to presume that once the warnings are given and there is a valid waiver, any statements by the suspect are voluntary and hence admissible in court. Thus, the warnings serve to discourage further judicial scrutiny of interrogation practices.

The police are largely free to violate Miranda rules because the Court has not required that they create an objective record of what transpires in the interrogation room. Few states require electronic recording of interrogations.

In essence, The Miranda warnings are bark with very little bite. Generally, though unwarned statements themselves cannot be used at trial, evidence derived from those statements ("fruits of the poisonous tree") can still be used at trial. Also, these unwarned statements can be used at trial to impeach the defendant. Finally, there is no penalty for the police if unwarned statements are taken, as long as they are not used at trial.

See Also: 2. Arrest Practices; 6. Interrogation Practices.

Further Readings

Covey, Russell Dean. "*Miranda* and the Media: Tracing the Cultural Evolution of a Constitutional Revolution." *Chapman Law Review,* v.10 (2007).

Dressler, Joshua, and George C. Thomas III. *Criminal Procedure: Investigating Crime.* St. Paul, MN: Thomson/West, 2007.

Feld, Barry C. "Police Interrogation of Juveniles: An Empirical Study of Policy and Practice." *Journal of Criminal Law and Criminology,* v.97 (2006).

Kamisar, Yale. "On the Fortieth Anniversary of the *Miranda* Case: Why We Needed It, How We Got It—And What Happened to It." *Ohio State Journal of Criminal Law,* v.5 (2007).

Kamisar, Yale, Wayne R. LaFave, Jerold H. Israel, Nancy J. King, and S. Kerr Orin. *Basic Criminal procedure,* 12th ed. St. Paul, MN: Thomson/West, 2008.

Kassin, Saul M., and Gisli H. Gudjonsson. "Psychology of Confessions: A Review of the Literature and Issues." *Psychological Science in the Public Interest,* v.5 (2004).

Leo, Richard A. *Police Interrogation and American Justice.* Cambridge, MA: Harvard University Press, 2008.

Leo, Richard A., and Welsh S. White. "Adapting to *Miranda*: Modern Interrogators' Strategies for Dealing With the Obstacles Posed by *Miranda*." *Minnesota Law Review,* v.84 (1999).

Rogers, Richard, Lisa L. Hazelwood, Kenneth W. Sewell, Daniel W. Shuman, and Hayley Blackwood. "The Comprehensibility and Content of Juvenile *Miranda* Warnings." *Psychology, Public Policy, and Law,* v.14 (2008).

Weisselberg, Charles D. "Mourning *Miranda*." *California Law Review,* v.96 (2008).

8

Plain View Doctrine

J.C. Oleson
University of Auckland

The Fourth Amendment of the U.S. Constitution safeguards against unreasonable searches and seizures, but is not implicated in all searches and seizures. The Fourth Amendment, for example, does not apply to searches and seizures conducted by private citizens or organizations, nor does it apply to information-gathering actions by government actors that do not constitute "searches" and "seizures" within the meaning of the Fourth Amendment.

Over time, the U.S. Supreme Court has developed a large body of technical case law to adjudicate disputes about search and seizure. In *Katz v. United States* (1967), the Court established the fundamental rule that the Fourth Amendment covers "reasonable expectations of privacy." Ascertaining reasonableness, however, can prove difficult. Fourth Amendment jurisprudence often relies upon specific facts and appeals to "reasonableness."

One especially contentious area of search and seizure is a doctrine that allows government actors who are lawfully present at a location to seize contraband or evidence left in plain view. Merely looking at something in plain view is not a "search" within the scope of the Fourth Amendment. The law has struggled to keep up with technology in these cases, since devices like night-vision devices, magnetometers, and thermal-imaging devices allow police officers to "see" objects that cannot be seen by the naked eye. As a general matter, and with a couple of important exceptions, the Court has upheld the warrantless use of surveillance techniques that merely enhance human senses, and has rejected as unconstitutional the use of extrasensory surveillance techniques. This is a frequently litigated area of law, however, because evolving technologies continue to extend what government agents can sense with "plain view."

The Fourth Amendment

The general principles governing search and seizure in all U.S. jurisdictions stem from the Fourth Amendment:

> The right of the people to be secure in their persons, houses, papers, and effects, against unreasonable searches and seizures, shall not be violated, and no Warrants shall issue, but upon probable cause, supported by Oath or affirmation, and particularly describing the place to be searched, and the persons or things to be seized.

The amendment is somewhat vague and does not define the terms *search* or *seizure*. Accordingly, part of the Supreme Court's challenge has been to determine which kinds of searches and seizures implicate the Fourth Amendment, and which do not. The Fourth Amendment applies only to searches and seizures conducted by governmental actors; private citizens and organizations that engage in searches do not trigger it. Furthermore, as Justice William Brennan explained in his dissent in *United States v. Jacobsen* (1984), because the Fourth Amendment applies only to searches and seizures, "an investigative technique that falls within neither category need not be reasonable and may be employed without a warrant and without probable cause, regardless of the circumstances surrounding its use."

As a general matter, for Fourth Amendment purposes, a "search" occurs whenever a reasonable expectation of privacy is infringed upon by a governmental actor. A "seizure" of property occurs whenever a government actor intentionally asserts dominion and control over an item of tangible personal property, thereby interfering with the owner's possessory interests in the property. Actual physical possession is not required.

A "seizure" of a person occurs whenever a government actor uses physical force or a show of authority to intentionally terminate or restrain a person's freedom of movement. Not all interactions between the police and others constitute searches. And, it is not a "seizure" when an officer approaches an individual in a public place and asks him questions, although a consensual encounter can become a seizure if a reasonable person would no longer feel free to leave.

The exclusionary rule provides the remedy for violations of the Fourth Amendment. If a police officer engages in a search and discovers incriminating material, but a court determines that the search violated the Fourth Amendment, the fruit of the illegal search cannot be used as evidence in any subsequent criminal trial. The exclusionary rule was first applied to the federal system in *Weeks v. United States* (1914), and later applied to the states in *Mapp v. Ohio* (1961).

Katz v. United States

In the seminal 1967 case *Katz v. United States,* Federal Bureau of Investigation (FBI) agents attached an electronic recording device to a public phone booth in Los Angeles, from which Charles Katz regularly placed bets in Miami and Boston. The Court rejected an analysis that focused on the qualities of the phone booth, and instead looked at Katz's expectation of privacy, stating famously that "the Fourth Amendment protects people, not places." The two-pronged test for determining whether a "search" has occurred asks (1) whether a person exhibited an actual (subjective) expectation of privacy that (2) society is prepared to recognize as a reasonable expectation.

Generally speaking, government actors must obtain a warrant in order to search or seize. Police must obtain advanced judicial approval of searches and seizures whenever possible. A search conducted without a warrant is presumed unreasonable. The product of such a search will be admitted into evidence only if it falls into one of the few established exceptions to the warrant requirement. Some searches and seizures are exempted from the warrant requirement because the type of government action in question has been upheld by the Supreme Court for pragmatic law enforcement reasons. Such exceptions to the warrant requirement include searches conducted incident to arrest (e.g., a protective sweep); searches under exigent circumstances (i.e., hot pursuit); consent searches; and seizures of limited intrusiveness and duration based on reasonable suspicion (i.e., a Terry stop).

Even without a warrant, searches of these kinds are typically deemed reasonable. Other searches and seizures are exempted from the warrant requirement because there can be no reasonable expectation of privacy under the circumstances, such as customs and border inspections; searches of "open fields," since there is no reasonable expectation of privacy on property that lies beyond the "curtilage" (the vicinity immediately surrounding a residence); and plain view searches.

The *Coolidge* Test

The examination of items left in plain view does not implicate the Fourth Amendment because there is no legitimate expectation of privacy under such circumstances. In the language of *Katz*, "What a person knowingly exposes to the public, even in his own home or office, is not a subject of Fourth Amendment protection." Thus, if, for example, an individual leaves contraband on his property where it can be observed from a public road, there is no objectively reasonable expectation of privacy. Similarly, if the individual discusses the details of a criminal conspiracy publicly—for example, in a restaurant—and is overheard by a police officer at the next table, there is no Fourth Amendment claim because there is no reasonable expectation of privacy under those circumstances.

In the 1971 case, *Coolidge v. New Hampshire*, the Supreme Court noted that the plain view seizure doctrine was already well settled:

> It is well established that under certain circumstances the police may seize evidence in plain view without a warrant. But it is important to keep in mind that, in the vast majority of cases, any evidence seized by the police will be in plain view, at least at the moment of seizure. The problem with the "plain view" doctrine has been to identify the circumstances in which plain view has legal significance rather than being simply the normal concomitant of any search, legal or illegal.

The plurality opinion notes that plain view seizure is permissible when the police have a warrant to search for one thing, and in the course of that search, come across contraband or other incriminating objects. Similarly, if an officer is in "hot pursuit" of a suspect and sees evidence in the course of that pursuit, that evidence may be seized. Under the same rationale, an incriminating object that comes into view when an officer is conducting a search incident to arrest also may be lawfully seized. The plurality opinion in *Coolidge* explains,

> What the "plain view" cases have in common is that the police officer in each of them had a prior justification for an intrusion in the

course of which he came inadvertently across a piece of evidence incriminating the accused. The doctrine serves to supplement the prior justification—whether it be a warrant for another object, hot pursuit, search incident to lawful arrest, or some other legitimate reason for being present unconnected with a search directed against the accused—and permits the warrantless seizure. Of course, the extension of the original justification is legitimate only where it is immediately apparent to the police that they have evidence before them; the "plain view" doctrine may not be used to extend a general exploratory search from one object to another until something incriminating at last emerges.

The test under *Coolidge* for a warrantless, plain view seizure, then, required four elements: (1) the prior government intrusion had to be legitimate, (2) the discovery had to be inadvertent, (3) the incriminating character of the object had to be immediately apparent, and (4) the officer had to have a lawful right of access to the object itself. In 1987, in *Arizona v. Hicks*, the Court held that probable cause was required to invoke the plain view doctrine; and in 1990, in a case called *Horton v. California*, the Court rejected the inadvertency prong of the *Coolidge* test.

The rule in *Coolidge* applies to seizures, not searches. Technically speaking, there is no plain view search doctrine, since anything that a police officer can view without a prior physical intrusion into a constitutionally protected area is not a "search" for Fourth Amendment purposes. That said, it might be a plain view search if an officer uses sophisticated equipment to make the observation, but as a general matter, it is not a search when a police officer sees incriminating objects in open fields, inside premises, inside vehicles, or upon an individual's person.

Covering the Five Senses

The police officer's ability to see incriminating objects does not impart a concomitant authority to touch them. That right exists only when officers immediately recognize plain view contraband or evidence after making a prior legitimate government intrusion (such as exigent circumstances or the execution of a warrant), as held in *Coolidge*. If police officers see contraband through the window of a dwelling, they can look, but they cannot touch without a warrant. The plurality opinion by the Court in *Coolidge* explains:

Incontrovertible testimony of the senses that an incriminating object is on premises belonging to a criminal suspect may establish the fullest possible measure of probable cause. But even where the object is contraband, this Court has repeatedly stated and enforced the basic rule that the police may not enter and make a warrantless seizure.

In *Arizona v. Hicks* (1987), the Court held that no seizure occurred when an officer called to the scene of a shooting recorded the serial numbers of stereo equipment in plain view that he believed was stolen, but the Court held that moving the stereo equipment to find the serial numbers constituted a search.

Just as what officers see in plain view where they are lawfully present is not considered a search, what they learn by using their other senses under those circumstances is not a search, either. The plain view doctrine has been expanded to cover other senses. Police also gather information by relying upon their sense of smell (such as detecting the odor of marijuana), hearing (such as overhearing incriminating remarks), and touch (such as feeling the shape of contraband while conducting a Terry pat-down search for weapons). The Supreme Court recognized an analogous "plain feel" doctrine in the 1993 case *Minnesota v. Dickerson*.

In summation, it is a long-settled matter that officers may engage in plain view observation (or smelling, listening, or touch) without intruding into a constitutionally protected area, for this does not constitute a "search" under the Fourth Amendment. Similarly, it is a settled matter that officers who have already legitimately intruded into a constitutionally protected area may there seize plain view objects without a warrant as long as they have probable cause to believe the objects are contraband or evidence. But what about using mechanical devices to increase an officer's ability to see something in plain view, such as a flashlight?

As a general matter, the Supreme Court has upheld the warrantless use of surveillance equipment that merely aid human senses (sense-augmenting surveillance) while rejecting the warrantless use of devices that reveal information that could not be discerned by any of the five senses (extrasensory surveillance).

Sense-Augmenting Surveillance

The Supreme Court has generally held that sense-augmenting surveillance does not implicate the Fourth Amendment when an officer would be justified in making the same warrantless observations without the sense-enhancing device. For example, an officer on public property has the right to look through a suspect's open drapes with a telescope because (1) he theoretically could have gathered the same information with unaided vision and (2) he has a right to make the observations from his location. Because sense-augmenting technology merely provides information that is theoretically available via the officer's own senses, it is deemed to be no more intrusive than information gathered by unaided senses.

The Supreme Court upheld the use of a flashlight to aid plain view observation in the 1927 case *United States v. Lee.* Noting that the Coast Guard boatswain had used a marine searchlight to pierce the darkness and reveal cans of alcohol in a motorboat, the Court distinguished his using a spotlight from a search. They wrote, "Such use of a searchlight is comparable to the use of a marine glass or a field glass. It is not prohibited by the Constitution."

It is now a well-supported rule that when officers are standing in a place where they have a lawful right to be, they may use artificial illumination to reveal the contents of vehicles, since there is a diminished expectation of privacy in vehicles. As the Court noted in *Cardwell v. Lewis* (1974),

> One has a lesser expectation of privacy in a motor vehicle because its function is transportation and it seldom serves as one's residence or as the repository of personal effects. A car has little capacity for escaping public scrutiny. It travels public thoroughfares where both its occupants and its contents are in plain view.

Even the use of flashlights to enhance plain view observations into buildings has been upheld. But not in all cases. Applying the two-prong *Katz* test means that courts must ask whether the owner of a property had an expectation of privacy that society is prepared to say is reasonable. Courts have split on whether shining a light into a premise constitutes a search. In making these decisions, they have typically relied on case-specific factors such as whether the building was a private residence—where Fourth Amendment protections are at their absolute zenith—or a commercial property; whether drapes were open or closed; the size of the opening through which the light was beamed; and the invasiveness of the search.

The use of other devices has also been upheld on the theory that sense-augmenting technology merely provides information that would otherwise be available through the officer's own senses. In *United States v. Knotts* (1983), for example, Minnesota narcotics agents, suspecting that Tristan

Armstrong was buying chloroform to use in the production of illegal drugs, arranged for a beeper (a battery-powered wireless transmitter) to be placed in a barrel of chloroform so that the location of the barrel could be tracked. The Supreme Court held that beeper surveillance did not constitute a Fourth Amendment search, since "[t]he governmental surveillance conducted by means of the beeper in this case amounted principally to the following of an automobile on public streets and highways." Because it did no more than an officer could legally do by tailing the suspect, it was merely a plain view observation, not a search.

The use of magnifying devices such as binoculars, field glasses, telescopes, and photo enlargements has usually been upheld. After all, in *United States v. Lee*, the Court approved the use of a searchlight by analogizing it to the use of a field glass.

In *Dow Chemical Company v. United States* (1986), the Supreme Court concluded that the Environmental Protection Agency's (EPA) use of aerial photography to inspect a Dow Chemical plant was not a search within the ambit of the Fourth Amendment, because the $22,000 aerial camera revealed minimal information and was therefore functionally "a simple fly-over with naked-eye observation." The same year, warrantless aerial surveillance was again upheld by the Court in *California v. Ciraolo*, when Santa Clara police, flying at an altitude of 1,000 feet, were able to look down and use "plain view" observation to see the marijuana plants that Dante Carlo Ciraolo grew in his backyard, concealed from the ground by two large fences. This did not constitute a search under the Fourth Amendment.

Still, the majority opinion in *Dow* implies that greater intrusiveness by sense-augmenting devices could be constitutionally problematic, if these devices should enhance human senses to a significant degree. The Court held,

> Here, EPA was not employing some unique sensory device that, for example, could penetrate the walls of buildings and record conversations in Dow's plants, offices or laboratories, but rather a conventional, albeit precise, commercial camera ... Although [the camera views gave] EPA more detailed information than naked-eye views, they remain limited to an outline of the facility's buildings and equipment. The mere fact that human vision is enhanced somewhat, at least to the degree here, does not give rise to constitutional problems.

Kenneth Troiano has argued that plain view surveillance should qualify as a "search" if the technology in question augments the senses so as to provide information that could not otherwise be obtained from a lawful vantage point. In *United States v. Kim* (1976), an appeals court applied similar reasoning, holding that the FBI's use of an 800-mm telescope did constitute a search. The court noted that even though the agents were a quarter mile away, their telescope allowed them to look through Kim's open windows and even identify the headlines of the newspapers he was reading. The *Kim* court wrote that "as the technological capability of law enforcement agencies increases, the Fourth Amendment must likewise grow in response. To permit governmental intrusions of the sort at issue in this case to remain uncontrolled would violate the basic foundations of privacy, security and decency which distinguish free societies from controlled societies."

Extrasensory Surveillance

Because extrasensory surveillance reveals information that is otherwise indiscernible to human senses, the Supreme Court tends to maximize Fourth Amendment protections and to hold that surveillance of this type is generally prohibited without a warrant. But the Court sometimes upholds extrasensory surveillance techniques, especially when the technique is unobtrusive and when it does not penetrate private residences, where subjective expectations of privacy are at their most reasonable. Particularly if the extrasensory techniques disclose very limited information, such as commercial use of Sensormatic detection devices that alert merchants only when their tagged property is removed from the store, courts may uphold the warrantless search as reasonable.

As a general rule, however, when government agents use magnetometers (such as those utilized in airports), x-ray machines, or weapons detectors, their use of these devices has typically been characterized as a search. By detecting fluctuations in magnetic fields, emitting x-rays to reveal concealed objects, or measuring the high-frequency waves emitted by living persons, these devices reveal information that could never be detected by plain view observation. Unlike flashlights or binoculars, these devices provide police officers with superhuman powers, allowing them to see through walls and clothing.

The same reasoning has been applied by the Court to thermal imaging devices. In *Kyllo v. United States* (2001), the Court examined the application of a thermal-imaging device used to scan the exterior of a townhouse. Government agents used the device to investigate suspicions that the occupants were growing marijuana inside the residence using high-intensity lamps that generate substantial heat. The majority held that warrantless use of the thermal imager violated the Fourth Amendment because it was an extrasensory device that disclosed heat signatures "otherwise imperceptible" to average human beings. The majority opinion in *Kyllo* explains, "Where, as here, the Government uses a device that is not in general public use, to explore details of the home that would previously have been unknowable without physical intrusion, the surveillance is a 'search' and is presumptively unreasonable without a warrant."

But not all warrantless extrasensory observations have been characterized as unconstitutional searches. As previously noted, the Court has been willing to uphold extrasensory techniques that are minimally intrusive and disclose only narrow classes of information. Thus, although the use of a narcotics-detecting dog is "extrasensory surveillance" (since humans cannot normally smell narcotics in sealed containers), in *United States v. Place* (1983) the Court held that such extrasensory canine assistance did not constitute a Fourth Amendment search. The Court wrote,

> A "canine sniff" by a well-trained narcotics detection dog ... does not require opening ... luggage. It does not expose noncontraband items that otherwise would remain hidden from public view, as does, for example, an officer's rummaging through the contents of the luggage. Thus, the manner in which information is obtained through this investigative technique is much less intrusive than a typical search. Moreover, the sniff discloses only the presence or absence of narcotics, a contraband item. Thus, despite the fact that the sniff tells the authorities something about the contents of the luggage, the information obtained is limited.

At the time, the Court characterized the canine sniff as *sui generis* (of its own kind), yet just one year later, the Court showed that the rationale of *Place* was not at all unique to canine sniffs. In the 1984 case of *United States v. Jacobsen*, when the employees of a private freight company noticed bags of white powder contained in a damaged parcel, they contacted the Drug Enforcement Administration (DEA). The DEA agent conducted a field chemical test to determine that the powder was cocaine, and then proceeded to get a warrant. The Court held that the warrantless field test was not an unlawful search or seizure within the meaning of the Fourth Amendment. Relying upon *Place*, the Court reasoned that government actions that can reveal whether a substance is cocaine, but reveal no other private fact, do not compromise any legitimate privacy interest.

Pro: Strengths of the Plain View Doctrine Compromise

The plain view doctrine accommodates two competing principles: (1) the interest of the public to be free of government intrusion and (2) the ability for law enforcement officers to effectively investigate and prosecute crime. Under this conception, the plain view doctrine represents a pragmatic compromise between a world in which the police are afforded plenary discretion to search and to seize at will and an alternative world in which a judicial warrant is required for every search and seizure, no matter how exigent the circumstances.

Although the plain view doctrine requires frequent refinement by Supreme Court case law, the doctrine makes an effort to balance the competing interests of individual privacy and effective policing. Allowing officers to seize contraband and evidence without a warrant, under certain conditions, has not been fatal to the Fourth Amendment's warrant requirement. Most citizens would prefer for police officers to be required to seek a warrant from a neutral magistrate in order to search private homes or seize personal papers. But perhaps not in all cases. Citizens may not want to exclude from trial the evidence discovered by a police officer while engaged in hot pursuit or while making an arrest. After all, like searches conducted incident-to-arrest, plain view seizure is a doctrine that applies only in a narrow class of circumstances. The doctrine becomes relevant only when an officer has already made a legitimate government intrusion, discovers an incriminating object, and has a lawful right to access in order to seize it.

Clear Guidance

Such a rule provides clear guidance to law enforcement agents. Police officers, in order to be effective enforcers of the law, tend to interpret established rules of search and seizure as liberally as possible. This is encouraged in society, as it means crimes can be effectively prosecuted. But society does not want to leave matters of search and seizure to the judgment of each police officer (who may not have a wholly objective view of the case under investigation). Therefore, a bright-line rule (such as the plain view doctrine), simple enough to be understood and applied by police officers, protects individual-liberty interests and allows police officers to know which seizures are constitutionally permissible and which are likely to result in the exclusion of seized evidence.

Con: Limitations of the Plain View Doctrine

Unfortunately, the plain view doctrine is part of a body of criminal procedure (search and seizure) that lacks a unifying jurisprudence. The plain language of the Fourth Amendment is unclear, and the efforts of the Supreme Court to establish a coherent set of organizing principles have been unsuccessful.

One of the problems with search and seizure generally (and with the plain view doctrine) is that the Court characterizes Fourth Amendment interests in a monolithic, bifurcated way. Acts are either "searches" and "seizures," implicating legitimate privacy interests, and therefore entitled to all the protections of the Constitution, no matter how compelling the countervailing law enforcement interest might be; or they are not "searches" and "seizures," and are therefore afforded no constitutional protections whatsoever. The Court's holdings that certain warrantless activities were permissible, in cases like *Terry* (warrantless, pat-down searches based on reasonable suspicion), *Place* (warrantless searches by drug dogs), and *Jacobsen* (warrantless field test for cocaine) might imply that Fourth Amendment interests actually do exist on a graduated continuum, but the Court continues to deal with search and seizure in a largely binary manner. And attempting to superimpose a sliding scale of Fourth Amendment interests over the *Katz* rule could produce an unenforceable standard—one that is too complicated for the police to understand or obey, and too difficult for courts to enforce.

Another limitation of the plain view doctrine is that it corresponds with a rather bourgeoisie view of what constitutes reasonable privacy interests. While the Supreme Court's cases may afford adequate Fourth Amendment protections to citizens who live in houses with drapes that can be drawn and walls that muffle the sound of interior conversations, citizens who live in tenements with paper-thin walls may find themselves exposed to plain-hearing searches. Homeless citizens who live out of their cars may find their privacy interests truncated under the rationale described in *Cardwell*, and those who are living on the street may find that they have little or no legitimate expectation of privacy.

Finally, the plain view doctrine is problematic because it is an 18th-century standard that is awkwardly applied to 20th- and 21st-century problems. The Fourth Amendment is not always easily adapted to evolving technologies. While it may seem straightforward to state, as did the Court in *Lee* in 1927, that using a searchlight to enhance an otherwise plain view observation does not constitute a "search," where does that logic lead? It seems disingenuous to suggest that the government's use of an 800-mm lens, allowing FBI agents to peer through the defendant's open window and read his newspaper headlines from a quarter-mile away, is not a search. Surely, *Katz* cannot stand for the proposition that citizens must either shutter every window and seal every crack of their homes, or else accept whatever high-tech snooping the government chooses to use. Perhaps that is why the district court in *Kim* held that the use of the high-powered lens was an illegal search. Still, it can be difficult to know what investigative techniques are permissible. Although the Supreme Court struck down the use of a device to read heat signatures in a home in *Kyllo*, it upheld aerial surveillance in *Dow* and *Ciraolo*, despite the fact that viewing buildings from above is hardly in the plain view of ordinary citizens. The gulf between the concept of the plain view doctrine and the reality of modern surveillance techniques is likely to grow. In particular, the dynamics of digital evidence searches (such as files on hard drives) appear especially incompatible with the doctrine.

See Also: 16. Vehicle Searches; 19. Warrants.

Further Readings

Amar, Akhil Reed. "Fourth Amendment First Principles." *Harvard Law Review*, v.107 (1994).

Amsterdam, Anthony G. "Perspectives on the Fourth Amendment." *Minnesota Law Review*, v.58 (1974).

Arizona v. Hicks, 480 U.S. 321 (1987).

California v. Ciraolo, 476 U.S. 207 (1986).

Cardwell v. Lewis, 417 U.S. 583 (1974).

Coolidge v. New Hampshire, 403 U.S. 443 (1971).

Dow Chemical Company v. United States, 476 U.S. 227 (1986).

Harris, David A. "Superman's X-ray Vision and the Fourth Amendment: The New Gun Detection Technology." *Temple Law Review*, v.69 (1996).

Horton v. California, 496 U.S. 128 (1990).

Katz v. United States, 389 U.S. 347 (1967).

Kerr, Orrin S. "Searches and Seizures in a Digital World." *Harvard Law Review*, v.119 (2005).

Kyllo v. United States, 533 U.S. 27 (2001).

LaFave, Wayne R. *Search and Seizure: A Treatise on the Fourth Amendment*. St. Paul, MN: Thomson West, 2004.

Mapp v. Ohio, 367 U.S. 643 (1961).

Minnesota v. Dickerson, 508 U.S. 366 (1993).

Moylan, Charles E. "The Plain View Doctrine: Unexpected Child of the Great 'Search Incident' Geography Battle." *Mercer Law Review*, v.26 (1975).

Swire, Peter P. "*Katz* is Dead, Long Live *Katz*." *Michigan Law Review*, v.102 (2004).

Terry v. Ohio, 392 U.S. 1, 20 (1968).

Troiano, Kenneth. "Law Enforcement Use of High Technology: Does Closing the Door Matter Anymore?" *California Western Law Review*, v.24 (1988).

United States v. Jacobsen, 466 U.S. 109 (1984).

United States v. Kim, 415 F.Supp. 1252 (D.Haw. 1976).

United States v. Knotts, 460 U.S. 276 (1983).

United States v. Lee, 274 U.S. 559 (1927).

United States v. Place, 462 U.S. 696 (1983).

Wallin, Howard E. "Plain View Revisited." *Pace Law Review*, v.22 (2002).

Weeks v. United States, 232 U.S. 314 (1914).

Wilkins, Richard G. "Defining the 'Reasonable Expectation of Privacy': An Emerging Tripartite Analysis." *Vanderbilt Law Review*, v.40 (1987).

9

Police Brutality

Lyndsay N. Boggess
Christopher Donner
Jonathan Maskaly
University of South Florida

Police officers serve a multitude of functions in society. They are the most visible component of the criminal justice system and are called on to handle a myriad of situations. Due to the sheer number of criminal statutes, it would be impossible for officers to enforce all laws all the time. Therefore, officers are given the ability to use discretion in the commission of their duties. Discretion is an individual officer's judgment as to the best course of action during police encounters.

Two common examples of discretion include whether or not to issue a traffic citation, or whether or not to make an arrest. Discretion, in and of itself, is not problematic within criminal justice. Uncontrolled discretion, however, can be problematic and may lead to poor police-community relations, corruption, brutality, and legal proceedings against the officer (both civil and criminal).

Police brutality is conceptualized in different ways in various social contexts; its meaning has also changed over time. The use of violence by officers has decreased in recent years, but police brutality takes many forms, including lethal and nonlethal force. Understanding the exact prevalence of police brutality is complicated because of the variability in defining police brutality, the difficulty in distinguishing between justified and unjustified force, and the lack of centralized reporting systems. The potential causes of brutality are varied, and efforts to reduce brutality are tied to these causes. Despite the negative connotations associated with police brutality, however, some researchers argue that police use of force can serve a purpose in reducing and controlling crime. This chapter will more closely examine the problem of police brutality, its causes, and attempts at reform.

Defining Police Brutality

Unwarranted police violence and the physical mistreatment of citizens are not uncommon in the history of U.S. law enforcement. Empirical and anecdotal evidence supports the "shoot first and ask questions later" philosophy held by many police officers until the early 20th century, when the criminal justice system began to pay closer attention to issues of police brutality. Police brutality is generally defined as the unlawful use of physical force by officers in the performance of their lawful duties, but the line between acceptable force and brutality can be unclear. That is, police have the authority to use reasonable and acceptable force to subdue offenders, initiate arrests, prevent escapes, and protect citizens; but when an officer uses force that exceeds the minimum amount necessary, or continues to use force after it is no longer necessary, the officer is engaging in brutality. When the use of force is within the amount necessary to overcome resistance and prevent additional violence, the use of force is considered justified; it is warranted based on the offender's actions and within the confines of allowable force. Unjustified force, on the other hand, refers to those circumstances when the force is disproportionate to the immediate threat. This distinction is often subjective, and poses serious problems for holding officers accountable for their behavior.

Police brutality often involves physical pain or a threat of pain or violence. The videotaped beating of Rodney King in Los Angeles in 1991 is often referred to as one of the foremost examples of extreme police brutality (though the accused officers were acquitted of any wrongdoing). Other examples include a Baton Rouge, Louisiana, police officer who was investigated by the FBI for using a Taser stun gun five times on a handcuffed man during an arrest for marijuana possession, and the death of a 15-year-old in Bay City, Michigan, who was also stunned by a Taser while handcuffed. Other cases of police brutality are less obvious, such as the Portland, Oregon, police officer who faced disciplinary action after he allegedly shot an unarmed teenage girl with a beanbag shotgun.

Police brutality, however, can also consist of verbal aggression or abuse. Abusive language is not only aggressive, but often offensive, including the use of insults, degrading language, or racially based epithets.

Police abuse of power sometimes occurs in the interrogation room. In the past, it was common for police officers to question suspects for extended periods of time without providing basic necessities, including food or water or an opportunity to sleep. In some instances, detectives made threats against the suspect or the suspect's family, or beat confessions out of them. These behaviors were essentially outlawed in 1936 when the Supreme Court ruled in *Brown v. Mississippi* that confessions obtained through physical torture would not be allowed in court. The ruling, however, did not completely end the use of brutality during interrogations. Considered by some as the most egregious case of police brutality, former Lieutenant Jon Burge was recently convicted on federal perjury and obstruction of justice charges related to the decades-long torture of suspects (almost all black males) in the Chicago Police Department between the early 1970s and 1991. Accusations include the use of electric shocks, burning, suffocation, and beating in order to force confessions. The allegations ultimately led to a moratorium on executions in Illinois after Governor George Ryan pardoned four men from death row whose confessions had been coerced under Burge.

Brutal police practices were further limited during the tenure of Chief Justice Earl Warren between 1953 and 1969. Under Warren, the Supreme Court began a "due process revolution" by placing the individual rights of defendants above the crime control goals of police. This Court emphasized the ideal that police strictly adhere to the law; they did not tolerate police abuses, ranging from coerced confessions to warrantless searches. The Warren Court upheld the notion that those accused of crimes still enjoyed constitutionally protected rights. Around the same time, the National Advisory Commission on Civil Disorders (better known as the Kerner Commission after the chair, Governor Otto Kerner Jr. of Illinois) investigated the use of "street justice" by police officers during the urban riots of the late 1960s. Aggressive police patrol techniques, brutality, harassment, verbal abuse, and discourtesy were cited as key sources of tension between the African American population and the police. Like the allegations against Jon Burge in Chicago, the Kerner Commission concluded that questionable police practices targeted minorities. In fact, the commission further concluded that the brutal treatment of minorities by police was one of the precipitating factors behind the riots.

Excessive physical force is typically dichotomized into deadly force incidents and nondeadly force incidents. A great deal of research shows incidents of nondeadly force occur more frequently than incidents of deadly force, but the ramifications of unjustified deadly force incidents are far greater.

Deadly Force

Deadly force is commonly defined as force that causes or intends to cause death or serious physical harm. Unjustified deadly force can represent the ultimate form of police brutality; however, research indicates that this does not occur frequently, and most officers can work an entire career without ever discharging their firearm. There are approximately 550 cases of deadly force per year, and less than one-third of those are considered unjustified. When deadly force is used, it is most often with a firearm, although police vehicles have also been used as instruments of deadly force.

Police are justified in using deadly force only in cases when it is necessary to prevent the suspect's escape, and the officer has probable cause to believe the suspect poses a threat of death or serious physical harm to the officer, other officers, or the community. The most influential case delineating the restrictions on the use of deadly force is *Tennessee v. Garner* (1985). In that case, a Memphis police officer shot and killed Edward Garner as he was fleeing the scene of a residential burglary, despite evidence that Garner was unarmed. The Supreme Court determined that deadly force may only be used when the suspect poses a serious threat and that the prevention of escape is not a sufficient justification for deadly force. More specifically, under *Garner*, deadly force can only be used in two situations: (1) when there is an immediate danger to the officer, other officers, or the community; or (2) when the suspect has demonstrated serious dangerousness in prior threats/uses of force. At the time of the *Garner* decision, 45 states followed some version of the "fleeing felon" rule— allowing the use of force (including deadly force) against a person suspected of committing a felony and clearly attempting to escape. The *Garner* decision mandated that all states modify their laws to comply with the new standard.

While the number of people shot at by the police is low, the number actually killed by police officers each year is even lower. Researcher Michael White found that police shootings result in a fatality in only 14 percent of incidents. Despite the small number of people actually killed, however, there is a higher percentage of African Americans. Research from criminology professor and author Michael White demonstrates that 81 percent of Philadelphia police shootings involved African Americans.

Deadly force can provoke intense community reactions, particularly when it is unjustified or has the appearance of being unjustified. For example, there was a strong negative reaction in the aftermath of the shooting of Oscar Grant in Oakland (2009) and the shooting of Shawn Bell in New York City (2006), and riots occurred after the shooting of Timothy Thomas in Cincinnati in 2001. Communities often respond negatively to police shootings; urban communities almost always respond negatively (and sometimes violently) to police shootings of minorities. Such actions damage police-community relations and can undermine citizens' perceived legitimacy of the police.

Non-Deadly Force

Though nondeadly force occurs more frequently than deadly force, it is still a rare occurrence. Nondeadly force is typically defined as any type of force that is not likely to result in the death or serious physical injury of the suspect. This type of force is typically relegated to incidents of restraining and repelling assaultive suspects, and includes the use of clubs or batons, chemical-irritant spray, less-lethal devices such as beanbag or rubber-bullet firearms, and electronic-shock devices (Tasers). The burden of proof for using nondeadly force is less than the strict requirements for deadly force set forth in the *Garner* decision.

The *Garner* decision set a clear standard for the use of deadly force, but questions about what constitutes excessive and unjustified nondeadly force remained unanswered until 1989. At that time, the Supreme Court decided *Graham v. Connor*, a case coming out of North Carolina that involved allegations of abusive police behavior against a diabetic man. In the case, a police officer stopped Dethorne Graham's vehicle as it left a convenience store parking lot. When Graham exited the vehicle he passed out on the curb and awoke only after being handcuffed and slammed onto the hood of the vehicle by the officer. When Graham explained that he fainted as a result of his medical condition and asked the officers to verify this on a diabetic card that he carried, the officer told Graham to "shut up" and shoved him head first into the patrol car. As a result of the officer's actions, Graham sustained a broken foot, multiple cuts, and a shoulder injury. Graham filed a lawsuit against the police alleging that the officer used excessive force during the stop.

In the *Graham* decision, the Supreme Court decided that all claims of excessive force against a free citizen (both deadly and nondeadly) during the course of an arrest, investigatory stop, or other seizure should be analyzed under the Fourth Amendment's reasonableness standard. Under this standard, the officer's actions must be considered as reasonable while taking into consideration the severity of the crime, if the suspect poses a risk to the officer, and whether or not he is actively attempting to flee the scene. The Court determined that there must be a balance between the government's interest in societal safety and the individual's interest in being protected from unreasonable seizures.

Prevalence of Police Use of Force and Brutality

Though ambiguity in defining justified and unjustified police use of force affects the ability to accurately keep statistics on incidents of police brutality, a number of private entities such as the American Civil Liberties Union (ACLU) have made efforts to track and record the prevalence of police brutality. One group spearheading this effort is the National Police Misconduct Statistics and Reporting Project (NPMSRP). The NPMSRP is a nonpartisan, nongovernmental project devoted to reducing the problem of police misconduct, especially brutality. The project gathers statistical data on police misconduct through reports published in U.S. media outlets. Utilizing a compilation of police reports, citizen complaints, and victim surveys, the NPMSRP statistics reveal that the rate of unjustified police force appears to be very low, occurring in less than one percent of all police-citizen encounters. According to 2009 NPMSRP statistics, there were a recorded 3,445 alleged incidents of police misconduct involving 4,012 officers, including 261 law enforcement leaders (police chiefs or sheriffs). Less than one percent of the incidents resulted in a civilian fatality, but they were nonetheless exceptionally costly, with more than $198 million spent in misconduct-related civil litigation. With respect to justified (i.e., nonelective) incidents of deadly force, White's research indicates that 86 percent of Philadelphia's on-duty and 79 percent of off-duty shootings were nonelective (after a more stringent administrative policy was instituted).

Upon closer examination, the 2009 NPMSRP data shows that citizens made formal complaints for nearly every type of deviant police behavior. The most common citizen complaint was non-firearm related excessive force (18.1 percent of all reports), followed by sexual misconduct complaints (11.9 percent of cases). Other complaints involved unwarranted shooting, assault, excessive force against animals, and the unwarranted use of electric shock or Taser. Unfortunately, there is no accurate data reflecting trends of police brutality. According to Tony Pate, a research associate in criminology, and Lorie Fridell, an associate professor of criminology, many departments do not keep precise records of police behavior, and a national reporting system of police brutality does not exist.

Furthermore, research indicates a small number of police officers are responsible for the vast majority of use of force and brutality incidents. This means most police departments are not wholly corrupt—rather, each department may have a few "rotten apples." For example, the Christopher Commission, which was responsible for investigating the Los Angeles Police Department (LAPD) after the videotaped beating of Rodney King, identified 44 officers with six or more citizen complaints for excessive use of force 1986–90. Sixteen of those officers had eight or more complaints, and one officer had 16 complaints. These 44 officers constitute less than one percent of the LAPD, but were responsible for over 15 percent of the department's use-of-force reports; they averaged 13 use-of-force incidents during the time period compared to just 4.2 for all other officers with at least one complaint. Although these statistics represent just one agency, research from other cities (New York, Chicago, and St. Petersburg, Florida) has validated the "rotten apples" phenomenon.

Research suggests that a majority of police-abuse incidents go unreported, and that the estimates gathered by the ACLU, NPMSRP, and other agencies are vastly underestimated. A 1982 federal study determined that 13.6 percent of survey respondents were dissatisfied with the police, but only 30 percent of these people filed a formal complaint. Citizens may be reticent to file such complaints because the process can be logistically difficult and time-consuming, they fear retaliation from the police, or they feel that the complaint would not be taken seriously. The substantiation rate of citizen complaints is even less; work from Pate and Fridell, published in 1993, demonstrate that these rates range between zero and 25 percent, with 10 percent or less being the norm.

Potential Causes of Police Brutality

There are a myriad of potential causes of police brutality, including police exposure to violence, officer workload, departmental management style and administrative policies, and the social and demographic characteristics of the police and citizens. Most research, however, focuses on three areas: the police subculture, inherent biases among individual officers, and job burnout and cynicism.

Police Subculture

The first potential cause of police brutality is the police subculture. Organizational research indicates that occupations develop their own culture, and no occupation has a subculture as clearly defined and studied as the policing subculture. Developed to help officers cope with powerful feelings of isolation from society, officers are first socialized into the police subculture during the hiring and training processes. The socialization process provides new officers with a set of rules, attitudes, and techniques specific to policing. The police subculture, also referred to as the *blue curtain*, values secrecy and emphasizes loyalty to the police as paramount; violating the code of silence among officers is tantamount to a criminal offense. The subculture also fosters a general mistrust of the public and an "us versus them" mentality, in which only the police understand the police. As such, police officers often turn to other officers for moral and emotional support and mechanisms to manage stress, and to mitigate the isolation created by their unique role in the community. The subculture is passed from one generation of officers to the next; and research indicates that the policing subculture is so powerful and prevalent, that officers are almost bound to adopt it.

The subculture has such a powerful effect on the beliefs and actions of police officers that it can reinforce deviant behavior. In fact, some researchers have argued that one of the most powerful motivators within a police agency is the peer influence exerted by other members of the subculture. The subculture serves two distinct purposes: to protect police officers from harm on the streets caused by citizens, and to deal with a punishment-centered management that does not understand the problems that officers face on the street. Supervisors are often the mediating entity between the officers and management. This mediating role means supervisors are responsible for enforcing departmental policy, but are still partially involved with the subculture. This dual status of supervisors could potentially create an atmosphere where force is seen as acceptable because subordinates are not punished for inappropriate use of force. The lack of punishment likely comes in the form of supervisors informally handling allegations of brutality instead of referring it to management.

Biases Among Individual Officers

A second potential cause of police brutality is inherent biases among police officers. Although many people do not like to discuss the presence of bias in law enforcement, it is necessary to acknowledge bias and implement training to alter it. Reforms in the hiring process have made efforts to exclude officers with the most egregious biases. However, no screening process can be expected to keep a department from hiring a select few who hold prejudicial attitudes or beliefs. Research indicates that some police officers view certain citizens—prostitutes, drug users, gang members, homosexuals, drunks, career criminals—as second-class citizens having little to add to society. These officers may be unable to separate their bias from their obligation to provide police services in an objective manner. These officers do not generally consider individuals in these groups worth protecting, or will utilize less-professional procedures than those used with other citizens. Anecdotal evidence and research indicates that some officers may even single out individuals from these groups for harassment and brutality.

Furthermore, although the United States has come a long way in providing equal protection and individual liberty for all citizens, some police officers hold negative attitudes toward people of certain racial and ethnic groups. Officers are expected to set aside any bias in order to provide fair and impartial policing, but evidence suggests that officers continue to use derogatory language toward these groups. The 1991 Christopher Commission's investigation of the Los Angeles Police Department (LAPD) found hundreds of improper communications between officers, including "If you encounter these Negroes shoot first and ask questions later" and "I almost got me a Mexican last night but he dropped the dam [sic] gun too quick." Although these messages may reflect coping strategies or joking as part of the police subculture, they are also clearly prejudiced, racially biased, and inappropriate comments. The Christopher Commission concluded that the LAPD did have an organizational culture that emphasized and rewarded aggressive policing, and in doing so, isolated the police from citizens, particularly within certain communities and especially among minority populations.

Burnout and Cynicism

A third potential cause of police brutality stems from cynicism and burnout within police officers. The police are frequently called on to deal with the worst situations in society, and often encounter depressing and emotionally traumatizing situations on a daily basis. At times, officers may see persons they perceive to be guilty acquitted, released for lack of evidence, or set free on legal technicalities. If an officer repeatedly observes these patterns of injustice, he may become cynical toward the criminal justice system and allow the negativity to influence his or her behavior. Such officers may develop beliefs and attitudes that support taking justice into their own hands or relying on street justice (defined as policing in accordance with the ends justifying the means) to compensate for the absence of adequate legal justice. In particular, if an officer encounters a person known to frequently commit crime but avoid legal punishment, the officer may use unnecessary or excessive force as a tool to relieve frustration with the system and gain justice for society.

Curbing Police Brutality

When police brutality occurs, it frequently appears in the media, drawing attention to the problem and encouraging reform. Fully eradicating police brutality from society is a seemingly impossible task, especially if society gives police officers authority and discretion. In recent years, many police departments have started addressing issues of unjustified force and brutality and changing departmental force policies. Some changes resulted from legislative or judicial mandates, while others have come through research recommendations or internal audits of department policy.

The two most common mechanisms for reforming police behavior are the utilization of citizen complaints and civilian review boards. Police departments allow citizens to file a complaint against an officer through some mechanism. Less serious complaints are investigated and handled by a supervisor, and more severe complaints are handled by an internal affairs department. While filing a citizen complaint is usually a straightforward process, filings are often met with resistance, due in part to the blue curtain. In 1998, Human Rights Watch reported that the process of filing a citizen complaint, in 14 departments examined, was difficult and intimidating. The unnecessary level of difficulty could artificially reduce the number of complaints by discouraging filing.

Civilian Review Boards

Another mechanism used to curb police brutality is civilian review boards. These boards review and handle all types of complaints against police officers through an impartial investigation. The review boards offer citizens from minority groups an alternate avenue of reporting police brutality. The boards permit members from minority groups to report instances of brutality to an impartial group of citizens separate from the police department.

The presence of minority citizens on review boards could increase reporting and help restore police-community relations. Additionally, these boards provide an opportunity for police procedures to be explained to citizens, to review departmental policies, and to initiate dialogue between the police and the community.

Police brutality can also be diminished through training reforms (academy, field, and in-service). Research indicates that police academy curricula turn out officers rife with tactical training and lacking in community relations training and communication skills. Most training overemphasizes the potential for danger and spends an inordinate amount of time on firearms, physical combat, and arrest training (skills used infrequently during a police career). This training focus reinforces the subculture premise that policing is inherently dangerous and citizens need to be physically subdued.

Early Warning Systems

Another mechanism to curb police brutality is through the use of early warning systems. According to the National Institute of Justice, an early warning system is a database management tool designed to identify officers with problematic behavior, allowing the department to intervene and correct performance. The system works by selecting problem officers, intervening with them, and monitoring their subsequent performance. Research in Minneapolis and New Orleans shows early warning systems significantly alter the behavior of both officers and supervisors. Additionally, the early warning systems encourage supervisors to monitor officers identified for the program, reinforcing the overall goals.

If officers are convicted of engaging in police brutality (either by an internal investigation or criminal trial), there are ramifications for the individual officer and the agency that depend largely on the severity of the incident. Specifically, punishments vary from remedial training for minor infractions to termination for major infractions. If the incident is determined to be criminal, the officer can be sentenced to state or federal prison, as was the case with Sergeant Stacey Koon from the Rodney King incident in 1991. Additionally, the officer can be sued civilly for financial compensation by the aggrieved party. The officer's supervisor and the chief of police can also be included in this lawsuit through vicarious liability statutes. Furthermore, if the officer's behavior shows a clear pattern or practice of brutality, the department can be ordered by the Department of Justice to enter into a consent decree, which forces the department to implement changes to prevent further federal regulation and oversight of the department. For example, cities such as Cincinnati and Los Angeles have been on consent decrees for force-related instances since 1982 and 2001, respectively.

Pro: Arguments Supporting Police Use of Heavy Force

Some argue that police use of heavy force serves an integral purpose in society. Herbert Packer, a Stanford University law professor, developed what he called a "crime control model" in the 1960s that privileges the rights of law-abiding citizens over the rights of criminals. One of the foundations of this model is that the most important task of the criminal justice system is the repression of criminal activity. Therefore, people subscribing to this model of criminal justice believe that police brutality is not only acceptable, but also necessary to effectively control crime. Advocates of the crime control model view crime as an encroachment on society's right to live in crime-free communities, and police are entitled to use any means necessary to repress the criminal conduct and preserve order for the greater good of society. This belief could allow police officers to act with impunity when controlling criminal conduct. Those subscribing to this view believe the police can and should use any means necessary, including any amount of necessary force in order to maintain order and apprehend all criminal suspects and bring them to justice as quickly as possible.

In 1982, criminologists James Q. Wilson and George Kelling published their views on the use of zero-tolerance policing as a means to maintain order in neighborhoods. In the groundbreaking article *Broken Windows* that appeared in the *Atlantic Monthly,* they argued that simply arresting gang members or other criminals is not sufficient to discourage crime and abate disorder. They refer to the history of policing when, in order to assert authority, officers routinely used violence on behalf of the community. The authors notes that at times, in the name of safety and protection of the community, individual rights should be minimized.

Additionally, the heavy use of force by the police has a potential deterrent effect on crime. In order to achieve deterrence, three factors are necessary: certainty of detection, severity of punishment, and celerity (swiftness) of punishment. Allowing police officers to use any method necessary to detain and bring suspects to justice would allow police officers to fulfill all necessary elements to deter future criminal behavior. The criminal would be deterred from committing crime under the knowledge that if caught by the police, immediate and severe punishment would be inflicted. This consequence would deter not only the offender from future offending (specific deterrence), but also other, uninvolved citizens learning of the harsh punishment (general deterrence). In fact, in a 1991 study of 57 U.S. cities, economist Dale Cloninger found an inverse relationship between the rate of civilian killing by police and the nonhomicide violent crime rate: for a one percent increase in police killings, violent crime decreases one-sixth of a percent.

An additional reason society may become more permissive of the heavy use of force by the police is out of concern for the police officers themselves. The neighborhoods in which police officers work make it necessary for officers to be willing and able to defend themselves from attack. Police officers may experience what researchers Carl Werthman and Irving Piliavin called "ecological contamination" in 1967, whereby officers respond to the ecological cues of the neighborhood and the behaviors of people within the neighborhood for self-preservation. For example, research in the late 1990s by urban sociologist Elijah Anderson suggests that residents in disadvantaged and high-crime communities value respect and honor above all else. In such communities, violence is often relied upon to maintain and establish respect. Police interactions in such communities, then, could effectively incorporate and utilize similar violent mechanisms in order to best convey their authority and establish respect, which could serve to diminish further uses of force and improve police community relations.

Con: Arguments Against Permitting Police Brutality

On the other hand, many more argue against permitting unjustified use of force by police, believing this brutal conduct has negative consequences for society. Specifically, allowing police officers to administer street justice circumvents the criminal justice process by convicting and punishing an offender without a criminal trial. The constitutional premise of the criminal justice system in the United States rests on the presumption of innocent until proven guilty, not innocent until arrested. Police brutality against suspects, defined as unjustified violence, can potentially cause a plethora of problems for police, including unnecessarily brutalizing innocent members of society. Additionally, excess force could lead to diminished trust in the police, especially with populations already lacking faith in the police (e.g., inner-city African Americans), making it more difficult to perform policing functions. Furthermore, these types of activities could bring negative media attention, further damaging the reputation of the police within society. An example of the power of the media coverage with police use of force can be seen in the "don't tase me bro!" incident from the University of Florida in 2004. Student Andrew Meyer was arrested during a forum with visiting U.S. Senator John Kerry, after he demanded access to a closed microphone, confronted the senator with questions, and then forcefully resisted officers who attempted to remove him. After the officers' decision to use a Taser gun on Meyer, controversy and media attention erupted. In addition to negative consequences for the policing profession, there could be negative consequences for individual officers, including civil liability suits, criminal prosecution, and job loss.

In addition to the diminished trust in the police on the societal level and the adverse consequences for police officers, police brutality also negatively impacts the victim, who will likely suffer physical injuries from the incident. The nature and significance of these injuries is dependent upon the type of force used against the suspect; damage could range from contusions on the minor level, to permanent physical disfigurement, mental damage, or death on the extreme level. All injuries from unjustified attacks could lead to diminished faith in the police, which could have additional consequences for the victim of the brutality, including increased victimization and retributive offending because of a reticence to call the police.

When the police brutalize members of society, regardless of the legal status of the suspect, the public's level of cynicism against the police is increased. This results in a loss of perceived legitimacy, which refers to the belief that an authority is appropriate, proper, and just. If people believe an authority is legitimate, they will voluntarily defer to the rules, decisions, and social arrangements of the authority.

Support of Research

Some argue the notion of police legitimacy is purely theoretical and cannot be empirically substantiated. However, research shows that police engaging in unjust practices (e.g., racial profiling, use of unnecessary force) lose public support from the loss of legitimacy. Conversely, when the police act in a fair and just manner, people more willingly defer to authority. Ultimately, this means that if police brutality was prevented and punished more severely (restoring the level of legitimacy), the public would be more willing to self-regulate behavior and enforcement techniques would not be as necessary, further reducing the need for police use of force.

Furthermore, many of the arguments made in favor of permitting police brutality have never been empirically validated. For example, research published in 2000 by Dan Nagin and Greg Pogarsky indicates certainty of detection routinely exhibits the strongest effect on deterring behavior. Therefore, it is difficult to claim that brutality would serve to deter crime when the variable shown to have the largest effect is unrelated to police brutality.

Additionally, the argument that allowing police brutality will lead to decreases in the crime rate is deeply flawed. Specifically, it appears crime was actually increasing during the period of time prior to the riots investigated by the Kerner Commission. Furthermore, research by John Eck and Edward Maguire indicates the 1990s New York City crime rate was not dropping at a rate significantly different than areas in other parts of the country (most with fewer uses of force and complaints). Finally, many of the conclusions drawn between elevated levels of police brutality and crime have failed to control for key variables likely to influence the relationship observed, such as the economy and community-level factors.

See Also: 1. Accountability; 2. Arrest Practices; 10. Police Corruption and Code of Silence; 15. Use of Deadly Force.

Further Readings

Adams, Kenneth. *Use of Force by Police: Overview of National and Local Data.* Washington, DC: National Institute of Justice, 1999.

Alpert, Geoffrey, and Lorie Fridell. *Police Vehicles and Firearms: Instruments of Deadly Force.* Prospect Heights, IL: Waveland Press, 1992.

Bratton, William. "Crime is Down in New York City: Blame the Police." In *Zero Tolerance: Policing a Free Society,* edited by Normal Dennis. London: IEA Health and Welfare Unit, 1998.

Christopher, Warren. *Report of the Independent Commission on the Los Angeles Police Department.* Los Angeles: City of Los Angeles, 1991.

Cloninger, Dale O. "Lethal Police Response as a Crime Deterrent: 57-City Study Suggests a Decrease in Certain Crimes." *American Journal of Economics and Sociology,* v.50 (1991).

Griffin, Catherine, and Jim Ruiz. "The Sociopathic Police Personality: Is it a Product of the 'Rotten Apple' or the 'Rotten Barrel?'" *Journal of Police and Criminal Psychology,* v.14 (1999).

Eck, John E., and Edward R. Maguire. "Have Changes in Policing Reduced Violent Crime?" In *The Crime Drop in America,* edited by

Alfred Blumstein and Joel Wallman. Cambridge, MA: Cambridge University Press, 2006.

Holmes, Malcolm. "Minority Threat and Police Brutality: Determinants of Civil Rights Criminal Complaints in U.S. Municipalities." *Criminology*, v.38 (2000).

Inciardi, James. *Criminal Justice*. Boston: McGraw-Hill, 2007.

Kappeler, Victor, Richard Sluder, and Geoffrey Alpert. *Forces of Deviance: Understanding the Dark Side of Policing*. Prospect Heights, IL: Waveland Press. 1998.

Lersch, Kim. "Police Misconduct and Malpractice: A Critical Analysis of Citizens' Complaints." *Policing: An International Journal of Police Strategies and Management*, v.21 (1998).

Nagin, D. S., and G. Pogarsky. "Integrating Celerity, Impulsivity, and Extralegal Sanction Threats Into a Model of General Deterrence: Theory and Evidence." *Criminology*, v.39 (2001).

National Police Misconduct Statistics and Reporting Project. www.injust iceeverywhere.com (Accessed October 2010).

Packer, Herbert. *The Limits of the Criminal Sanction*. Palo Alto, CA: Stanford University Press, 1968.

Pate, Anthony, and Lorie Fridell. "Toward the Uniform Reporting of Police Use of Force: Results of a National Study." *Criminal Justice Review*, v.20 (1993).

Pate, Anthony, Lorie Fridell, and Edwin Hamilton. *Police Use of Force: Official Reports, Citizen Complaints, and Legal Consequences*. Washington, DC: The Police Foundation. 1993.

Punch, Maurice. "Rotten Orchards: Pestilence, Police Misconduct and System Failure." *Policing and Society*, v.13 (2003).

Seron, Carroll, Joseph Pereira, and Jean Kovath. "Judging Police Misconduct: 'Street-Level' Versus Professional Policing." *Law and Society Review*, v.38 (2004).

Skogan, Wesley, and Tracey Meares. "Lawful Policing." *Annals of the American Academy of Political and Social Science*, v.593 (2004).

Skolnick, Jerome. *Justice Without Trial: Law Enforcement in Democratic Society*. New York: Macmillan College Publishing Company, 1994.

Skolnick, Jerome, and James Fyfe. *Above the Law: Police and the Excessive Use of Force*. New York: The Free Press, 1993.

Stock, Harley, Randy Borum, and Dennis Baltzley. "Police Use of Deadly Force." In *Lethal Violence: A Sourcebook on Fatal Domestic,*

Acquaintance, and Stranger Aggression, edited by Harold Hall. Boca Raton, FL: CRC Press, 1998.

Terrill, William. "Police Use of Force and Suspect Resistance: The Micro Process of the Police-Suspect Encounter." *Police Quarterly,* v.16 (2003).

Tyler, Tom. "Enhancing Police Legitimacy." *Annals Of the American Academy of Political and Social Science,* v.593 (2004).

Tyler, Tom. "Psychological Perspectives on Legitimacy and Legitimation." *Annual Review of Psychology,* v.57 (2006).

Tyler, Tom, and Cheryl Wakslak. "Profiling and the Legitimacy of the Police." *Criminology,* v.42 (2004).

Van Maanen, John. "Observations on the Making of Policemen." *Human Organization,* v.32 (1973).

Walker, Samuel, Geoffrey Alpert, and Dennis Kenney. *Early Warning Systems: Responding to the Problem Officer.* Washington, DC: National Institute of Justice, 2001.

Werthman, Carl, and Irving Piliavin. "Gang Members and the Police." In *The Police: Six Sociological Essays,* edited by David Bordua. New York: John Wiley, 1967.

White, Michael. "Assessing the Impact of Administrative Policy on Use of Deadly Force by On- and Off-Duty Police." *Evaluation Review,* v.24 (2000).

White, Michael. "Hitting the Target (or Not): Comparing Characteristics of Fatal, Injurious, and Non-Injurious Police Shootings." *Police Quarterly,* v.9 (2006).

Wilson, James, and George Kelling. "Broken Windows: The Police and Neighborhood Safety." *The Atlantic Monthly,* v.249 (1982).

10

Police Corruption and the Code of Silence

Cara Rabe-Hemp
Illinois State University

Corruption continues to be one of the most persistent problems faced by American police departments in the 20th century. In addition to undermining the integrity of police and the criminal justice system, corruption allows criminal activity to thrive. Former *New York Times* reporter, David Burnham, argues in his book, *The Role of the Media in Controlling Corruption*, that police corruption is a multimillion-dollar secret tax imposed on taxpayers every year. The most damaging cost of police corruption may be the detriment to the public confidence in the police, impacting the ability of police and citizens to work together to fight crime in their communities.

The code of silence—the refusal of officers to testify against other officers—is one of the major factors protecting police corruption. Proponents argue the code of silence is integral to police work, due to the high level of danger and unpredictability, the impossible mandate set for police, and the unforgiving and unsupportive nature of the public and police administration. By comparison, opponents argue that the code of silence breeds police secrecy as well as public distrust of the police, diminishing the perceived competency of the criminal justice system. Before these arguments can be assessed, a description of the nature of police corruption, as well as its theories, types, and levels, must be introduced. The triumphs and challenges for preventing and controlling corruption in the modern century are also discussed.

Defining Police Corruption

Police corruption takes place when an officer misuses his or her authority and official capacity to bring about personal gain. Police corruption takes place anytime an officer receives advantage or reward for: (1) doing something that he or she is required to do under duty anyway; (2) doing something that an officer is prohibited from doing on duty; (3) exercising police discretion, but for improper reasons; or (4) employing illegal or immoral means to achieve police goals. Defining police corruption this way embodies the variety of behaviors typically defined as police corruption and the rewards associated with corruption, which may be personal in nature—including money, gifts, power, and prestige, or organizational rewards such as promotion, approval of administrators, and colleague's support.

Types of Police Corruption

In their book, *Police in America* (2008), Sam Walker and Charles Katz describe four general types of police corruption: taking gratuities, taking bribes, theft or burglary, and internal corruption.

The most common form of police corruption involves gratuities—small tips or discounts on good purchased. While taking gratuities may be a violation of policy in some departments, it is not illegal. For this reason, whether to define the acceptance of gratuities as corruption has been and continues to be hotly debated. Many believe police should never be allowed to receive gratuities because of the slippery slope to more serious forms of corruption. Others argue that gratuities are a way of building positive social relationships between the police and public, and should be encouraged. Much of the debate is focused on whether the motive in giving a gratuity is to covertly buy additional police protection. Preferential treatment to businesses that offer gratuities may lead to an environment conducive to police corruption.

Police corruption may also involve taking bribes—the payment of money or other consideration to police officers with the aim of subverting the criminal justice system. Bribes may take place as a pad or regular periodic payment to overlook criminal behavior, or as a score or one-time payment intended to avoid arrest or overlook criminal behavior.

Theft or burglary—the taking of money or property by the police while performing their duties—is another form police corruption. Narcotics arrests are especially tempting. The 1985 River Cops case in Miami revealed that a large number of officers had stolen and sold cocaine. Officers were caught keeping money, weapons, and valuables to sell for profit. Due to the nature of police work, the opportunity for this type of police corruption is abundant.

The final type of police corruption is internal corruption, when officers pay members of their departments for special assignments or promotions. Internal payoffs may not be as common as they were in the early 1900s, but they still exist.

Corruption, in comparison to other types of misconduct such a brutality or deviance, always involves a benefit for the police officer in exchange for abuse of the officer's power. Although brutality has been utilized to further the goals of corruption, it does not involve personal gain.

The History of Police Corruption in America

The American police experience with corruption has been unique, and the history of corruption in the United States has influenced the character and structure of law enforcement in many ways. In the political era of policing (1840–1930), urban police officers bought their jobs, their assignments, and promotions. Officers could expect to recoup the costs and make a profit from graft. The vice laws—those regulating alcohol, gambling, and prostitution, were the most common, supplemented by ignoring building and health codes, Sabbath closings, and traffic laws. Despite several postwar police scandals that led to extensive reform (e.g., Gross Commission, 1953; Los Angeles, 1951; Oakland, 1955), corruption was not eliminated from American policing.

Real progress in understanding and dealing with corruption began in the 1960s, when police began to understand that the problem was systematic, not just the result of a devious few. Previous to this time, police departments suggested that the problem of corruption was the occasional "rotten apple," the uniformed officer who accepts an occasional bribe. Defining corruption in this way did not explain the pervasiveness or the organization of corruption in many departments.

Today, police corruption is explained in many levels. Type I, or "rotten pockets," are small groups of officers, typically assigned to enforce vice laws, who engage in low-level corruption. Type II, or pervasive unorganized corruption, occurs when a large percentage of the department is corrupt, but the actors work independently. This level of corruption does not require organizational support within the department. Many officers may be involved in corrupt behaviors, but not in concert. Finally, Type III, or pervasive, organized corruption, includes situations in which corruption is widespread within the agency and the actors collude to achieve their goals. This level of corruption entails the entire hierarchy of the police department participating in corruption, or the agency's complete tolerance and lack of control of corruption.

The 1970s Knapp Commission: Meat Eaters and Grass Eaters

The 1970s presented a new inducement with police corruption: the buying, selling, and stealing of narcotics. The War on Drugs has significantly increased the opportunities for corruption, due to the financial payouts that far exceed other previous forms of corruption. The Knapp Commission identified payoffs to officers as high as $80,000 in drug cases. The five-member Knapp Commission, chaired by Whitman Knapp, a federal judge, was organized in 1970 to investigate corruption allegations leveled at the New York Police Department (NYPD). In the first-ever televised hearings, Detectives Frank Serpico and David Durk claimed widespread corruption in the NYPD ranging from organized shakedowns of bar owners and construction contractors to payoffs from gamblers and drug dealers to criminal activity from NYPD officers. The commission's findings of systematic corruption in the agency led to a dozen indictments and the resignation of the police commissioner of the time.

The Knapp Commission report introduced two types of corrupt officers: "meat eaters" and "grass eaters." Grass eaters are passive officers who only engage in corruption when propositioned from the public. By comparison, meat eaters actively seek out opportunities to engage in corrupt and criminal behavior. For example, in 1979, a federal prosecutor indicted the entire Philadelphia police force for their corrupt methods and unwillingness to participate in the investigation of corruption. The Chicago police department also faced major scandals during this time.

The 1990s and Beyond

In the 1990s, a commission was assembled to examine the infrastructure and ethos of the Los Angeles Police Department (LAPD) in the wake of the 1991 beating of Rodney King by LAPD officers and the subsequent public riots over the officers' acquittal. The blue-ribbon panel issued over 400 recommendations, including increased supervision, better screening of job candidates, and racial sensitivity training. Despite all the attention police corruption has received and the efforts by police administrators to detect and eradicate corruption, there are still a number of recent examples of police corruption.

The Mollen Commission was created in 1993 to investigate allegations of corruption in the 75th precinct. Former police officer Michael Dowd testified before the commission about how he received $4,000 per week in return for protecting illegal drug operations. In addition, he testified to robbing crime victims, drug dealers, and arrestees of drug money; accepting money and drugs; and using drugs and alcohol while on duty.

The LAPD Ramparts Division scandal in the late 1990s was one of the largest police corruption scandals in history. Over 70 officers from the elite anti-gang squad were investigated for their roles in widespread corruption, including committing crimes, covering up unjustified beatings and shootings, planting evidence, and committing perjury. The Ramparts scandal highlights the convergence of brutality and corruption that characterized the 1990s.

After Hurricane Katrina in 2005 in New Orleans, there were allegations that police officers participated in the large-scale looting that followed the flooding. In addition, over 200 officers abandoned their posts during the disaster; they were fired or suspended.

Theories of Police Corruption

The most commonly used theoretical frameworks for explaining police corruption are sociological, sociocultural, and organizational.

Sociological theories emphasize the code, solidarity, and norms of the police culture that contribute to the opportunity for police corruption. The occupational subculture is a major factor not only in creating police corruption by initiating police officers into corrupt activities, but also by sustaining and covering up corrupt activities by other officers. As officers' exposure to the police subculture increases, they become more permissive toward deviant and corrupt police behavior. This process of socialization acculturates rookie officers to the norms and values of the police culture through early academy and field-training experiences. Police isolation also contributes to an unwritten rule of police culture—in the rare event that a fellow officer's misconduct is reported to outsiders, the informant faces serious isolation and repercussions. These theories also recognize that certain structures in the United States tend to encourage and sustain corruption, such as the criminal law, cultural conflict, and the local political culture. For example, the criminalization of activities that many people consider legitimate and culturally appropriate, combined with lax criminal standards, creates unguided police discretion and potential for police corruption. Due to the tradition of local control for police functions, the community and its political environment are influential in establishing attitudes toward corrupt activities. It is a commonly reported finding that disadvantaged communities—those with a high population turnover or language barrier— have greater police corruption.

The sociocultural perspective focuses on the interaction between the individual and the culture. These theories attempt to explain why some officers become corrupt while other officers do not. Historically, individual officer explanations, while popular and common with police officials, have been challenged by police researchers who claim that individual explanations for police corruption provide police officials with easy solutions to police corruption, allowing them to ignore more systematic and difficult issues. In his 1974 book, *Police Corruption: A Sociological Perspective*, Lawrence Sherman suggests that deviant officers pass through various stages of rationalization to more serious misdeeds in a systematic and gradual way, progressing through the "moral career." The first stage includes the acceptance of minor gratuities such as free meals, and progresses to actively seeking bribes. Once officers get past the first moral crisis in their identity, the initial corruption becomes the foundation for justifying future, more egregious behaviors. Eventually, the corrupt acts are initiated by the officer. It becomes easier to rationalize new and less ethical behaviors. At this point, the moral career of the corrupt officer is complete. Sloppy recruiting and the development of a police personality are also sociocultural theories of police corruption.

The organizational analysis of police corruption speculates that the bureaucratic and quasi-military structures of police departments provide a setting that is tolerant of police corruption. The inflexibility of the traditional police bureaucracy, resulting in the reliance on the authoritarian rank hierarchy, enables the emphasis on cover-ups and lying. Corruption flourishes in departments in which the organizational culture tolerates or ignores it. Without at least implicit approval by an organization, corruption could not exist for long. In a 2000 study entitled *The Measurement of Police Integrity*, Carl Klockars was able to demonstrate that different police agencies have very different environments of integrity. The bureaucratic structure is difficult for outsiders to permeate. This research suggests that while police officers view the seriousness of various forms of corruption similarly, officers in organizations that do not tolerate corruption are less likely to engage in corrupt behaviors.

Preventing and Controlling Corruption

The responsibility for combating police corruption lies with the police themselves. The status of the profession demands that police self-regulate. The control of corruption involves two distinct tasks: (1) preventing corruption in the first place, and (2) reducing or eliminating it once it exists. Fortunately, police agencies have numerous methods at their disposal to control police corruption internally.

Positive Leadership

Experts agree that successful control of corruption begins with police leadership, namely the attitude of the chief. Effective chiefs show support by example and support, defining the culture of the department and setting the policies and procedures for fighting corruption. Most historical examples of successful corruption control involve strong chiefs, including William Parker in Los Angeles, O.W. Wilson in Chicago, and Patrick Murphy in New York City.

Administrative Rulemaking and Corruption Investigations

The second step in the process involves clearly defining what actions will not be tolerated. Effective anticorruption policies must be clear, comprehensive, and systematically distributed. Mechanisms for detecting and punishing corrupt behavior, as well as for rewarding good behavior, must be established.

Dealing with police corruption requires meaningful investigations of suspected corruption by training investigators. Internal affairs units receive, process, and investigate allegations of police corruption.

Community Policing

The philosophy of community policing requires that police be more transparent and open. Secrecy is seen as an impediment to the police–community partnership. As police officers increase their interaction with the public, a greater trust and rapport will lessen the need for secrecy.

External controls imposed on a department provide another layer of control, including the following:

- **Special Investigations.** In pervasive police corruption scandals, special investigations or "blue-ribbon committees" are common. Examples include the Knapp Commission (1970), the Mollen Commission (1992), and the Commission on Police Integrity (1997). Most external forms of police accountability lack the intimate knowledge of the police subculture to break the code of silence. Despite this difficulty, they have been effective at drawing attention to the problems of relying on internal control for police accountability.
- **Criminal Prosecution.** The use of criminal prosecution to decrease police accountability is complicated by the fact that not all corrupt activities are criminal. Because cases against police officers are usually difficult to win, prosecutors contend that it is best to pursue only the cases with the greatest chances of conviction, which are typically the most egregious. This leads to the common finding that most criminal prosecutions involve the severe end of the corruption scale.
- **Media and Public Opinion.** Police corruption flourishes in a local political culture that tolerates it. In those cultures, mobilizing public opinion can be an effective means of bringing attention to police corruption.

Code of Silence

The ability of police administrators, reformers, and researchers to evaluate and control police corruption has depended largely on their ability to break through the code of silence—the refusal of officers to testify against other officers. In his classic study of the police subculture, *Violence and the Public* (1970), William Westley reports that officers were willing to lie to cover up an illegal activity by another officer. Four decades later, research suggests that not much has changed. The code of silence admonishes officers to never, regardless of the seriousness of the alleged corruption, provide information to outsiders (superiors and citizens) that would bring harm to a fellow officer. The code of silence is enforced by threats to shun informing officers, the fear of drawing attention to missteps, and the fear of backup being withheld in emergency circumstances.

In policing, the code of silence has three sources: defensiveness, professionalization, and depersonalization. Defensiveness reflects the "us versus them" attitude between the police and the public, and is an adaptation to perceived hostility from the outside world. The mistrust of the public has long been reinforced by the traditional or professional model of policing, which holds that police are experts at fighting crime and the public has little knowledge or authority to contribute to police work. The belief that outsiders of the police profession do not understand the challenges officers face is inculcated in police officers early in their training and socialization process. Once in the field, solidarity and the resulting code of silence is culturally transmitted when trainers frequently inundate officers with stories of how officers protect each other, not only against the public, but also against capricious and out-of-touch police administrators. Professionalism also provides police with a common definition of real police work and how citizens should view that work. In other words, officers protect each other in order to insulate themselves from challenges to their authority by citizens. The depersonalization of citizens whom police perceive as challenging and disrespectful leads to police abuse and brutality.

Proponents, mostly officers, argue the code of silence is integral to police work, due to the high level of danger and unpredictability, the impossible mandate set for police, and the unforgiving and unsupportive nature of the public and police administration. By comparison, opponents argue that the code of silence breeds police secrecy and public distrust of the police, diminishing the perceived competency of the government.

Pro: Arguments in Favor of the Code of Silence

There are several factors contributing to the development and necessity of the code of silence in policing. First, policing is a dangerous occupation that depends on the unquestioning support and loyalty of police peers. The danger and stress of police work make solidarity and the resultant code of silence an important part of the coping mechanisms utilized by police. In this way, the code of silence is reinforced through practices that encourage mutual protection and assistance. The trust that police maintain is necessary to ensure the officers' safety. Assurance of peer loyalty gives officers the moral support to perform their duty.

The second factor that confirms the need for the code of silence is the contradiction between the police goals of enforcing the law and maintaining order, while maintaining the constitutional rights of citizens. Herman Goldstein, author of *Police Corruption: A Perspective on Its Nature and Control* (1975), concludes that the demands placed upon the police are so diffuse and contradictory, their mandate is unachievable. This leads officers

to feel vulnerable in making decisions that will be perceived as rule violations. Policing is dictated by rules and regulations, and violating policy can
be grounds for police discipline. Policing is fraught with the potential for
mistakes, with the need for split-second decisions that are unfairly criticized
by outsiders. These reciprocal efforts also protect police officers from the
whims of departmental brass.

Third, the code of silence is necessary for protecting police from an unsupportive public. Police officers believe that the public does not understand or support what they do, and are reluctant to share their feelings with
outsiders. For this reason, the police have been said to hold the "us versus
them" attitude that differentiates police from citizens. Police are under constant review by citizens, many of whom do not hesitate to report what they
consider to be deviant to the media, or other authoritative bodies.

Fourth, the code of silence is essential due to the fact that police depend
on one another, sometimes in life-or-death situations. The highly unpredictable and dangerous environment in which police work occurs leads to a
general suspicion of citizens. The need for this suspicion is confirmed by officer experience, which frequently involves daily, often adversarial confrontations with citizens who are criminal or in need. Officers learn that their
fellow police are the only people who can be counted on in problematic
situations. Eventually, officers equate the very essence of survival with the
unquestioned support and loyalty of colleagues. Loyalty to officers also has
the positive benefits of bolstering self-esteem and confidence.

The fifth factor that confirms the need for the code of silence is that the
police have the right to step out of legal and ethical bounds, breaking departmental policies and even laws to achieve a moral outcome. In fact, to be
a good police officer, many police officers believe they have to violate some
of the rules they are supposed to follow. Called *noble cause corruption*, officers violate the civil right of citizens to achieve a moral remedy. According
to Michael Coldero and John Crank in their book *Police Ethics: The Corruption of Noble Cause* (2000), noble cause corruption is a more significant
problem than economic corruption, and is increasing among U.S. police
departments today. One reason for this growing problem is the widespread
tolerance among citizens for the violation of due process and citizens' rights
in order to arrest criminals.

Finally, the police code of silence is an extreme version of a phenomenon
that exists in all organizations, but has been exaggerated in policing to sati-
ate the entertainment media and its fascinated public. Sociologist and police
scholar Albert J. Reiss Jr. has suggested that his Yale University students

share a set of understanding about student corruption in cheating, which is rarely reported by classmates. Regardless of the organization, peers are encouraged to confide in one another, limit information to superiors, and avoid becoming an informant or whistleblower.

Con: Arguments Against the Code of Silence

While proponents of the code of silence suggest that it protects the police from an unsupportive public, most public opinion polls suggest that the public is overwhelmingly supportive of the police. In fact, the police rank highly compared to other occupations in terms of perceived honesty and integrity. Opponents of the code of silence argue that it erodes this public trust of the police and breeds police secrecy, diminishing the perceived competency of the government.

The code of silence is costly to individual officers through loss of integrity and police isolation, intense in-group dependence, and suspicion and distrust of citizens and administrators. The harm inflicted to a police officer's credibility is devastating. When peers systematically ensure that cops keep silent about illegal or unethical behavior, corruption allows criminal activity to thrive. For example, the Knapp Commission reported that the most serious forms of corruption flourished when officers guilty of minor transgressions refused to report the serious crimes for fear of exposing their own petty criminality. For example, in its investigation of alleged corruption in the NYPD, the Mollen Commission reported in 1994 that the police code of silence facilitated corruption by creating the ideal that loyalty to other officers was more important than stopping corruption and by fostering behaviors that thwarted the control of corruption.

Enormous pressure is placed on officers not to discuss police behaviors outside the ranks. This omnipresent suspicion, coupled with long and irregular work hours, serves to isolate police from the rest of society. This isolation makes officers overly dependent on policing for their self-identity. Having identified themselves as a group, individual officers who then betray the group also betray their own group identity. Officers who do not reciprocate or are not loyal to this code are ostracized within the police subculture. Honest officers cannot act without fear of reprisal in this atmosphere, and face the decision of becoming corrupt themselves, staying quiet, or leaving the agency. All of these options lead to negative outcomes for the police organization. This is especially true if administrators participate in and thereby encourage corruption. When this occurs, the honest officer truly is alone.

Police misconduct not only affects the officer in question, but also the reputations of police officers and police agencies in general. The eventual cost of police coverups is public distrust of police testimony. In the late 1990s, during the Rampart division scandal, hundreds of drug convictions were threatened due to allegations that corrupt officers planted illegal evidence on offenders. The result was a tarnished reputation for the LAPD and a lack of trust in the criminal justice system. Exposing corruption impacts how the community views police, which impacts officer morale.

While the code of silence shields police from public scrutiny, it also restricts the public's knowledge of police activities. Without public information regarding police policies and practices, the public is educated about policing from the often-inaccurate images provided by the media. Most modern police innovations, including community policing and problem-oriented policing, rely on citizens' assistance to decrease crime. Citizens won't help the police if they harbor a lack of trust, and trust is the first step toward working together to fight crime in communities.

Police corruption also undermines legitimate attempts at curbing crime by concealing or strengthening criminal enterprises. Police corruption consists of those actions that violate the very laws entrusted by police officers to uphold. The code of silence encourages and facilitates corruption through eroding communities and the governments that oversee them.

Despite the fact that many organizations have a code of silence, police are asked to be held to a higher standard of honesty and care for the public good than the general citizenry due to the unique power and prestige associated with their position. No other profession has the power to so immediately deprive citizens of life and liberty. Defining police corruption this way makes it harder to forget the psychological and social effects police corruption has on victims and their communities.

Conclusion

In conclusion, the vast majority of police officers perform their difficult jobs in an ethical and professional manner. Police corruption occurs when an officer uses power and authority for personal gain. The implications of police corruption are far-reaching, as it imposes costs on the police department, criminal justice system, and society. While corruption may not ever be completely eradicated, research suggest that the opportunity structure inherent in the nature of police work must be addressed, along with hiring quality, ethical recruits, and systematic accountability for both officers and administrators to lessen the harmful effects of corruption. There are some indications that the changing structure of modern police departments through the increased recruitment of women and minorities, and adoption of community policing principles, has lessened the reliance of loyalty to other officers and strengthened the loyalty for the ethical canons of the profession.

See Also: 1. Accountability; 4. Entrapment; 5. Internal Review Practices; 9. Police Brutality; 12. Police Strikes and Blue Flu; 18. Vigilantes.

Further Readings

Barker, Thomas, and David Carter, eds. *Police Deviance.* Cincinnati, OH: Anderson Publishing, 1996.

Bayley, David. *Police for the Future.* New York: Oxford University Press, 1994.

Bracey, Dorothy. "Police Corruption and Community Relations: Community Policing." *Police Studies,* v.15/4 (1992).

Brown, Michael. *Working the Street: Police Discretion and the Dilemmas of Reform.* New York: Russell Sage, 1981

Burnham, David. *The Role of the Media in Controlling Corruption.* New York: John Jay College, 1977.

Christopher, Warren. *Report of the Independent Commission on the Los Angeles Police Department: Summary.* Los Angeles: Commission, 1991.

Crank, John, and Michael Caldero. *Police Ethics: The Corruption of Noble Cause.* Cincinnati, OH: Anderson Publishing, 2000.

Daley, Robert. *Prince of the City: The Story of a Cop Who Knew Too Much.* Boston, MA: Houghton Mifflin, 1978.

Goldstein, Herman. *Police Corruption: A Perspective on Its Nature and Control.* Washington, DC: Police Foundation, 1975.

Haarr, Robin. "They're Making a Bad Name for the Department: Exploring the Link between Organizational Commitment and Police Occupational Deviance in a Police Patrol Bureau." *Policing: An International Journal of Police Science and Management,* v.20/4 (1997).

Ivkovic, Sandra. *Fallen Blue Knights.* Oxford: Oxford University Press, 2005.

Kania, Richard. "Should We Tell the Police to Say Yes to Gratuities." *Criminal Justice Ethics,* v.7/2 (1982).

Klockars, Carl. *The Measurement of Police Integrity.* Washington, DC: National Institute of Justice, 2000.

Knapp Commission. *Report of Police Corruption.* New York: George Braziller, 1973.

Maas, Peter. *Serpico.* New York: Harper Torch, 1997.

Martin, Susan. *Breaking and Entering: Police Women on Patrol.* Berkeley, CA: University of California Press, 1982.

Mollen Commission. *Commission Report.* New York: The Mollen Commission, 1994.

Muir, William. *Police: Streetcorner Politicians.* Chicago: University of Chicago Press, 1997.

Neiderhoffer, Albert. *Behind the Shield: The Police in Urban Society.* Garden City, NY: Doubleday, 1967.

Palmiotto, Michael. *Police Misconduct: A Reader for the 21st Century.* Upper Saddle River, NJ: Prentice Hall, 2001.

Parks, Bernard. *Ramparts Area Corruption Incident: Public Report.* Los Angeles: Los Angeles Police Department, 2000.

Prenzler, Timothy, and Mackay, Peta. "Police Gratuities: What the Public Think." *Criminal Justice Ethics,* v.14/1 (1995).

Punch, Maurice. *Control in the Police Organization.* Boston: MIT Press, 1983.

Ruess-Ianni, Elizabeth. *Two Cultures of Policing: Street Cops and Management Cops.* Brunswick NJ: Transaction Books, 1983.

Sherman, Lawrence. *Police Corruption: A Sociological Perspective.* Garden City, NY: Doubleday, 1974.

Skolnick, Jerome. *Justice Without Trial: Law Enforcement in Democratic Society.* New York: John Wiley and Sons, 1966.

Skolnick, Jerome, and James Fyfe. *Above the Law.* New York: Free Press, 1993.

Stoddard, Ellwyn. "The Informal Code of Police Deviancy: A Group Approach to Blue-Coat Crime." *Journal of Criminal Law, Criminology, and Police Science,* v.20/3 (1968).

Walker, Samuel, and Charles M. Katz. *The Police in America: An Introduction.* Boston: McGraw Hill, 2008.

Westley, William A. *Violence and the Police.* Cambridge, MA: MIT Press, 1970.

Wilson, James Q. *Varieties of Police Behavior: The Management of Law and Order in Eight Communities.* Cambridge, MA: Harvard University Press, 1978.

11

Police Privatization

Luke Perry
Southern Utah University

Privatization of policing services involves taking policing activities performed by governments and turning them over to private corporations, organizations, and individual citizens. Modern efforts toward police privatization take several forms. Entire police departments can be privatized, but this is rare; most communities are hesitant to relinquish all public control of policing services. More commonly, police departments have experimented with variants of privatization. One example is termed *contracting out*. Police departments retain funding responsibility, but hire providers to perform specific services. Departments in several states use private security firms in support roles. Parking control, traffic direction, special-event security, crossing-guard duties, laboratory services, and communications-system maintenance are types of services that police departments have contracted out. A second variant of privatization is termed *load shedding*, where police departments shift specific services and funding to the private sector. Examples of load shedding include permitting alarm companies to respond to subscriber alarms, and privatized police services on certain college and university campuses.

The historical relationship between public and private policing in the United States has culminated in some related trends in American politics over the last century, and has generated both support and criticism surrounding modern efforts toward police privation and related ethical concerns. The future prospects for police privatization are intricately wound in American politics and economics, and present some important questions about the nation's ideological future.

Politics, Privatization, and Policing

Ronald Reagan famously stated in his first inaugural address that government was not the solution to social problems; government was the problem. Republicans took control of the U.S. House and Senate in 1994 for the first time in 50 years, an event referred to as the Republican Revolution. Reagan's tenure reopened the question of which functions should be the responsibility of government. Privatization was a key component of Reagan's policy agenda and that of the Republican Party. The 1980s and 1990s constituted a significant period of change in public administration as different types of government services were privatized at the federal, state, and local level. During this time, public policing lost market share to a growing private security industry, and a number of different nongovernmental organizations became increasingly responsible for policing functions. This transformation blurred distinctions between public and private control of policing services, and resulted in an overall reduction in public policing.

Historical Fluctuations of Private Policing in America

In some ways, these modern developments paralleled earlier periods of policing in America, which was localized in sections of major cities during the 18th and 19th centuries. The system was premised on contractual agreements between clients, who sought protection or investigation; and independent agents, who provided these services for a fee or a reward. The system was highly decentralized and market-based, and the providers of policing services exercised extensive control over the amount of work involved and the methods employed.

The establishment of local police departments was deeply connected to the rampant threats to social order that persisted throughout the 19th century. Publicly supported, salary-based, bureaucratically organized policing developed in urban areas after the Civil War. The role of the police gradually shifted from retrievers of property to peacekeepers. The first public police department was developed in New York in 1845, and other cities quickly followed suit.

Industrialization in the antebellum period produced dominant industries such as coal, steel, oil, and the railroads, which laid the foundation for decades of capitalist development. Large numbers of unskilled laborers congregated in company towns under a paternalistic relationship between entrepreneurs and the working class.

Labor strikes and labor militancy unfolded in the final decades of the 19th century, which were met by unreliable and occasionally hostile responses from local law enforcement agencies. Private security firms were employed to break strikes and engage in espionage. Spying on laborers was undertaken to infiltrate developing labor organizations and remove potential union leaders. Congressional committees were established to investigate these policing practices, while related reports criticized the private protection of corporate assets to the detriment of employee security and property. Government reaction to private policing helped shape a political consciousness that identified and sought to reform the perceived dangers of private policing, particularly as it related to corporate interests.

The size of local police departments grew in conjunction with the population growth of urban centers. Patronage dominated the hiring and promotion of police officers. Corruption was endemic in the political organization of cities in the early 20th century. Reformers sought to neutralize patronage and corruption, particularly as it was connected to organized crime. The quasi-military police bureaucracy was transformed into a legalistic and technocratic bureaucracy. Law was increasingly viewed as external and impersonal, and police officers were increasingly held accountable to bureaucratic authorities rather than political authorities. Police chiefs were previously appointed by elected city officials and expected to be loyal to their boss, not the law. Merit became increasingly important in the evaluation of police officers. The rational allocation of police services displaced allocations based on political demands. Order increasingly became a public commodity as professional norms solidified and legitimacy was enhanced.

Meanwhile, private policing declined in the 1920s and the 1930s. Antilabor efforts shifted from private security firms to federal agencies, including the Bureau of Immigration and the U.S. Army. Advances in transportation and communication facilitated the creation of the Federal Bureau of Investigation in 1908. This added a new national component to existing public policing services, which were predominately local.

Private policing became a multi-million dollar industry in the 1960s. The number of employees at private policing firms doubled, which was a much faster growth rate than their counterparts experienced in the public sector. During the 1970s, a growth in related research helped to spotlight the existence of private policing, which challenged conventional assumptions that

policing was exclusively public. Private policing became increasingly understood as an important phenomenon that should be recognized and studied.
The Department of Justice hired research corporations such as RAND and
Hallcrest to examine the extent, scope, nature, and effectiveness of private
policing. The issue of public versus private policing services increasingly
became viewed as a matter of efficiency.

Organizational Design of Public Policing

Private services have never entirely gone away, even though police services
have largely been publicly provided for over a century. Law enforcement
responsibility is now divided between federal, state, and local governments.
The system is highly fragmented and consists of many different small, autonomous organizations that vary in nature and scope. Most law enforcement
occurs at the local level. There is little integration among the many parts
of the system, which fits with democratic values of decentralized power,
authority, and decision making, the dominant ideology in law enforcement.
Changes in the structure and organization of policing impact performance.
There are two dominant ways in which scholars of public administration
approach the organizational design of predominately public organizations,
such as police departments: public-choice theory and interorganizational
theory.

Public-Choice and Interorganizational Theories

Public-choice theory supports a mix of public and private organizations
that produce and consume public services. This theory assumes that people
are self-interested and make rational decisions. Market mechanisms produce
competition, which generates greater internal efficiency than government
bureaucracies. The citizenry is viewed as the best judge of whether services,
such as policing, are fulfilling the interests of the community. A multiple-
provider arrangement prompts public administrators to justify their choices
in terms of efficiency and the extent to which public decisions fit with local
preferences. In the 1960s and 1970s, public-administration scholars sought
to develop a more systematic view of the relationship between existing circumstances and organizational design.

Interorganizational theory focuses on how environmental conditions set
parameters and develop criteria for effective facilitation of services, such
as policing. Universal assumptions about human nature are displaced by a

mode of analysis that seeks to enhance organizational design, as it exists. Analysis seeks to understand the network in which services are being provided and determine what organizational interactions are most relevant to desired outcomes.

Public-Interest, Economic, and Management Dimensions

In addition to broad theoretical frameworks, the configuring of public organizations, such as police departments, can be understood through several dimensions. The public-interest dimension, as applied to the American context, posits a notion of public control that requires democratic governance to exercise power with accountability to the masses. There is an expectation of leadership through which social problems are diagnosed and publicly engaged. In exercising power, leaders should consider whether the actions taken are sufficient to produce the desired results. Separation of powers permeates all levels of government, and by design, intends to keep power limited to avoid abuse.

The economic dimension, as applied to the American context, expects a certain degree of efficiency from public organizations in addition to the advancement of public welfare. Relevant economic considerations include the type of market involved, and the cost, supply, and demand of the services being produced in this market.

The management dimension focuses on the administrative system in which the managers of public organizations operate. In the American context, there is an expectation that management has the capacity to adapt to unfolding trends and related challenges that emerge in a dynamic and social environment. Budgets, personnel, procurement, regulatory processes, and information systems are central to the process of management. How these three dimensions are prioritized and blend together shapes how public organizations will function and are understood by outside observers.

Politics, history, theory, and analysis combine to shape current perspectives toward police privatization. Since 1980, privatization has moved from the intellectual fringe to the center of debates over public policy and law enforcement. Privatization has been advocated for a variety of government services, even policing powers, which were long considered beyond the scope of these efforts, given their unique authority. The end of the 20th century is regarded as an era of increased collaboration between private security firms and public law enforcement, reflecting changes in the preferences of the citizenry. The issue of police privatization remains highly contentious.

Pro: Arguments in Support of Police Privatization

Supporters of police privatization favor public-choice theory over inter-organizational theory. Related arguments tend to prioritize the economic dimension of public administration over the public interest and management dimensions. Support of police privatization is based in the view of reducing costs, boosting efficiency, encouraging competition, and promoting democratic governance.

Reducing Costs and Gaining Efficiency

Three-strikes laws and mandatory sentences for repeat offenders were implemented in the 1990s in response to high crime rates. Compared to the 1980s, the median sentence that prisoners served rose in every category of serious crime except for aggravated assault. Serious crime fell in the late 1990s to a 25-year low, but the financial costs were incredibly high. According to the Bureau of Justice Statistics, government expenditures on criminal justice between 1982 and 2006 grew by 422 percent at the local level, 548 percent at the state level, and 749 percent at the federal level. In this time, direct expenditures on corrections grew 660 percent to approximately $70 billion. Direct expenditures on police grew 420 percent to approximately $100 billion. As of 2010, America had the largest prison population in the world as measured by a percentage of the total population.

This situation has generated public pressure for public administrators to reduce the costs of criminal justice services, and privatization viewed as a viable solution. Ideologically, the basic tenets of privatization date back to *laissez-faire* economics as created by Adam Smith and engaged by prominent 20th-century scholars, such as Friedrich von Hayek and Milton Friedman. *Laissez-faire* economists advocate a very limited role for government in society, akin to present day libertarianism. Government should not perform unnecessary activities because restraint is vital to preserving individual freedoms, promoting economic growth, restoring trust in government, and addressing perceptions that contemporary society is over-regulated.

The 1970s and 1980s witnessed deregulation and privatization of publicly controlled elements of transportation, housing, environmental protection, energy, communication, business, and health. The Reagan administration cited British privatization and deregulation efforts undertaken by Margaret Thatcher's government from 1979 to 1990 as evidence of the economic feasibility and political popularity of these reforms. Proponents supported deregulation and privatization as an important means to promoting the economic interests of government, particularly in terms of efficiency, competition, innovation, and deficit reduction. Hundreds of federal prisons, state prisons, juvenile detention facilities, and holding centers for illegal immigrants are now operated by the private sector. Most facilities are located in politically conservative regions of the country, such as the southwest and southeast. Texas, for example, has the largest number of private prisons.

Similar approaches can be applied to policing. Nonvital functions do not require the full range of skills acquired by trained police officers. Contracting out allows other agencies to perform functions that do not involve crimes or emergencies, better enabling the publicly funded police force to attend to such matters. As it is, police spend a fraction of their time dealing with crime-related matters, but private companies operate in an open market that promotes competition and have the potential to offer services at a cheaper price than government can provide. Staff performing these functions can be paid less than full-time police officers. Minimizing costs through contracting out is viewed as beneficial to bureaucrats as well. Contracting services to private firms forgoes a degree of authority and control, but if the services are provided at a cheaper rate than public alternatives, this leaves bureaucrats with more money in discretionary budgets to use as they see fit.

Competitive Pressures Beneficial to Democracy

From a political perspective, supporters of privatization view competitive pressures as more beneficial to democratic governance. Government holds an exclusive monopoly on services, including policing, which are managed by a bureaucratic hierarchy. Citizens of respective communities are presumed to be the best judge of their policing services. Privatization gives citizens a dominant voice in shaping the quantity and quality of the services being provided by private companies. This perspective seeks to combine Smith's vision of *laissez-faire* economic philosophy with Thomas Jefferson's conception of democracy.

The Constitutional Convention (1787) resulted in a system of federalism, in which powers are shared between different levels of government, including federal, state, and local. Alexander Hamilton and Thomas Jefferson, two prominent constitutional founders, developed different visions of American political development in the new republic. Hamilton advocated the creation of a national government to mitigate internal strife, promote economic growth, develop international prominence, and ensure national security. Jefferson believed that states should retain a significant portion of political power because democracy works best when public authority is closely connected to the people.

Jefferson envisioned a small, predominately agrarian society with states and localities exercising the bulk of government power. Hamilton envisioned a commerce-based society with a strong national government that was able to exercise leadership and promote American interests abroad. Debates over these competing visions of development have persisted throughout the country's history. In line with Jefferson, prominent 20th-century Republicans advocated devolution, the process of devolving federal power to states and local governments. The intention was to limit the growth of the federal government, particularly the welfare state, in hopes of preserving and expanding Jefferson's vision of democracy.

As a whole, proponents of police privatization view it as a means to cut costs, increase efficiency, provide police officers with more opportunities to deal with crime-related matters, and promote values of democratic governance. These perspectives are shaped by the prominent role private police services once had in American society, a resurrection of *laissez-faire* economic philosophy, an emulation of modern British privatization efforts, the practical challenges of financing the contemporary criminal justice system, and the desire to lessen the mundane tasks of policing in order to maximize the crime-fighting efforts of police officers.

Con: Arguments in Opposition to Police Privatization

Critics of police privatization believe that policing fundamentally belongs in the public sector because of its inherent focus on general welfare and the collective good. In this view, the basic purpose of government is to provide order and security. Police departments nationwide are responsible for fulfilling this objective on a daily basis through timely and direct interaction with people who threaten shared peace and prosperity, as collectively codified and protected through law. Opponents argue that transitioning enforcement responsibilities to the private sector jeopardizes the very nature of modern law enforcement by granting authority to the private actors public law is designed to regulate. This makes it more difficult for the governed to control citizens and control itself, a prominent concern of James Madison, the leading architect of America's political system.

Profit Motivations, Ethics, and Accountability

Traditional norms of public policing question the core motivations of private corporations entrusted with policing functions. Making money is the fundamental motivation of every for-profit company. Private companies, by design, provide goods and services in exchange for market-orientated compensation. Business administrators seek to act in the best interest of their respective companies and shareholders by maximizing financial profits and minimizing costs. Opponents of privatization believe that in contrast, public administrators are concerned, first and foremost, with service to their constituencies; and that while members of government disagree about the best way to serve, constituent service is the primary motivation of public administrators throughout the political spectrum. Critics of police privatization believe that the production of police services should prioritize effectiveness, not profit.

Concerns about profit-motivated policing raise larger questions about the ethics of private policing. Policing in an ethical manner is essential to maintaining the public trust and preserving America's strong tradition of rule of law. Ethical behavior is a product of evaluating a range of competing choices and making ethical decisions. Professional roles and responsibilities of policing are enshrined in codes of conduct, statements of ethical principles, and oaths of office developed and adhered to by public police departments. Critics of police privatization question the premise that profit-based policing is compatible with the ethical norms of public departments, and suggest that the prospects for corruption are increased in a more decentralized, private policing model as compared to a more standardized public policing model.

Philosophical concerns regarding law enforcement are commonly translated into practical considerations through the notion of accountability. When public functions are shifted to private actors, hence becoming private actions, public accountability is inherently reduced. Such changes can even help to shield private actors from traditional mechanisms of private accountability if they are permitted to assert government immunities. This is particularly problematic in considering how policing differs from nearly all other public services. Police have the right, and at times, the obligation to use force, including deadly force. Federal and state laws especially sanction this authority. Critics do not believe it is prudent to transfer this unique authority to private entities performing quasi-governmental functions. Under these circumstances, incompetent behavior or the abuse of power can result in the greatest of injustices: the unwarranted loss of life.

Use of Force, Violations of Human Rights, and Social Control

Concerns surrounding government-sanctioned use of force were heightened by the actions of private security firms in the war on terror. Private contractors were involved in the physical, psychological, and sexual abuse of prisoners in places such as Iraq's Abu Ghraib prison in 2004. Private contractors have also been implicated in the deaths of detained suspected terrorists and the killing of innocent civilians in Afghanistan and Iraq. Billions of dollars of Pentagon contracts related to fighting terrorism were allotted without a full, open process of competition. These no-bid contracts generated criticism for their lack of transparency and the perceived misuse of public funds. Critics of police privatization cite these injustices in their resistance of increased privatization of policing. If profound violations of human rights have occurred in recent privatization of military functions, it is plausible that similar violations of individual freedoms could occur with additional privatization of police functions.

A related concern is the increased specialization and technical proficiency of social control within American society. New surveillance techniques, such as video monitoring and DNA testing, are more penetrating and intrusive than in the past. Distance, darkness, and physical barriers have been overcome. Information can be easily stored, retrieved, analyzed, and communicated. These forms of control are often involuntary and undertaken in a decentralized manner. Such advancements in surveillance, coupled with the recent growth of private undercover operations, has created a new vision of freedom. The convergence of public and private policing makes it more difficult for citizens to understand and monitor constraints on individual freedoms. The distinction between the public and private sector has blurred, joint operations are more frequent, and relevant professionals regularly circulate between the public sector and the private sector. Critics such as criminology expert Gary Marx, a well-known author, lecturer, and professor emeritus of sociology at MIT, believe these developments negatively impact privacy and the preservation of limited and transparent governance.

Quality and Costs of Services

Critics of police privatization question the assumption that competition for services will inevitably enhance the quality of the services being provided. The hiring of police officers typically occurs through a statutory framework that requires a specific set of qualifications. Candidates are psychiatrically evaluated prior to being offered a position and receive extensive training, which includes how to effectively deal with people in difficult situations, criminal law, physical fitness, and marksmanship. Training of private security guards is limited. Without sufficient training, serious mistakes become more likely. Investing in rigorous training could remedy this problem, but would limit the ability of private security firms to offer services at a reduced cost, which is a major selling point. Fundamental questions remain regarding who is responsible for oversight and how this process will occur.

Critics of police privation raise doubts about cost reductions related to privatization. Evidence is mixed as to whether privatization actually results in lower costs of services. What public policing lacks in efficiency, it makes up for in the perpetuation of a mostly transparent, dependable, and formalized policing model that clearly identifies rank, procedure, and oversight procedures, among other issues. By nature, markets are inherently unpredictable and inconsistent. Shifts in the health of the market can significantly impact economics and politics, as witnessed in the recession of 2006.

Critics of police privatization reject the *laissez-faire* perspective that privatization will inevitably lead to positive gains in policing, and other publicly controlled entities, in favor of a more nuanced approach that recognizes the associated risks to long-term stability as markets fluctuate.

Whereas privatization flourished in era of economic growth in the 1980s, it may flounder after what some analysts are calling the worst economic downturn since the Great Depression. The economic downturn of the late 2000s resulted in costly and unpopular federal provisions for economic stimulus, as well as bailouts of banks and car manufacturers deemed "too big to fail." Arguably, *laissez-faire*-inspired deregulation was intimately involved in both the boom and the bust. This is ironic, considering that government programs typically constitute long-standing public responses to past shortcomings and failures of predominately market-based interactions. Critics of privatization couple conventional backlash toward economic deregulation with concerns that privatized policing could resurface in ways that mirror the shortcomings of its 18th and 19th-century roots.

Legality

Critics of police privatization also question the legality surrounding police privatization. Private actors are not bound to the same constitutional, statutory, and oversight restrictions as members of government. The responsibilities of public organizations merely change rather than disappear. Increasing privatization of policing services will complicate, rather than simplify, existing organizational arrangements. This contradicts the implicit assumption articulated by supporters of privatization that privatization is a simplifying tool for public policy. Whereas supporters of police privatization emphasize the influence citizens can have over police services in an increasingly privatized approach, critics believe that an increasingly private supply of police services is inconsistent with the principle of separation of powers. The actions of private actors engaged in policing activities are rarely challenged by reviewing courts, typically only when gross conflicts of interests are evident.

In short, critics of police privatization are concerned about reduced accountability, reduced quality, abuses of power, confusion, systematic instability, and potential illegality. These perspectives are shaped by the prominent role public policing has had over the last century; a rejection of several assumptions made by *laissez-faire* economics; recent experiences with private security contractors in the war on terror; and a fundamental belief that order and security, the most important collective good, should be legislated and enforced by the public sector. Critics support interorganizational theory over public-choice theory. Related arguments tend to prioritize the public interest dimension of public administration over the economic and management dimensions.

Looking Forward

America experienced wild fluctuations in political power during the early 21st century. The Republicans dominated the 2000, 2002, and 2004 national elections. President George W. Bush was the first Republican two-term president since Ronald Reagan, whose presidency served as an ideological model for the Bush administration, including widespread support of privatization, deregulation, and devolution. Bush's popularity dropped from record-high ratings in his first term to record-low ratings in his second term. Democrats took control of Congress in 2006 and won the White House in 2008 with the election of Barack Obama, then suffered resounding defeats in the 2010 elections during the largest turnover of congressional seats since 1948.

It remains to be seen whether the era of privatization that characterized the 1990s Republican Revolution will persist or dissipate. It is unlikely that police departments will fully privatize in large numbers. However, as states struggle with diminished revenues from the most recent recession, contracting out will likely continue, and load shedding may grow as they deal with challenging budget realities. These developments raise timely and important questions about the ideological future of American politics, the appropriate role of government in American society, and the positive and negative aspects of privatizing police services.

See Also: 1. Accountability; 10. Police Corruption and Code of Silence; 18. Vigilantes.

Further Readings

Fixler, Phillip, and Robert Poole. "Can Police Services be Privatized?" *Annals of the American Academy of Political Science and Social Science,* v.498 (July 1988).

Gilmour, Robert, and Laura Jensen. "Reinventing Government Accountability: Public Functions, Privatization, and the Meaning of 'State Action.'" *Public Administration Review,* v.58/3 (May/June 1998).

Henig, Jeffrey. "Privatization in the United States: Theory and Practice." *Political Science Quarterly,* v.104/4 (Winter, 1989–1990).

Maguire, Edward, and William King. "Trends in the Policing Industry." *Annals of the American Academy of Political and Social Science,* v.593 (2004).

Marx, Gary. "Recent Developments in Undercover Policing." In *Punishment and Social Control,* edited by Thomas Bloomberg and Stanley Cohen. New York: Aldine de Gruyter, 1995.

Reiss, Albert. "Police Organization in the Twentieth Century." *Crime and Justice,* v.15 (1992).

Shearing, Clifford. "The Relation between Public and Private Policing." *Crime and Justice,* v.15 (1992).

Spitzer, Steven, and Andrew T. Seull. "Privatization and Capitalist Development." *Social Problems,* v.25/1 (October 1977).

Wise, Charles. "Public Service Configurations and Public Organizations: Public Organization Design in the Post-Privatization Era." *Public Administration Review,* v.50/2 (March/April 1990).

12

Police Strikes and Blue Flu

Dennis Bulen
Wright State University

T he police are the entity of local government empowered to enforce laws, protect people and property, and preserve civil order. What separates the police from other representatives of the government is the authorization for the legitimized use of force, including deadly force. The police are the most highly visible representatives of the government. Police officers wear a uniform that is easily recognizable by the citizenry, they drive vehicles that are readily identifiable, and they are the first resource to be considered by the citizenry in times of need. America's police officers form the "thin blue line" between the public and the criminal element. Police officers are the first responders when the public peace has been breached. The police are expected to professionally, impartially, and objectively investigate criminal activity and successfully aid in the prosecution of those who stand accused of statutory violations, all within the confines of due process.

Historically, there have been conflicts between the police and their municipal employers. These conflicts traditionally have arisen from grievances not addressed by city leaders, generally wage disputes. As a result of these disputes, as well as police objection to the arbitrary nature of their government's decision making, the police have developed a variety of job actions in an attempt to persuade city administrators to accept their position. Job actions are defined as a deliberate disruption of normally assigned duties. Job actions can include ticket-writing slowdowns, ticket blitzes, and slow responses to service calls. The most drastic type of job action is a strike, a work stoppage caused by the mass refusal of police officers to work. A lesser response used by police to bring their grievances to the city administration is called the *blue flu,* an organized tactic with the goal of immobilizing the police department. Blue flu is initiated when a substantial number of police officers call in sick. This term was coined in 1967 as a result of the rank-and-file members of the Detroit Police Department walking off the job. The etymology of blue flu was taken from the traditional color of the police uniform.

Early History of Police Strikes

The use of the strike as a labor tactic has a long history. In ancient Egypt under Pharaoh Ramses III, the artisans of the Royal Necropolis at Deir el-Medina organized the first strike in recorded history. The use of the English word strike first appeared in 1768, when sailors struck in support of demonstrations in London. The sailors removed the topgallant sails of merchant ships in port, rendering the ships immobile.

Between 1919 and 1965, there were few attempts by police to unionize and initiate job actions. This was due to legislative and judicial actions prohibiting municipal employees from striking.

The first major police strike in the United States was conducted by the Boston Police Department in 1919; it was the first attempt by U.S. police to organize and possibly the most famous police strike in American history. In the years following World War I, inflation dramatically eroded the value of a police officer's salary. From 1913 to May 1919, the cost of living rose by 76 percent, while police wages rose just 18 percent. Police officers worked long, 10-hour shifts and often slept over at the station without pay in case they were needed. Officers were not paid for court appearances, and they also complained about the conditions of police stations, including the lack of sanitation, baths, beds, and toilets.

In early 1919, the nation saw a number of strikes in which workers sought to increase wages that had not been adjusted for postwar inflation. The American Federation of Labor began to take an active role in unionizing police departments. The Boston Commissioner forbade the creation of a police union. However, on August 15, the Boston police formed a union despite the directives from the police commissioner. Officers who were identified as union activists were suspended by the commissioner. The Boston mayor ordered an outside committee to investigate the possibilities of improving working conditions and averting a strike, but the commissioner refused their recommendations. On September 9, Boston Police Department officers went on strike. After four days of strike action, approximately 1,000 rank-and-file officers were fired. The replacement officers received the pay increase, the equipment allowance, and the time off that the striking officers had requested.

Modern History of Police Strikes

Several U.S. cities experienced police strikes during the 1960s and 1970s. During this time, other types of job actions occurred, including ticket blitzes, ticket writing slowdowns, slow response to nonemergency calls, and blue flus. All of these job actions were attempts to bring grievances to the attention of city management. The police officers, whether represented by a recognized bargaining unit or not, sought fair treatment from cities. When officers perceived they were not being treated fairly, they felt the only remaining recourse was to take some type of job action. In the most severe cases, police officers went on strike.

In 1967, Detroit Police Department rank-and-file officers began to take action over wages. The city had made a nominal wage offer that the officers unanimously rejected through the Detroit Police Officer's Association (DPOA). The DPOA was not a union, but functioned as an *ex officio* union. The DPOA took a firm stand in rejecting the city's offer. The city administration, relying on the Hutchinson Act, which prohibits strikes by public employees in Michigan, took an equally firm stand, believing they had no obligation to negotiate with the DPOA.

The officers' first attempt to gain some leverage with the city administration was with a ticket slowdown. This action, endorsed by the DPOA, gave strength and credibility to the DPOA as the bargaining unit for the Detroit police officers. The police commissioner issued a directive stating the ticket slowdown would not be tolerated. When the rank-and-file ignored the directive, police supervisors were given a directive to suspend three officers in each precinct for dereliction of duty. Punitive transfers were used in an attempt to coerce the officers to resume ticket production. The officers' response was immediate. Officers began to call in sick with the "bluebonic plague," sparking the beginning of the blue flu. The police administration ordered the department to work 12-hour shifts, cancelled all vacations, and immediately suspended all emergency leaves. The city administration filed for a temporary injunction against the DPOA and ordered all officers who called in sick to report to the medical section. Officers who violated the court order were threatened with contempt of court. The president of the DPOA issued a back-to-work order and the officers complied, returning police operations to normal. Within two days, a second blue flu began, precipitated by the police administration's reaction to officers picketing police headquarters. The Detroit mayor and the DPOA president agreed to a 10-day truce, at which time officers reported to duty. The city administration and the DPOA began negotiations to reach a wage agreement.

During the 1970s, police strikes were most common in states where public employees had little or no statutory protection that addressed bargaining rights. These strikes were staged by nonunion police officers attempting to obtain union representation. A police strike is a major crisis for the community, the citizenry, and the police.

In August 1975, approximately 90 percent of the rank-and-file officers of the San Francisco Police Department struck over the city's refusal to grant a pay increase the officers believed they had earned and deserved. The San Francisco Police Officers Association (SFPOA) was recognized by the city as the official representative and bargaining unit of the rank-and-file, and functioned as a union. Less than five percent of the department—primarily minority officers—were represented by Officers for Justice, which was not recognized by the city as a bargaining unit.

Several events took place that polarized the striking officers and the San Francisco Board of Supervisors. A survey of other service departments in San Francisco revealed that street sweepers, pickup truck drivers, gardeners, and plumbing supervisors were all paid more than police officers. In March 1975, the Civil Service Commission endorsed a pay increase of 12 percent for the deputy sheriffs. The Board of Supervisors rejected the proposal and passed a lesser pay increase. When the Deputy Sheriffs Association voted to strike, the Board of Supervisors quickly reached an agreement with the sheriff's deputies. The city of San Francisco adopted a charter amendment in 1952 that outlined the pay formula to be applied annually to police officers. This charter provision was not binding, but had been followed since its adoption. In August 1975, the Civil Service Commission certified the wage increase for the police at 13.05 percent as outlined in the charter. The Board of Supervisors again rejected the increase. When officers began to talk openly about a strike, the mayor threatened to fire any officer who participated. Several attempts by the SFPOA to bring the wage issue to the attention of the full Board of Supervisors were rejected. On August 18, 1975, the San Francisco Police Department went on strike.

In early 1978, the Memphis Police Association began contract negotiations with city officials. In 1978, Memphis police officers were represented by two police unions. The Memphis Police Association was the official bargaining unit for the rank and file. Fifteen percent of the Memphis Police Department were African American; the Afro-American Police Association represented these and other minority officers in the areas of promotions, fringe benefits, and job transfers. Initial negotiations were generally unsuccessful, which resulted in a growing discontent among union members within the Memphis Police Department. City officials responded by taking a harder line in the negotiations. In August 1978, the Memphis Police Association called a general walkout and left the policing of the city to supervisory personnel. Court-issued injunctions were ignored by striking officers. The strike lasted eight days, after which the city acquiesced to the demands of the Police Association to take no punitive action against the striking officers. However, the city made no concessions relating to salary increases or contract renewals.

The Legality of Police Strikes

Police officers have the same constitutional protections of freedom of speech and freedom of association rights as any other citizen. However, the U.S. Supreme Court has upheld the restriction on the right to strike by public employees, including police officers. These laws denying police officers the right to strike originated in the need to protect the legitimate state interest of maintaining needed governmental services. These laws also sought to preserve a system of government in the sphere of public employment and the prohibition of practices not compatible with the public employer-employee relationship.

The first executive expression directed at the right of the police to strike was issued by Massachusetts Governor Calvin Coolidge during the Boston Police Department strike of 1919. His now famous proclamation, "there is no right to strike against the public safety by anybody, anywhere, anytime" set the standard for tolerance for police actions: There would be no tolerance.

Some states prohibit all strikes by public employees, under laws such as the Taylor Law in New York. Other jurisdictions impose strike bans only on certain categories of workers, particularly those regarded as crucial to a safe society. Police and firefighters are among the groups commonly barred from striking in these jurisdictions.

Pro: Arguments in Favor of the Right of Police to Strike

One of the fundamental human rights is the right to organize, a freedom of association that has been reaffirmed nationally and internationally. The First Amendment to the U.S. Constitution prohibits Congress from abridging the freedom of speech, abridging the right of people to peaceably assemble, and abridging the right of the people to petition the government for redress of grievances. While the First Amendment applied to the federal government, the Fourteenth Amendment, through the Due Process Clause, selectively applied this Bill of Rights to the states. At both the state and federal level, the courts have applied these rights to the actions of local jurisdictions in areas such as demonstrations, marches, and public meetings. The right of police officers to petition the government to which they are employed for redress of grievances falls within the spectrum of this First Amendment protection.

The right of employees to organize, negotiate working conditions, and address grievances is a derivative of the right to freedom of association. The Universal Declaration of Human Rights initially proclaimed this basic human right of freedom of association in 1948. All workers have the right to organize, select leadership, develop a program to defend and forward their interests, and make demands on their employers. In such circumstances, employers have a duty to recognize and negotiate in good faith with their employees' representatives with a view toward arriving at mutually acceptable solutions to issues raised. Should negotiations fail, the employees have a right to organize a campaign designed to produce concessions, including withdrawing their labor. In short, they have the right to strike. Once an employee association is formed, management loses its right to act unilaterally.

The U.S. Supreme Court has ruled on the constitutional duty of the government to protect an individual. In *DeShaney v. Winnebago County* (1989), the Court ruled that a social service agency had no substantive constitutional duty to protect a child. By extension, there would be no constitutional duty for the police to protect its citizenry. Substantive due process prohibits the government from infringing on fundamental constitutional liberties. It does not protect individuals from other individuals, or put the government in a position whereby it has to anticipate criminal activity. The police are not liable, either civilly or criminally, to the victims of crime. If this were the case, the police and the municipality would be sued every time a criminal offense occurred in their jurisdiction.

In a ruling rendered in 2005, the Supreme Court again ruled that police have no constitutional duty to protect. In the case of *Castle Rock v. Gonzales* (2005), the court ruled that the police have no constitutional duty to protect a person from harm. This case was unique in that attorneys for Gonzales framed their argument as a procedural due process violation. Procedural due process refers to the procedural limitations placed on the manner in which a law is administered, applied, or enforced, and prohibits the government from arbitrarily depriving individuals of legally protected interests without first giving them notice and the opportunity to be heard. The court ruled that there is no due process protection for processes. Even though the police have policies and procedures in place for responding to calls for service, they have no constitutional duty to protect the citizenry, nor does the citizenry have any constitutional right to that protection. There is no duty established to the citizenry at large. If the police are not available, no constitutional duty has been breached.

Citizen Opinion

Research indicates that citizens are not overwhelmingly opposed to police officers having the right to strike, and even that the citizenry sometimes offers strong support for the idea that police officers have this right. As long as the citizens themselves do not feel personally threatened, they tend to view the strike in a labor-versus-management context. This research seems to challenge the thin blue line thesis, which suggests the police are the last line of defense before anarchy, and the citizenry lives in fear of victimization. In reality, citizens may not even be aware of a police presence. The Kansas City Preventative Patrol Experiment found that decreasing or increasing patrols had no effect on crime, on citizens' fear of victimization, and on community attitudes toward the police. Researcher Erdwin Pfuhl suggested in 1983 that police may have less influence on the incidence of crime than they have influence on the weather. The general absence of significant criminal activity during police strikes suggests that contemporary police policies and procedures do little to control or prevent crime. While the presence of police may influence an individual's actions, a police presence may not influence society at large. Based on this research, there is no apparent relationship between police presence and criminal activity. Police strikes appear to have neither a significant nor systematic impact on rates of reported crime.

Supporters of the police right to strike believe that police should have the same rights as any other member of society, which include having their concerns heard and addressed. If the concerns are not addressed adequately through meaningful negotiation, then steps must be taken to force a compromise. Withholding labor is the ultimate weapon of working people to force the employer to reach an agreement, and a strike may be the only avenue for police officers to get their concerns addressed.

Con: Arguments Against Police Strikes

It is illegal in all 50 states for police officers to participate in a strike. Police officers take an oath to uphold the laws of the United States and the laws of the individual state and municipality in which they work. Therefore, it is hypocritical of the police to be charged with enforcing the laws, but be allowed to violate a law when the violation fits their needs. This is no different than a police officer having the authority to arrest a violator for driving under the influence, while simultaneously having permission to do the same. Both of these circumstances create a breach of the public trust.

The justification for prohibiting police strikes is normally based on the concept that police services are necessary for the health and safety of the community. Legislatures have prohibited strikes by some public employees, including police officers, if the strike would invariably result in imminent danger to the citizenry. The police offer is the last vestige of protection to the community. Without a police presence, the citizenry would be the unwilling victims of criminal activity. Communities where police are on strike are viewed as targets for criminal activity; therefore, the citizenry suffers an increased fear of victimization.

Collective Bargaining and Binding Arbitration

There are alternatives for addressing grievances and reaching a fair settlement without resorting to a strike. The bargaining interactions between the police and the city have wide-ranging political ramifications for both parties, and the outcome should therefore reflect a fair settlement. Collective bargaining agreements outline the procedure for dispute resolution between parties. The duty to bargain is an important right granted to employees in the state bargaining process. Employees have the right to organize, but equally as important, the public employer is required to bargain with representatives of the employee organization. The increased participation by employees in the dispute resolution process may reduce the incidents of labor-management conflict by bringing the employees' perspective into the decision-making process.

Collective bargaining statutes outline the process for certification of bargaining units. This recognition of the bargaining unit formalizes the negotiation process by giving a legitimate face to both sides, and the recognized negotiators become the official voice of the bargaining units. It is through these negotiators that information if certified and passed to employees. Collective bargaining is a form of shared management; a fundamental tenet of American democracy is the participation in the decision-making process. Both sides get aggressively involved in the process in order to garner a maximum return, both economically and politically. Issues from both sides can be brought to the negotiating table, discussed, and resolved. Collective bargaining in large police agencies is significantly correlated to pay benefits, hazardous duty pay, shift differential pay, and educational incentive pay.

A form of binding arbitration, which interjects an arbitrator's version of a fair settlement, is a proven format for reaching a negotiated agreement. Cities that adopt either bargaining agreements or a form of compulsory arbitration experience significantly fewer police strikes than cities without this option. Cities that have duty-to-bargain rights, with or without binding arbitration, also experience fewer police strikes. However, the arbitration provision significantly reduces police strikes. Lobbyists for the powerful organizations Fraternal Order of Police and the Police Benevolent Associations can lobby state lawmakers to enact a form of binding arbitration.

There are four reasons why the arbitrator must address the fairness concerns of both parties. The first reason is that the arbitrator in this type of adversarial proceeding is supposed to offer a fair hearing to both sides. Second, arbitration laws should require the arbitrators to apply evaluative criteria to resolve a disputed point. Third, both the city and the police department bargaining unit have an equal voice in the selection of the individual arbitrator to resolve a specific impasse. Fourth, both the city and the police department bargaining unit can influence the availability of future work opportunities for an arbitrator by informing other unions and employers of the arbitrator's perceived competence and fairness.

Reduction in police strikes may be accomplished with the enactment of compulsory arbitration laws and formalized grievance procedures. Most grievances can be resolved without going to arbitration, but as long as arbitration is available, strikes are unlikely.

Community Support

An alternative to initiating a strike is the garnering of community support for the issues at hand. In general, the public supports the police, and believes they serve a vital function in society. Historically, the police have been successful in mobilizing citizens when support was needed. Informational pickets have been used successfully to inform the citizenry of the concerns of the police. Off-duty officers can form picket lines outside police headquarters and hand out information sheets that outline their concerns. Police spokespersons can use public service announcements through the media to explain and justify their issues to the public and express how a failure to reach an agreement with the city would be detrimental to citizens. Every police department has a public information officer who has connections to the media, and continuous interviews and articles in the newspapers and other media can keep citizens informed of the issues.

One simple method of community involvement is to ask citizens to attend community meetings and ask about the progress of police negotiations. As community leaders look to commerce for political and economic support, the police can seek support in that quarter as well. The police can form alliances with businesses for support of their issues and use these alliances to leverage support from the city. Allying with businesses provides benefits for police support, as cities that are perceived to have problems with the police are not attractive to commerce; businesses view these issues as roadblocks to relocating to the city, new business development, or current business expansion.

As city leaders serve the people, ultimately, city leaders must answer to the citizenry for actions taken, or a lack of action. The police should also monitor the electoral process, as would any other organization with a vested interest in the management of the city. Candidates who are sensitive to the issues important to the police can be actively courted and supported. Candidates who are not sensitive to the issues important to the police can be actively challenged by the police. These are all nonconfrontational approaches designed to inform the community of the issues facing the police and garner support for their positions.

Altering Enforcement Strategies

Police officers have a wide range of discretion when enforcing the laws and ordinances of their jurisdiction. Officers can alter their enforcement strategies to bring attention to their issues. One such strategy is a ticket blitz, in which officers write tickets at a greater volume than normal. For example, police officers could issue citations for speeders at five miles per hour over the posted limit when the departmental norm is to issue at nine miles over the posted limit. The result would be an outcry from the citizenry, who will then want the city administration to address the issues with the police so enforcement would return to normal.

A second enforcement strategy is a ticket slowdown, when the police only issue citations in circumstances where there is a threat of serious physical injury if no enforcement action is taken. The result of a ticket slowdown is a reduction in revenue for the city, which can have a very detrimental effect on the city budget. A third strategy is to slow down the response to nonemergency calls for service. This strategy leverages the frustrations of citizens, who then apply pressure on the city to address this issue.

It is illegal for the police to strike. While issues will inevitably arise between the police and the city, there are mechanisms that can be implemented to address these issues without resorting to a job action that eliminates or limits police available to respond to calls for service. The police should lobby their state legislatures to enact some form of binding arbitration to resolve these conflicts, whereupon both parties would be assured of a fair and equitable resolution.

See Also: 1. Accountability; 5. Internal Review Practices; 11. Police Privatization.

Further Readings

Adams, R. "The Human Right of Police to Organize and Bargain Collectively." *Police Practice and Research*, v.9/2 (2008).

Anderson, R., T. Bartell, F. Gehlen, and T. Winfree. "Support Your Local Police: On Strike?" *Journal of Police Science and Administration*, v.4/1 (1976).

Bennett, W., and K. Hess. *Management and Supervision in Law Enforcement*. Belmont, CA: Wadsworth-Thomson, 2001.

Bopp, W., P. Chignell, and C. Maddox. "The San Francisco Police Strike of 1975: A Case Study." *Journal of Police Science and Administration*, v.5/1 (1977).

Briggs, S., J. Zhao, S. Wilson, and L. Ren. "The Effect of Collective Bargaining on Large Police Agency Supplemental Compensation Policies: 1990–2000." *Police Practice and Research*, v.9/3 (2008).

Bureau of Labor Statistics. *Analysis of Work Stoppage*. Bulletin 2066. Washington, DC: U.S. Government Printing Office, June 1980.

Castle Rock v. Gonzales, 545 US 748 (2005).

City of San Diego v. American Federation of State etc. Employees, 8 Cal. App 3d (1970).

Delaney, J. "Strikes, Arbitration, and Teacher Salaries: A Behavioral Analysis." *Industrial and Labor Relations Review*, v.36/3 (1983).

DeShaney v. Winnebago County, 489 US 189 (1989).

Feuille, P., J. Delaney, and W. Hendricks. "Police Bargaining, Arbitration, and Fringe Benefits." *Journal of Labor Research*, v.4/1(1985).

Frances, Russell. *A City in Terror: Calvin Coolidge and the 1919 Boston Police Strike*. Boston: Beacon Press, 1975.

Giacopassi, D., R. Anson, and G. Donnenwerth. "A Comparison of Racial Attitudes: Right of Police to Strike." *International Journal of Comparative and Applied Criminal Justice*, v.4/2 (1980).

Goldstein, H. *Policing in a Free Society*. Cambridge, MS: Ballinger, 1977.

Hebdon, R., and R. Stern. "Tradeoffs Among Expressions of Industrial Conflict: Public Sector Strike Bans and Grievance Arbitrations." *Industrial and Labor Relations Review*, v.51/2 (1998).

Hobgood, W. "Should Police Be Permitted to Organize and Bargain Collectively?" *FBI Law Enforcement Bulletin*, v.50/1 (January 1981).

Ichniowski, Casey. "Arbitration and Police Bargaining: Prescriptions for the Blue Flu." *Industrial Relations*, v.2/2 (Spring 1982).

Ichniowski, C. "Police Recognition Strikes: Illegal and Ill-Fated." *Journal of Labor Research*, v.9/2 (1988).

Kelloway, E., L. Francis, V. Catano, and K. Dupre. "Third-Party Support for Strike Action." *Journal of Applied Psychology*, v.93/4 (2008).

Klockars, C. *Thinking About Police: Contemporary Readings*. New York: McGraw-Hill, 1983.

Lundman, R. *Police and Policing: An Introduction*. New York: Holt, Rinehart, and Winston, 1980.

Nichols, J. "Management and Legal Aspects of Police Strikes." *The Police Chief* (December 1972).

Pfuhl, E., Jr. "Police Strikes and Conventional Crime." *Criminology*, v.21/4 (1983).

Ritchey, F., M. Wilson, R. Hamby, and B. Trigg. "Public Perceptions of a Police Strike in a Southern City." *Journal of Police Science and Administration*, v.11/1 (1983).

Schofield, D. "Law Enforcement and Government Liability: An Analysis of Recent Section 1983 Litigation." *FBI Law Enforcement Bulletin,* v.50/1 (January 1981).

Winfree, T., and F. Gehlen. "Police Strike: Public Support and Dissonance Reduction During a Strike by Police." *Journal of Police Science and Administration,* v.9/4 (1981).

13

Profiling

Phillip Chong Ho Shon
University of Ontario Institute of Technology

There is relative consensus in the findings of previous and current research in police studies that vehicle drivers of color receive disparate treatment from the police. Across various jurisdictions, from New Jersey, Maryland, Missouri, Michigan, and San Diego, officers appear to be disproportionately targeting drivers of color for official post-stop activities such as field interrogations, searches, and sanctions in the form of citations. Furthermore, it has been reported that black motorists are more likely to be stopped for nonmoving violations, highly suggestive of equipment violations as a pretext for searches and general harassment. If such disparities in the application of the law and coercive actions of the state are supported by official statistics, then citizens' perceptions of such disparities and their prevalence are given additional support.

Citizens of color—in particular, young African American and Hispanic men—are more likely to perceive that the actions of police lack legitimacy. These types of encounters, directly and indirectly, when accumulated over time, are likely to further entrench the siege mentality between the police and the public, while eroding support of the police and trust in formal criminal justice institutions. It has also been argued that the unwelcome attention that African American males receive from the police is explained as a function of their overinvolvement in crime and because the racial background of the locations in which they are stopped is inconsistent with the residential population. Simply put, more persons of color are pulled over because they are noticeably out of place. Thus, it is not surprising that drivers of color have been disproportionately targeted for stops in predominantly white communities.

Accounts of why such disparities exist in police practices have been manifold as well, principally related to an agency's purpose and locale of operation. For instance, one primary reason that African American and Hispanic men have been disproportionately targeted on interstate highways is explained by the flawed intelligence reports disseminated by the Drug Enforcement Administration (DEA) to state police agencies during the War on Drugs. As part of Operation Pipeline, the DEA trained state agencies to spot "drug couriers" on roadways based on superficial characteristics in an attempt to intercept the flow of illegal narcotics. That minority drivers were disproportionately targeted during the 1980s and 1990s is thus attributable to this broad mission directive of the DEA. Others reasons behind the disparity refer to the practice of race-based deployment strategies, where assignment of officers to segregated areas results in a differential stratification of enforcement, the homogenous racial composition leading to an imbalance in the outcomes of activities.

Other explanations posit racial animus for the inequitable treatment that persons of color receive from the (white) police. Simply put, some officers make it their business to stop, interrogate, and search motorists of color for no other reason than pure bigotry, whether conscious or unconscious. Other psychological explanations resort to the presence of cognitive bias and the use of stereotyping against African Americans, because they are most visibly different and most commonly portrayed as criminals, images that are reified daily in the mass media. Some have argued that this tendency to equate color with criminality is a logical effect of the conditions of police work, in that the police form unconscious biases against persons they repeatedly encounter in situations that involve violence. While this type of explanation is in agreement with the current work on the formation of police personalities that is often attributed to work conditions, street experience, and peer socialization, it unduly diminishes a phenomenon that is institutional, structural, and pervasive to one that is unobservable and psychologically reductionistic.

Thus, while previous and current works have highlighted inequitable patterns in police behavior that warrant organizational reform—ones that target, punish, and cast a suspicious light on minority citizens—explanations of such discrepancies in traffic data is inadequate, given the role of the police in a democratic society. Ascribing disparate police treatment of minorities as a function of racial bigotry, cognitive bias, differential suspicion, stereotyp-ing, and race-based deployment unfairly militates against the professional-ism of the police. Explanations of police behavior that unjustifiably dimin-ish the capacity of the police to form humanistic philosophies of human behavior; understand the complex social organization of cities; and practice a professional, moral theory of policing unfairly robs the perspective and agency the police possess. Thus, theories of police behavior that are unduly psychological reduce police officers to cultural dopes who—consciously, unconsciously, or subconsciously—absorb their ecological street experience without critical reflection, blindly imbibing the inaccurate media portrayals and the inconsistent psychology of the public.

Contemporary patterns of racial profiling cannot be intelligibly discussed without a historical examination of the role of white supremacist ideology on the creation and sustenance of predominantly white communities. The historical origins of what are termed *sundown towns* provides a basis for the argument that predominantly all-white communities are an effect of ex-clusionary ideology that have been implemented as *de facto* social policies in communities across America.

The Rise of Sundown Towns

According to the 2000 Census, there were 59,614 residents in Terre Haute, Indiana: 86.3 percent white, 9.8 percent African American, and 1.2 percent Asian. Yet, just west of the Wabash River in West Terre Haute, a town of 2,330 people, 97.6 percent of the population were white, with one African American resident.

For residents of west and central Indiana from the early 1900s through as recently as the 1970s, it was common knowledge that blacks, Jews, or any-one of ethnic descent or color were not welcome to reside in or even travel through the town. This type of community is what author James Loewen defines as a *sundown town*: "any organized jurisdiction that for decades kept African Americans or other groups from living in it and was thus 'all white' on purpose." Such towns are notorious for the "Don't Let the Sun Go Down on You" signs that stood at their perimeters. And while towns such as West Terre Haute may appear to be anomalies, Loewen contends that they are scattered all across America and reflect the pervasive yet invis-ible character of racism in America.

The rise of all-white communities began after the post-Reconstruction period between 1890 and 1940, when racist ideology suffused the Democratic Party. Loewen describes this period as "the nadir," the lowest point of race relations in America, when whites across America systematically began to create and adopt formal and informal policies to exclude African Americans and others in order to create racially homogenous communities. Loewen states that while African Americans were found to be living in remote and unlikely places such as Wyoming, Idaho, and Maine after the Civil War, the census shows that there was a dramatic declination—a virtual disappearance—in the number of African Americans residing in the same communities across the United States after 1890. He attributes this sudden exodus to whites' use of threats, arson, and lynching against blacks, which was spurred on by the success of driving out the Chinese in the Pacific Northwest. Thus, that African Americans began retreating to cities where there was relative strength and safety in numbers accounts for the migration patterns of African Americans from rural to metropolitan areas at the end of the 19th century. This migration pattern of African Americans thus actually precedes the Great Migration from the south and serves as the incubation period of urban ghettos that 20th-century sociologists have described and studied.

What is especially notable is that this trend flourished, particularly after World War II, and continued thereafter in the emergence and proliferation of suburbs. Loewen writes that this was no accident, but "on the contrary, all-white suburbs were achieved" by forcibly removing African Americans from desirable locales through the Federal Housing Authority's official promulgation of segregationist policies, as well as other unofficial tactics to thwart African American home buyers, such as "steering, lying, stalling, special requirements imposed on blacks, missed appointments, and wrong addresses" by realtors.

If real estate agents were covert agent provocateurs in the formation and maintenance of sundown suburbs, Loewen writes that the police served as overt first responders to such exclusionary policies. Tactics included escorting persons of color to a town's boundaries; when in cars following black motorists, performing traffic stops as pretexts for vehicle searches; and in the name of protecting their communities from "criminals," systematically punishing black drivers through official sanctions and generalized harassment. Criminologists are well acquainted with the racist origins of policing; however, the systemic nature of racism—which is rooted in beliefs about the superiority of whiteness and has suffused the infrastructure of American cities and police departments—is glossed over in favor of individual and departmental pathologies.

The White Supremacy–Racial Profiling Nexus

This poignant moment in American history has the potential to overcome a tendency in criminology to explain a phenomenon using theoretical generalities. The history of sundown towns exemplifies the white supremacist ideology that permeated the politics, labor movement, and racial identities of immigrants, which culminated in racial conflicts across major U.S. cities during the latter half of the 19th-century throes of industrialization, immigration, and imperialism. The rise of white supremacy as a social movement also led to, but did not stop with, the violent expulsion of blacks from their rural communities across America. In major, early 19th-century cities that bulged with added production and immigrants during the industrial revolution, one group, more than any other, was denied entry into the emerging labor economy. Thus, the same national-level sentiment that drove blacks from their rural homes also excluded them from participating in the newly emerging urban labor market. And as historians have shown, labor unions and recently arrived immigrants—in particular, the Irish—were at the forefront of denying membership to blacks as a way of solidifying their own identities in the new world. Later immigrants from southern and eastern Europe learned and made a choice to maintain a white identity after witnessing the consequences of being black in 19th-century America.

Social Consequences

The social consequences of this late 19th-century white supremacist movement have been chronicled in various disciplines. Sociologists have researched how the economic discrimination that black men faced in cities drove them to seek alternative employment in crime or underemployment in servile jobs, if not outright joblessness. Some have shown that hustling as a distinctly African American illegal enterprise developed and flourished during this period in American history. Sociological research in the 20th century continues to highlight the persistent effects of racial discrimination in the segregation of African Americans in housing, their prospects for employment, access to social services, and even sociolinguistic patterns. Such consequences have had a corrosive effect on the marrigeability of black men, further eroding the cohesiveness and tenure of black families. Viewed in such light, the black criminality that is often cited as a cause of differential police behavior is seen as an enduring effect of racial discrimination, not its cause. Crime as a persistent justification of racism, and particularly differential treatment of citizens of color, therefore, is not tenable.

"Out-of-Place" Policing

If criminological theory has overlooked racism as a cause of crime by ignoring the connection of historical contingencies that have marginalized African Americans, then contemporary police studies have progressed little, for accounts such as "out-of-place" policing also conflate cause and effect. That blacks are "out of place" is not a cause of police behavior as much as it is a product of white supremacist ideologies that initially spawned sundown towns and predominantly white suburbs, molding the perception of whites to interpret the presence of blacks in their communities as an unnatural act. The fact that blacks continue to remain incongruent in such communities is a testament to, and an effect of, the unwillingness and failure of law enforcement to intervene during the inception of sundown towns, and the consequences of contemporary police behavior in sustaining such shameful legacies, not its cause. Some police scholars such as Neil Websdale have argued that contemporary police in poor, minority neighborhoods and predominantly white suburbs—even under the auspicious rhetoric of community, problem-oriented, zero-tolerance policing—continue to be the hegemonic vestiges of antebellum "slave patrols," which were established back in the early 18th-century south to control slaves and prevent them from rioting.

Traffic Encounters

If the premise that white communities are artificial products of white supremacy is accepted, then the disparities in traffic encounters that occur primarily in white suburbs adjacent to major cities with a substantial black population are explained. For instance, Kenneth Novak, Albert Meehan, Michael Ponder, Jeff Rojek, and colleagues all examined the traffic encounters in predominantly white suburbs adjacent to metropolitan areas, such as St. Louis, Missouri, and Kansas City, Kansas. Their research site was located in a blue-collar, predominantly white suburb (three percent African American) next to a major urban center (75 percent African American). They concurred that motorists of color were disproportionately pulled over and searched. Although previous researchers have noted the existence of racial profiling, most have been unable to expound on the possible causes of this disparate treatment of citizens of color, with the exception of Meehan and Ponder. They argue that the practice racial profiling "reflects community-wide practices of segregation that creates the gestalt for all citizens, including the police, of who belongs and who does not belong in certain places" and that "racial profiling by the police appears to reflect community practices of racial segregation." In other words, the whiteness of the background makes color visible in the foreground.

The contemporary patterns of police behavior and residential homogeneity are thus consistent with the racial threat hypothesis, which posits that the presence of "threatening" minorities predicts the use of coercive control mechanisms that ultimately preserve the existing social order. Disproportionately targeting drivers of color for minor infractions and pretexts for searches (racial profiling) can be conceptualized as a coercive control mechanism that preserves the whiteness of communities by unfairly punishing drivers of color.

Pro: Arguments in Favor of Profiling Research

The disparate treatment that citizens of color receive from various law enforcement agencies often garner sensationalistic media coverage, especially if such encounters result in the fatal shooting of an unarmed citizen. However, recent scholarly attention has changed the tone of the discourse to one that is more bureaucratic and academic in tenor. Moreover, the body of racial-profiling research has spawned a parallel course that has become increasingly methodological. The empirical findings of racial disparity in traffic encounters have been challenged, contested, and at times dismissed as the product of flawed research design. Police administrators, when faced with such patterns in their agencies, have denied the existence of such practices, or have attributed its occurrence to a few bigoted individuals. However, the heart of the methodological debate emanates from those who find flaws with the benchmark, baseline, base rate, or denominator, for the actual roadway usage of drivers of color is different from estimates calculated from census data alone. This argument has merit, for denominators constructed from census data draw upon the residential population and not necessarily the driving population, who may use certain roads for work-related, recreational, and transactional purposes.

To remedy such limitations, researchers have developed more methodologically sophisticated techniques to arrive at a valid measure of actual roadway composition, such as using trained observers to estimate the racial and ethnic composition of drivers, conducting surveys at exit points of interstates, examining official data from accidents, obtaining estimates of traffic-violating behaviors through a rolling roadway composition method, and compiling internal departmental communications. By incorporating these multiple measures of actual roadway usage, composition, and rule-breaking behavior on roads, it is hoped that a more accurate view of frequency and patterns of driving behavior will provide a valid benchmark for comparison, as well as illuminate patterns in police behavior that are not evident through use of internal data alone.

Some departments have been amenable to changes. Such changes that seek to reduce the problem of racial profiling have been implemented at the structural and individual level. On a macro level, policies such as mandatory collection of racial data on traffic encounters have been adopted by some states; some departments have initiated independent citizen review boards to investigate and adjudicate allegations of police misconduct. Some departments have implemented comprehensive auditing and early warning systems to monitor problematic officers. On a micro level, some departments have increased cultural and sensitivity training for their officers.

Con: Research on Racial Profiling Is Insufficient

The current works on and theories of racial profiling presuppose the empirical fact of racial segregation and neglect to fully examine why neighborhoods and communities tend to be predominantly white in the first place. This tendency to naturalize the racial distribution of communities without critical reflection is reflected in a prevalent attitude among police: that police officers who stop black motorists in a predominantly white neighborhood are doing legitimate police work. Such official actions do constitute good police work for detecting persons and elements that are out of place, the principle of incongruity that shapes police work. If police officers are unable to spot such incongruities, then by definition, they would be incompetent.

Previous and current studies of racial profiling also place an undue amount of blame on police organizations and prejudiced police officers as causes of their own misbehavior, and the corrosive effects they engender in the perceptions of minorities. But the discrimination minority drivers face on public roads at the hands of the police is only one way of framing the research agenda and the problem. The other is to examine the implications of white motorists who do not face such intrusive police action. What the current research implicitly overlooks is the privilege and reification of driving while white: unlike motorists of color, who must negotiate public roads with the double burden of official suspicion and accusatory glances from locals, white motorists carry no such baggage. Such views have the potential to weaken the voices of minority drivers who report experiences of racial profiling, while entrenching the attitudes of whites (who witness such police action) that their accounts are simply the grumblings of oversensitive minorities. Thus, the inordinate focus on minority drivers renders them into the foreground, while white privilege is pushed into the background; whites are thus absolved from formulating the problem as a larger social, historical, and structural one. If disparities in traffic enforcement appear, the problem is likely to be conceptualized as an organizational one, with reforms sought at the individual and agency level.

Existing police scholarship does not conceptualize the predominance of whites in communities, or the preconditions that legitimize intentionally biased policing, as problematic. Although the socially carcinogenic consequences of residential (minority) segregation have been documented, how and why predominantly white communities are formed while African Americans remain segregated in inner cities has yet to be fully explored. The existing accounts remain one-sided, and fail to ask the history and genealogy of segregation. The history of race and race relations in America, in particular the ascendency of whites as a national social movement in late 19th-century America, could provide that missing genealogical link in the racial profiling puzzle.

Changing the current patterns of racial profiling necessitates a meaningful and honest dialogue about the role of race and race relations in the United States. First, law enforcement agencies and the communities they serve must acknowledge the existence of a history that is reproduced in present traffic enforcement patterns. Second, an agency empowered to investigate and penalize entities that possess the capacity to systematically deny qualified applicants desirable housing in predominantly white communities can be established to mitigate discrimination. Examples of these entities include political arms, such as local commerce boards; commercial organizations, such as developers and homebuilders; and other organizations such as neighborhood and realty associations. Thus, integrated housing is argued as a way to alter the structural conditions that permit racial profiling to occur and persist.

Third, if federal and state funds are withdrawn from departments that serve primarily white communities and demonstrate a continuing disparity in their treatment of persons of color, basic social reorganization goals may be easier to achieve. Fourth, some scholars have argued that white residents in sundown towns— not just the police—ought to be the targets of sensitivity training and education as to the history of racial profiling and discrimination. Combating racial profiling seeks changes at all levels of society, and not just police departments; in other words, social justice reforms that reorganize the basic patterns of society are seen as critical in changing criminal justice policy and organizations.

See Also: 1. Accountability; 2. Arrest Practices; 16. Vehicle Searches; 20. Zero Tolerance Policing.

Further Readings

Alpert, Geoffrey P., Roger G. Dunham, and Michael R. Smith. "Investigating Racial Profiling by the Miami-Dade Police Department: A Multimethod Approach." *Criminology,* v.6/1 (2007).

Anderson, Elijah. *Code of the Street: Decency, Violence, and the Moral Life of the Inner City.* New York: W.W. Norton, 1999.

Barlow, David E., and Melissa Hickman Barlow. "Racial Profiling: A Survey of African American Police Officers." *Police Quarterly,* v.5/3 (2002).

Batton, Candice, and Colleen Kadleck. "Theoretical and Methodological Issues in Racial Profiling." *Police Quarterly,* v.7/1 (2004).

Brunson, Rod K. "'Police Don't Like Black People': African-American Young Men's Accumulated Police Experiences." *Criminology and Public Policy,* v.6/1 (2007).

Buerger, M., and A. Farrell. "The Evidence of Racial Profiling: Interpreting Documented and Unofficial Sources." *Police Quarterly,* v.5/3 (2002).

Devey-Tomaskovic, Donald, Marcinda Mason, and Matthew Zingraff. "Looking for the Driving While Black Phenomena: Conceptualizing Racial Bias Processes and Their Associated Distributions." *Police Quarterly,* v.7/1 (March 2004).

Engel, Robin S., and Jennifer M. Calnon. "Comparing Benchmark Methodologies for Police-Citizen Contacts: Traffic Stop Data Collection for the Pennsylvania State Police." *Police Quarterly,* v.7/1 (March 2004).

Engel, Robin S., and Jennifer M. Calnon. "Examining the Influence of Drivers' Characteristics During Traffic Stops With Police: Results From a National Survey." *Justice Quarterly,* v.21/1 (2004).

Entman, R. "Representation and Reality in the Portrayal of Blacks on Network Television News." *Journalism Quarterly,* v.71 (1994).

Harris, David A. "The Importance of Research on Race and Policing: Making Race Salient to Individuals and Institutions Within Criminal Justice." *Criminology and Public Policy,* v.6/1 (2007).

Independent Commission on the Los Angeles Police Department. *Report of the Independent Commission on the Los Angeles Police Department.* Los Angeles: LAPD, 1991.

Jones-Brown, Delores. "Forever the Symbolic Assailant: The More Things Change, the More They Remain the Same." *Criminology and Public Policy,* v.6/1 (2007).

Langan, Patrick A., Lawrence A. Greenfeld, Steven K. Smith, Matthew Durose, and David J. Levin. *Contacts Between Police and the Public: Findings From the 1999 National Survey.* Washington, DC: Bureau of Justice Statistics, 2001.

Lange, James E., Mark B. Johnson, and Robert B. Voas. "Testing the Racial Profiling Hypothesis for Seemingly Disparate Traffic Stops on the New Jersey Turnpike." *Justice Quarterly,* v.22/2 (2005).

Loewen, James W. *Sundown Towns: A Hidden Dimension of American Racism.* New York: Touchstone, 2005.

Lopez, Haney. *White by Law: The Legal Construction of Race.* New York: New York University Press, 1996.

Lundman, Richard J., and Robert L. Kaufman. "Driving While Black: Effects of Race, Ethnicity, and Gender on Citizen Self-Reports of Traffic Stops and Police Actions." *Criminology,* v.41/1 (2003).

Maanen, J. V., and P. K. Manning. *Policing: A View From the Street.* Santa Monica, CA: Goodyear Publishing, 1978.

Martinez, Ramiro. "Incorporating Latinos and Immigrants Into Policing Research." *Criminology and Public Policy,* v.6/1 (2007).

Massey, Douglas S., and Nancy A. Denton. *American Apartheid: Segregation and the Making of the Underclass.* Cambridge, MA: Harvard University Press, 1993.

Mastrofski, Stephen D., Michael D. Reisig, and John D. McCluskey. "Police Disrespect Toward the Public: An Encounter-Based Analysis." *Criminology,* v.40/3 (2002).

Meehan, Albert J., and Michael Ponder. "How Roadway Composition Matters in Analyzing Police Data on Racial Profiling." *Police Quarterly,* v.5/3 (2002).

Monkkonen, Eric. *Police in Urban America, 1860–1920*. New York: Cambridge University Press, 1981.

Muir, W. K. *Police: Street Corner Politicians*. Chicago: University of Chicago Press, 1977.

Niederhoffer, A. *Behind the Shield: The Police in Urban Society*. Garden City, NY: Anchor Books, 1967.

Novak, Kenneth J. "Disparity and Racial Profiling in Traffic Enforcement." *Police Quarterly*, v.7/1 (2004).

Oliver, M. B. "Portrayals of Crime, Race, and Aggression in Reality Based Police Shows: A Content Analysis." *Journal of Broadcasting and Electronic Media*, v.38 (1994).

Roediger, David R. *How Race Survived U.S. History: From Settlement and Slavery to the Obama Phenomenon*. New York: Verso, 2008.

Rojek, Jeff. "The Influence of Driver's Race on Traffic Stops in Missouri." *Police Quarterly*, v.7/1 (2004).

Rubinstein, J. *City Police*. New York: Doubleday, 1973.

Skolnick, Jerome H. "Racial Profiling—Then and Now." *Criminology and Public Policy*, v.6/1 (2007).

Smith, Michael R., Matthew Makarios, and Geoffrey P. Alpert. "Differential Suspicion: Theory Specification and Gender Effects in the Traffic Stop Context." *Justice Quarterly*, v.23/2 (2006).

Spitzer, Eliot. *The New York City Police Department's "Stop and Frisk" Practices: A Report to the People of the State of New York From the Office of the Attorney General*. New York: New York State Attorney General, 1999.

Stewart, Eric A. "Either They Don't Know or They Don't Care: Black Males and Negative Police Experiences." *Criminology and Public Policy*, v.6/1 (2007).

Tyler, Tom R. *Why People Obey the Law*. Princeton, NJ: Princeton University Press, 2006.

Websdale, Neil. *Policing the Poor*. Boston: Northeastern University Press, 2001.

Weitzer, Ronald, and Steven A. Tuch. "Perceptions of Racial Profiling: Race, Class, and Personal Experience." *Criminology*, v.42/2 (2002).

Wilson, William J. *When Work Disappears: The World of the New Urban Poor*. New York: Vintage, 1996.

14

Riot and Demonstration Responses

Jeff Shantz
Kwantlen Polytechnic University

F ew events reveal the social constructedness or relativity of deviant labels and criminalization processes like political actions, demonstrations, and riots, and the policing practices associated with such events. Policing demonstrations and protests is also one of the most controversial and politically charged aspects of police roles. Even understandings and representations of the character and cause of so-called riots are politically contested and constructed. For police and government authorities, demonstrators or protesters are unequivocally responsible for initiating riots and bear responsibility for any and all violence that results. In addition, riots and protests are understood as largely negative events that threaten social order. On the other hand, many protesters speak of "police riots" to denote their view that the political protest took a violent turn or became a full-blown riot through unjustifiable actions of the police. For many protesters, riots are precipitated by aggressive, violent, illegitimate, or intrusive policing practices, impeding rights to assembly and expression. Even more, for political organizers, protests (even riots) may be viewed as positive, legitimate expressions of dissent or necessary challenges to authority, injustice, or exploitation maintained within the status quo. Rather than events to be feared, such actions might be welcomed as part of the process of social change.

A fundamental difference between liberal democracies and more totalitarian regimes is that liberal democracies are expected to be more tolerant of dissent and protests. Totalitarian regimes, conversely, approach all dissent and protest as inherently criminal. In totalitarian or authoritarian states, the police, state militias, and even private paramilitary groups exhibit consistently repressive and typically violent approaches toward dissent and protest.

At the same time, in liberal democracies, the police have a particular responsibility to maintain self-control and control of their fellow members, especially since they are entrusted with carrying deadly weapons. Police riots can contribute to a divide between civilians and police and encourage distrust of police. However, it is expected that special training in riot conditions can limit violence inflicted by police on civilians. Additionally, jurisdictions that expect high police accountability and strong civilian oversight of police assume fewer instances of police violence against demonstrators.

Critical theorists view policing of demonstrations as a manifestation of class struggle. Such theorists argue that policing emerges with nation-states to protect the material and social interests of powerholders. Policing of protests emerges where powerholders seek to control and regulate other groups. For proponents, the police strive to defend social order and protect all citizens from crime.

Overview of Riots and Demonstrations

Demonstrations and Protests

Political demonstrations occur for various reasons, including lack of access to political and/or economic decision-making channels; dissatisfaction with ruling elites or authorities; desire for social transformation; or more simply, to publicly register dissent with ruling practices. Demonstrations can be directed toward radical, even revolutionary, ends such as the overthrow of a state or property owners, as in the revolutions in France and Russia that overthrew the feudal order of landed property and governance. They can also be more modest in character and mobilized toward less dramatic ends, as when people seek social reforms or policy changes, or simply seek to publicly display their disagreement with rulers or governments.

Demonstrations also take on a variety of forms. They can vary in terms of duration, intensity, range of activities involved, levels of organization, aggression, motivation, and composition of participants and supporting groups. They can involve participation from different backgrounds, often the working class, peasantry, or poor; religious groups; ethnic and racial minorities; and even disaffected members of elite groups.

Some demonstrations are relatively spontaneous, unplanned, and brief. This can occur in immediate response to the passage of a particular piece of legislation or a court decision that is viewed as unsatisfactory. It can also occur where workers respond to notice of impending job loss or workplace closure. Most are planned and address long-standing grievances, concerns, or economic or political policies and practices.

Protests often reflect a gap between goals and opportunities, or between expectations or hopes and people's means to achieve those goals. Protests and riots occur where there is a sense that social change cannot be achieved through discussion, debate, and democratic dialogue. Government or police responses that seek to prevent or crack down on public expressions of dissent will often intensify those expressions, giving rise to riots, violence, rebellion, and even revolution.

Conventional political protests in the contemporary period in Western liberal democracies rarely involve acts of violence or property destruction. Direct-action protests, which have become more prevalent in the period of globalization, do involve the targeting of specific corporations or symbols of corporate power, as in the attacks upon Starbucks coffee shops and Nike stores during the Seattle protests against the World Bank meetings in 1999.

Police Riots

The special term *police riot* is often used to describe confrontations between police or other security forces and civilians, in which police aggression or the use of disproportionate or improper force against civilians triggers a violent response or leads civilians to physically defend themselves against police. The term is also used to describe a civilian riot sparked by a police attack on civilians, or cases in which police provoked aggressive actions by civilians. One such attempt received notoriety during demonstrations against meetings involving business leaders and the governments of Canada, the United States, and Mexico over the proposed Security and Prosperity Partnership (SPP) in Montebello, Quebec, in August 2007. There, it was revealed that members of the Quebec Provincial Police acted undercover to infiltrate a protest and attempted to provoke otherwise peaceful demonstrators to throw rocks at police. The plan, however, was thwarted by a vigilant union organizer.

Police riots, or perceptions that a riot was initiated by policing practices, can lead to more widespread violence and even retaliation against authorities. In specific cases, such as the Soweto Uprising in South Africa on June 16, 1976, police riots have resulted in community violence and the collapse of state order. In Toronto, after a June 15, 2000, police riot to break up a homelessness protest, membership in the direct action group that organized the demonstration grew by the hundreds.

The term *police riot* is avoided by public officials, since it suggests that police have acted in a way that encourages violence, threatens public order and the safety of civilians, and may in fact be criminal. Civilians and police often offer widely divergent interpretations of such events and disagree over the legitimacy of police use of force.

Riots typically require both aggressive protesters and aggressive police. Contexts with lower degrees of police oversight and control and a history of more aggressive policing experience riots more frequently. Riots have been more common in the United States, continental Europe, and Latin America than in countries like Canada or Sweden.

The way in which demonstrations, political mobilizations, or riots are handled and controlled greatly influences whether or not full-scale riots will result from a precipitating event. Social regulation breaks down and new forms of socialization and collective sentiment among rioters emerges, supportive of riotous activities. As a result, there have been shifts toward more tolerant, softer forms of policing in some Western democracies, although more aggressive forms of policing have characterized recent antiglobalization protests.

Police and military partake in the escalation of violence from their side. In the United States, cities with fewer riots are those with more racially integrated police forces. Race riots are typically sparked by incidents involving police in a minority neighborhood. Usually there is a real or perceived misconduct or act of aggression by police in the area.

Even with regard to looting in specific riots, most acts of looting and community violence were not random or senseless, but in fact were directed at businesses that had histories of cheating or taking advantage of local residents. The Kerner Commission, investigating race riots in the 1960s in the United States, noted that almost every such eruption in the 1960s and 1970s was sparked by a specific act of police violence in communities that had long suffered under such violence for generations. Despite this, the riots of the 1960s were used as justification for the militarization of policing in local areas. A similar process has occurred in the context of alternative globalization demonstrations and calls for tighter security and policing of such demonstrations.

The Social Underpinnings of Demonstrations and Riots

The vast majority of people regularly conform to social norms. Notions of normalcy and morality are supported by various social, cultural, political, and economic sanctions. Ongoing socialization engenders habitual responses to authority that favor deference. To break through layers of socialization requires significant shifts in perception. Given the levels of injustice worldwide, it is surprising that protest is not a more regular feature of social life. Even more curious is the relative infrequency of occurrences in which ordinary people challenge authorities and political or economic elites. Even fewer are those who directly resist the undertakings of governments in a forceful manner.

Given the inhibition experienced by people in violating even minor or insignificant social rules or conventions, it is clear how difficult it might be to resist the demands of the state. It requires courage and a sense of purpose. One must overcome internal as well as external barriers to action.

Much research suggests that social structuring emerges within protests and riots such that participants develop their own moral sense, or what sociologist Emile Durkheim terms a *conscience collective*, a set of shared values. Thus, myths and rumors can be taken up by riot participants to justify involvement in riots and to explain why a riot started in the first place. This conscience collective can express a strong "us versus them" sentiment, in which protesters come to view opponents harshly as enemies to be contested and overcome. For activists, resistance to the state or police—the representatives of state authority—can be viewed as conforming to a higher moral or ethical standard, and is viewed as part of the process of broader social transformation and positive social change.

The "us versus them" sentiment is also a well-researched and long-recognized characteristic of police subcultures. Thus, harsh actions by police can initiate a cycle of escalation as each side reinforces polarized sentiments, increasing solidarity and a sense of aggrievement both among protesters and police.

Policing demonstrations can contribute to a sense of social cohesion and group identity on both sides. Often it is the presence of mass and/

or aggressive policing that spurs protesters to become more aggressive or even militant. It can play into the constitution or identification of "us versus them" sentiments, in which police and protesters harden within oppositional stances.

One part of policing riots is working to dispel the rumors that can spark riots. Policing practices that are not aware of this conscience collective can escalate aggression within riots by violating the sense of solidarity and self-defense within rioters. For protesters, even peaceful demonstrations can be spurred into riots when police act overzealously or irresponsibly.

Examples of Policing Demonstrations

Police have, since the earliest days of modern policing, regularly been deployed to disperse striking workers and break up picket lines. Much research shows that during the 19th century, many of the gatherings against which police were deployed that were identified as "riots" were actually simply gatherings of striking workers. Targeting of such "riots" was more than an issue of public order. Rather, the suppression of strikes offered examples of policing to benefit economic interests. Police strikebreaking under the guise of riot control was an effort to defeat working-class resistance to employers.

The first modern police forces in the United States were developed in urban centers in the industrialized northeast. Their main emphasis was maintaining urban order in the face of class conflict as cities grew through waves of migrants seeking employment. In American history, numerous cases show that local business people have had influence, even control, over directing police against striking workers. The earliest forms of policing in the south involved slave patrols dating back to 1712 in South Carolina. The function of these patrols was to maintain discipline over slaves and prevent slave riots. Black people caught violating any laws were summarily punished.

State forces were formed to deal with striking workers. The Coal and Iron Police were created in Pennsylvania in 1866 to control striking coal and iron workers. In 1905, a state police agency was formed for strikebreaking. These official state forces gave legitimacy to strikebreaking that private security, which lacked state authorization as keepers of the public order, could not claim. Strikebreaking and union busting has also been a function of private police and security, most notably reflected in the history of the famous Pinkerton agency founded in the mid-19th century. In

July 1934, striking longshore workers were involved in several engagements with police who attempted to break the strike. In response to the killing of two picketers by police, area unions initiated a general strike of all workers in the area. The result was the Big Strike of San Francisco. During the 1945 strike of United Auto Workers members against Ford in Windsor, Canada, picketers prevented police from dispersing the picket line to open the plant by creating a vehicular barricade surrounding the factory with parked cars, taxis, and buses.

Social and Political Demonstrations and Clashes

The extensive and often militant social and political struggles of the 1960s impelled states to re-think methods of social control. The transformation of urban police forces from community forces managed at local levels in towns and cities in America to militarized forces organized along national lines and standards related to changes during the 1960s in which "law and order" became a matter of national politics. Much of the impetus for this change came from the visible social conflict and protests of the 1960s, beginning with civil rights marches and boycotts and followed by antiwar movements and student protests. The period of conflicts included the numerous urban uprisings and race riots in cities such as Detroit, Washington, D.C., and the Watts area of Los Angeles.

Antiwar demonstrators opposing the Vietnam War frequently clashed with police and were subjected to baton blows, tear gas, and mass arrests. Often, police claimed the protesters were rioting. An infamous clash between antiwar and student protesters and police came during the mass protests during the August 1968 Democratic Convention in Chicago. National television coverage showed shocking instances of protesters being run down and severely beaten with batons. One protester was killed during the conflict. Two years later, in Kent, Ohio, after several days of antiwar protests, fires, and bottle-throwing by Kent State student demonstrators, city officials were fearful that local police forces would be inadequate to handle the disturbances. National Guardsmen were called in to maintain order. On May 4, 1970, Guardsmen fired into the tumultuous crowd on campus, killing four people. The resulting protests across the nation galvanized millions of students at hundreds of universities.

The violence in Chicago and Kent State radicalized many in these movements, who began to view America as a police state rather than a functioning democracy, and led to militant factions splitting from the main student organizations such as Students for a Democratic Society. Some went underground to wage violent campaigns against government targets through groups like the Weather Underground.

Calls for Reform

Images of the violent policing of civil rights marches, such as under Bull Connor's Birmingham, Alabama, Police Department forces in 1963, caused American society and foreign audiences to recoil, providing an impetus for others to join the movement, and leading for calls for restraint on local police and transformations in the structure of society itself. The use of police dogs and water cannons against nonviolent protesters, consisting largely of regular citizens from the local community rather than militant activists and organizers, shifted public opinion against police and southern governments and reinforced protesters' claims of injustice, racism, and inequality.

The most common recommendations were an expansion of police forces and the militarization of police through provision of advanced technology, weapons, and training. Key in the expansion of U.S. police power was the Law Enforcement Assistance Administration (LEAA), which was organized to extend policing along national lines through new technologies and strategies. Due in part to LEAA policies, military technology and weaponry, originally developed for use in warfare, were developed throughout U.S. police departments as police organizations adopted a largely paramilitary character.

In response to growing social movements, increased use of police was also requested to restore order. Part of that response has been the reconstruction of police forces and policing to maintain public order while limiting popular mobilization. Demands for greater democratization and equality in the 1960s and 1970s, as well as challenges to existing authority systems, were even met by a call for a "moderation of democracy" by the global-membership Trilateral Commission, which met in Kyoto in 1975 to discuss the "excesses of democracy" affecting many of the members' industrial nations.

The period of alternative globalization protests has seen a number a dramatic clashes between police and protesters. The protests against the World Trade Organization (WTO) in Seattle in November 1999 gained the nickname The Battle in Seattle. Demonstrations in Quebec City (2001), Genoa (2001), Miami (2003), and London (2009) saw running street battles between demonstrators and police. The Genoa and London protests also saw the death of civilians due to police actions.

Practices of Policing Demonstrations

States and ruling elites have a range of strategies to control or defuse opposition from citizens. At various points in dealing with demonstrations, police have played upon the moral inhibitions people feel in resisting state demands. In specific contexts, such as antipoverty demonstrations in Toronto, Canada, since at least 2003, police have approached elderly demonstrators and parents with younger children present, questioning their responsibility and judgment by virtue simply of their being present at a political demonstration. In addition, police have suggested that participants might be at risk of violence or physical harm. Even more, police have, as in Toronto, threatened parents with loss of children and the possible intervention of children's service agencies if parents remained at the demonstration site with their children.

Containing Space

Some demonstrations can be defused simply by providing a contained space in which they might occur. People can gather, blow off steam, feel a sense of empowerment or public engagement, and then disperse. Attempts can also be made to police demonstrations ahead of time by warning organizing groups of police intentions to be proactive in making arrests. More recently, particularly as part of policing alternative globalization demonstrations, preemptive arrests have become more regular features of policing demonstrations. Police will sometimes attempt to infiltrate groups and influence the planning and organizing for actions in a way that is less likely to threaten social order.

Riot Control Measures

Police and security forces also use a range of riot control measures to contain, disperse, discourage, or arrest civilians involved in protests or riots. Typically less lethal weapons, such as batons and clubs, have been used initially to disperse demonstrations or crowds. During alternative globalization demonstrations since the 1990s, riot police have made regular use of pepper spray, tear gas, rubber bullets, tasers, and mounted police. During the Quebec City demonstrations against the meetings of the Organization of American States (OAS) in 2001, police regularly ran through crowds with water cannons to cause them to disperse. In addition, thousands of canisters of tear gas were fired into neighborhoods near the meeting sites to disperse crowds. During the violent protests against the Group of Eight summit in Genoa, Italy, in 2001, police used armored vehicles to disperse crowds. After an Italian police vehicle was violently attacked by protestors, including Carlo Guiliani, who attempted to throw a fire extinguisher into the vehicle, police fired back with live ammunition, striking and killing Guiliani.

Riot police wear protective equipment such as helmets with face visors, body armor, and occasionally gas masks, when tear gas or other such agents are used. Other equipment includes extended riot batons and large Plexiglas riot shields. This equipment is designed to protect officers from direct contact as well as thrown objects such as bottles, rocks, and sticks. The equipment also provides ballistic protection.

In the era of globalization protests, police have moved from attempting to restrain protesters directly by using traditional means such as batons, riot squads, and pepper spray, which failed during the Seattle protests of 1999 and the demonstrations against the IMF and World Bank in 2000, to developing containment strategies prior to demonstrations against such entities as the World Bank or WTO. During the protests against the OAS in Windsor, Ontario, in 2000, a security fence closed off several city blocks around the convention center reserved for the meetings. Official delegates were flown to the meeting site by helicopter from Detroit. Protesters who approached the fence were then pepper sprayed. The fence, sealing off several city blocks around the convention site, reappeared as a crowd control technique during the 2001 protests against the OAS in Quebec City. There, protesters were bombarded by thousands of canisters of tear gas over three days of demonstrations. Water cannons and rubber bullets were also deployed.

Recent Transformations

In recent years, the policing of riots and demonstrations has undergone a substantial transformation in a very short period of time. Police and activists now engage in a dialectical process of preparation, response, and innovation in relation to each others' actions and expectations of action. During alternative globalization protests, activists have begun to expect or anticipate heavy police use of force, including tear gas and rubber bullets. As a result, many have taken to dressing themselves in often-elaborate homemade armor, including hockey pads and equipment, army surplus helmets, and shields fabricated from garbage can lids. Some have created suits of rubber inner tubes to protect themselves from baton blows. Swimming goggles to protect against pepper spray and gas masks to guard against tear gas have become staples of activist attire.

Commentators have suggested that many of the protests against corporate globalization have involved police riots. During the weeklong protests against the WTO in Seattle in 1999, conference proceedings were disrupted when an estimated 75,000 protestors, who clogged streets and wrote graffiti on buildings, shut down the summit's opening ceremonies and prevented delegates from gathering. While the majority were nonviolent protestors, a small group instigated some violence and looting, leading the Seattle police and National Guard to declare a state of emergency and issue curfews and initiate arrests, tear-gassing, pepper spraying, and even shooting rubber bullets at nonviolent protestors.

A 2009 inquiry report into policing of the G-20 meeting in Britain protests concludes that senior police officers risk losing the consent of the British public unless they abandon misguided approaches to public protests that are considered "unfair, aggressive and inconsistent." The report of Her Majesty's Inspectorate of Constabulary (HMIC) calls for a softening of the policing approach and advocates an "approachable, impartial, accountable style of policing based on minimal force and anchored in public consent." The report argues that public order training should be overhauled, with a new emphasis on educating the 22,500 officers trained for protests in communication and diplomacy rather than in riot scenarios. Additionally, use of forward intelligence teams (FITs) who follow, film, and photograph protesters, identifying activists and storing their information on databases, raises fundamental privacy issues.

Pro: Arguments in Favor of Policing Demonstrations

Criminalizing violent opposition to the state is viewed positively by authorities. It is, for police, simply a matter of meeting their professional obligations. Policing demonstrations is seen as a necessary aspect of preserving and supporting social and political order. Such conflict, if it spread, could result in violence, injuries, or even deaths, as is sometimes the case within riots, and was seen in larger race riots in various periods of American history. Protests, and especially riots, can incur large economic costs in property damage, vandalism, and theft. Even higher are the individual and social costs in personal injuries or loss of public services.

For authorities, there is a concern that protests will be used as cover for criminal activities, as when nonprotesters take advantage of political protests or riots to loot, steal, or shoplift. Looting of shops by nonaggrieved people has been observed within various riots, including the Detroit riot of 1967 and the Los Angeles riot of 1992. During the WTO protests in Seattle in 1999, observers noted the occurrence of people not involved in the protests breaking into stores and looting goods.

Governments, local or national, would be brought to crisis, and innocent nonparticipants would suffer through a withdrawal of social resources or a disruption of necessary services or provisions. Such desperation has often accompanied or followed periods of uprising, rebellion and, most extensively, revolution. If order is not restored, the riot can escalate, including dramatic actions such as gunfire, arson, and violence.

In some cases, protesters can represent a violent minority that may seek to subvert the needs and wishes of larger sectors of society. In some cases, such as protests by neo-Nazis or ethnonationalist groups, demonstrations may be the opportunity to engage in violent acts against minorities. Violence can circumvent political discussion and debate within contexts of political openness and democracy where such means are available to the population at large. Violence can also be used to silence political minorities or oppressed groups who are subjected to aggressive targeting by majority group members or members of extremist groups who act within the cover of a mass demonstration. For authorities, appropriate policing can protect innocent bystanders or groups that would otherwise be targeted. It can also secure a space in which vulnerable minorities can organize and carry out demonstrations.

For some, policing can serve to protect the protest message by preventing aggressive voices from drowning out less aggressive expressions of dissent. Violence can serve to deflect attention from the significant details of an issue, substituting debate over violence or property destruction for discussion and analysis of the issues. Such distraction can weaken the social visions of the mass of protesters.

Less aggressive policing practices can also be beneficial. Restrictive practices can lead to broader rebellion as larger sections of the citizenry become frustrated or indignant as a result of perceived restrictions on rights to assemble or freedom of expression. Officials are expected, by nonviolent observers, to maintain the safety of political protests. A public backlash can emerge in response to aggressive policing. Citizens in liberal democracies generally expect freedom of speech, expression, and assembly to be respected and upheld, at least where protests are peaceful and orderly. Permissive policing can reinforce a sense of democratic openness and participation in society. It can send a message to uninvolved observers that their society is one in which diverse opinions can be expressed, even forcefully, and in which rights to assembly and free speech are respected and preserved. This can lessen feelings of dissatisfaction and alienation, thereby lessening the likelihood of growing dissent and more aggressive and larger future protests.

Within popular discourse, citizens are understood to surrender voluntarily some of their authority and rights and delegate them to the state. In exchange, they expect the police to protect them and their property. Failure to police demonstrations, particularly aggressive ones, would be viewed as an abandonment of the state's responsibility to its citizens. In this view, the police are seen as a politically neutral force that uses its powers solely to enforce laws within a specific sociolegal context.

Con: Arguments Against Policing Demonstrations

For critics, policing of demonstrations provides a mechanism for elites, those who control wealth and resources, to suppress attempts by non-elites to redistribute wealth and resources. Such policing provides a powerful agency for maintaining inequalities of wealth and power in class societies. Critical theorists seek to determine whose order is being maintained, and what that order looks like in terms of inequality, liberty, or exploitation. In the view of critics, policing of protests reinforces and extends unequal class structures in society by focusing on activities predominantly of the poor and working class rather than the activities of elites, such as corporate crime, pollution, ecological destruction, or workplace injustice.

Historically, the most aggressive policing has occurred during demonstrations organized by working class, poor people, and racialized minorities, including indigenous people in the United States and Canada. Only with the antiwar protests of the 1960s was such aggressive policing deployed against middle class or privileged students. During the alternative globalization protests of the 21st centuries, aggressive policing has been directed at diverse groups, reflecting the plural composition of those movements.

Policing of demonstrations reinforces existing unequal property rights and the limited political processes of parliamentary democracy as the preferred or privileged form of political expression. Forms of politics outside of such legitimized, and hierarchical, channels are treated as deviant, threatening, and even criminal. Very early in their history, police were deployed by commerce to harass picket lines and break workers' strikes. The strikes were a response to exploitation and economic deprivation, yet police were not deployed against employers to end such harmful conditions. In these instances, police strikebreaking protects the interests of industrialists. Such actions served to break working-class resistance to the power of capital. Use of police to break strikes also defines collective organizing and assembly by workers as a criminal, rather than economic or political, act.

Protesters are sometimes presented by police as dangerous individuals who belong to fringe groups or are disaffected members of society and pose a threat to normal societal functioning or a certain way of life. In some cases, terms like *professional protesters* are used to disparage organizers and suggest they are not raising legitimate concerns, but rather acting out of self-interest. All actions are called into question by focusing on the most extreme and aggressive members as being typical of the movement as a whole. In Toronto, the former chief of police identified direct-action antipoverty groups as "terrorists" and attempted to make simple membership in the groups illegal.

For some critics, governmental or state violence against demonstrators or political opponents is viewed as an act of state terrorism, designed to strike fear into potential protesters, dissidents, or even observers. Such aggressive policing and state violence is intended to send a message to future activists that violence from political demonstrations will not be tolerated.

The focus on policing can serve to shift attention toward technical processes and tactics, rather than the pressure needed to expand social justice and end inequalities. For protesters, there is the concern that riots will provide police with an opportunity to crack down, and even inflict violence, against protest organizers who have long been targeted for repression or retribution. Criminalizing protests is a method that states and ruling elites have used to maintain power, status, and authority; sustain existing social structures; and control opposition or rebellion.

Police have the authority of the courts and criminal justice system, and often government, to support and sustain their definitions of situations. Charges of participating in a riot or counseling to riot are often laid against protesters. Such charges are not laid against police, regardless of their actions before, during, or after the outbreak of a riot.

❖

See Also: 9. Police Brutality; 15. Use of Deadly Force.

Further Readings

Beene, Charles. *Riot Prevention and Control: A Police Officer's Guide to Managing Violent and Non-Violent Crowds.* Boulder, CO: Paladin, 2006.

Boykoff, Jules. *The Suppression of Dissent: How the State and Mass Media Squelch American Social Movements.* New York: Routledge, 2006.

Capeci, Dominic J., and Martha Wilkerson. "The Detroit Rioters of 1943: A Reinterpretation." *Michigan Historical Review*, v.16/1 (1990).

Capeci, Dominic J., and Martha Wilkerson. *Layered Violence: The Detroit Rioters of 1943.* Jackson: University Press of Mississippi, 1991.

Carter, Stephen L. *The Dissent of the Governed: A Meditation on Law, Religion, and Loyalty.* Cambridge, MA: Harvard University Press, 1998.

Davenport, Christian, ed. *Paths to State Repression: Human Rights Violations and Contentious Politics.* New York: Rowman and Littlefield, 2000.

Davenport, Christian, Hank Johnston, and Carol Mueller, eds. *Repression and Mobilization.* Minneapolis: University of Minnesota Press, 2005.

della Porta, Donatella, and Herbert Reiter, eds. *Policing Protest: The Control of Mass Demonstrations in Western Democracies.* Minneapolis: University of Minnesota Press, 1998.

Ewens, William L. *Becoming Free: The Struggle for Human Development.* Wilmington, DE: Scholarly Resources, 1984.

Freeman, Jo, and Victoria Johnson, eds. *Waves of Protest: Social Movements Since the 1960s.* New York: Rowman and Littlefield, 1999.

Goldstein, Robert Justin. *Political Repression in Modern America from 1870–1976.* Urbana-Champaign: University of Illinois Press, 2001.

Grimshaw, Allan. "Lawlessness and Violence in America and Their Special Manifestation in Changing Negro-White Relationships." In *Racial Violence in the United States*, edited by A. Grimshaw. Chicago: Aldine, 1969.

James, C. L. R., George Breitman, and Edgar Keemer. *Fighting Racism in World War II.* New York: Pathfinder, 1980.

Janowitz, Morris. "Patterns of Collective Racial Violence." In *The History of Violence in America: Historical and Comparative Perspectives*, edited by Hugh Davis Graham and Ted Robert Gurr. New York: Praeger, 1969.

Johnson, Marilynn S. "Gender, Race, and Rumours: Re-Examining the 1943 Race Riots." *Gender and History*, v.10/2 (1998).

Langlois, Janet, L. "The Belle Isle Bridge Incident: Legend Dialectic and Semiotic System in the 1943 Detroit Race Riots." *Journal of American Folklore*, v.96/380 (1983).

Lewis, Paul, and Sandra Leville. "'Aggressive' Policing of Protests Condemned in Post-G20 Inquiry." (November 25, 2009). http://www .guardian.co.uk/politics/2009/nov/25/police-could-lose-public-consent (Accessed February 2010).

Lynch, Michael J., and Raymond Michalowski. *Primer in Radical Criminology: Critical Perspectives on Crime, Power and Identity.* Monsey, NY: Criminal Justice Press, 2006.

Reimam, Jeffrey. *The Rich Get Richer and the Poor Get Prison: Ideology, Class and Criminal Justice.* Boston: Allyn and Bacon, 2006.

Reiner, Robert. *The Politics of the Police.* Sussex, England: Wheatsheaf, 1985.

Schulhofer, Stephen J. *The Enemy Within: Intelligence Gathering, Law Enforcement, and Civil Liberties in the Wake of September 11.* Washington, DC: The Century Foundation, 2002.

Schultz, Bud, and Ruth Schultz. *The Price of Dissent: Testimonies to Political Repression in America.* Berkeley: University of California Press, 2001.

Shah, Anup. "WTO Protests in Seattle, 1999." http://www.globalissues .org/article/46/wto-protests-in-seattle-1999 (Accessed September 2010).

Shantz, Jeff. "The Criminalization of Dissent." *Social Anarchism*, v.34 (2003).

Shantz, Jeff. *Living Anarchy: Theory and Practice in Anarchist Movements.* Palo Alto, CA: Academica, 2009.

Shantz, Jeff. *Radical Ecology and Social Myth: The Difficult Constitution of Counter-Hegemonic Politics.* Saarbrucken, Germany: VDM Verlag, 2009.

Shantz, Jeff. "'They Think Their Fannies Are as Good as Ours': The 1943 Detroit Riot." *Studies in the Literary Imagination*, v.40/2 (2007).

Simon, David, R. *Elite Deviance.* Boston: Allyn and Bacon, 2008.

Tepperman, Lorne. *Deviance, Crime, and Control: Beyond the Straight and Narrow.* Oxford: Oxford University Press, 2006.

U.S. Army Military Police School. *Riot Control.* Amsterdam: Fredonia Books, 2002.

Waddington, David P. *Policing Public Disorder: Theory and Practice.* London: Willan, 2007.

15

Use of Deadly Force

Ivan Y. Sun
University of Delaware

The police represent the legitimate force of governmental control in society. Police officers are charged with enforcing substantive criminal laws, preserving public order, and protecting the citizenry from crime. To achieve these functions, the police are empowered with the legal authority to use coercion, intrude into citizens' private lives, deprive citizens of their liberty through detention or arrest, and employ physical and even deadly force if necessary. The critical role of coercion in the profession has led to the development of a force-centered definition of police that views the police as the main, and sometimes the only, mechanism for the state to distribute nonnegotiable force in handling emergencies in a society.

There are various types of police force, which can be roughly classified into two groups: nondeadly force and deadly force. The difference between the two lies in the likelihood of causing serious bodily harm or death, with the latter having a greater chance than the former. Use of deadly force thus refers to the application of force that is likely to have lethal consequences for the subject. Sometimes, citizens may be seriously wounded or killed by nondeadly force, but it is rarely, if ever, the intention of the police.

Policy change and legal justification for the use of deadly force has evolved over the past several decades. The frequency of police use of deadly force is dependent on several groups of factors. There are differing views on police use of deadly force; proponents view deadly force as an occasional necessity in extreme cases, while opponents note that deadly force is used unevenly across social groups. In either case, the use of deadly force is a hotly contested issue.

The History of Policy Governing Use of Deadly Force

Police use of deadly force became a central theme in U.S. policing after officers began carrying firearms in the 1850s. Since then, many police departments have prescribed the circumstances under which deadly force could be used. Such departmental policies and regulations largely followed the legal traditions for justifiable use of force. These traditions could be traced back to the early Middle Ages, when virtually all felonies were punishable by the death penalty; consequently, killing those fleeing from suspected serious crimes was viewed as appropriate and acceptable. As a result, police use of deadly force was guided mainly by the so-called *fleeing felon* rule, which authorized officers to apply deadly force as a legitimate means of apprehending individuals who were fleeing from suspected felonies.

From Fleeing Felon to Defense of Life Rule

The common law, fleeing felon doctrine endowed the police with broad authority to use all necessary means, including deadly force, to apprehend fleeing suspects. Given this broad power, incidents that involved an officer shooting unarmed people, and firing shots at the back or side of suspects or even innocent citizens, were not unheard of. Although police use of deadly force was relatively rare throughout U.S. history, it became the major source of conflict between the police and citizens, especially racial minorities. Reformers thus called for more limits on police use of deadly force.

Two critical events contributed directly to the abolishment of the fleeing felon policy. First, in 1972, the New York City Police Department (NYPD) replaced the permissive fleeing felon standard with a more restrictive defense-of-life rule. The new doctrine permitted the use of deadly force only if the arresting officer's life, a citizen's life, or another officer's life was in danger. The adoption of the new policy drew national attention, since the restrictive rule reduced NYPD's firearms discharges by 30 percent. As a result, more and more departments began to implement the new shooting policy in the 1980s.

Second, in its decision on *Tennessee v. Garner* (1985), the U.S. Supreme Court ruled that the fleeing felon standard was unconstitutional because it violated the Fourth Amendment's guarantees against unreasonable seizure. This decision officially ended the use of the fleeing felon rule. The Court noted that, "Deadly force may not be used unless it is necessary to prevent escape and the officer has probable cause to believe that the suspect poses a significant threat of death or serious physical injury to the officer or others." Thus, a purse snatcher (such as Edward Garner, the suspect in the case) who appears to be unarmed and attempts to flee the scene by jumping over the backyard fence should not be shot in the back because the suspect did not pose any immediate danger or threat to the responding officers or the public.

The defense-of-life rule was extended in *Graham v. Connor* (1989) with the introduction of the concept of reasonableness. Specifically, whether the officers' actions were "objectively reasonable" in light of the facts and circumstances confronting them, without regard to their underlying intent or motivation, became an important factor in deciding whether the force was justified. The Court commented that: "The reasonableness of a particular use of force must be judged from the perspective of a reasonable officer on the scene, and its calculus must embody an allowance for the fact that police officers are often forced to make split-second decisions about the amount of force necessary in a particular situation."

The implementation of the defense of life policy involves both substantial and procedural changes in regulating police shooting behavior. Substantially, the new policy limits the use of deadly force to defend officers and others from immediate threats of death or serious physical injury. In most jurisdictions, officers are also prohibited to fire warning and call-for-assistance shots or shoot from moving vehicles. Procedurally, officers who are involved in using firearms are required to complete incident reports that are reviewed internally by higher-ranking supervisors. These substantial and procedural improvements over the fleeing felon standard have greatly enhanced the accountability of police shooting behavior. The control of police use of deadly force has been one of the most successful areas in regulating police discretionary behavior over the past three decades.

The Force Continuum

Another important development in terms of regulating police use of deadly force is the concept of a use of force continuum. The concept or model was first developed in the late 1980s and now has been widely adopted by law enforcement agencies throughout the country. While there is no consensus about what a force continuum entails or how many different types of force should be included, the most common model presents various forms of force in a stair-step fashion, ranking force from low coercive (e.g., verbal command and threatening); to medium (e.g., search and seizure and physical restraint); to high coercive (e.g., arrest and deadly force). For example, the San Diego police use a five-category continuum (officer presence, verbal commands, control/compliance, soft impact, and lethal force), while the St. Petersburg police employ a nine-category model (officer presence, verbal direction, restrain devices, transporter, takedown, pain compliance, countermoves, intermediate weapons, and lethal force).

The force continuum is important because it clearly displays the possible force options that are available to officers in controlling situations, with each level of force matched by a corresponding level of subject resistance. However, the force continuum does not require officers to progress through each level before reaching the final level of force (i.e., deadly force). Instead, based on the subject's actions, officers should move along the force ladder by either escalating or de-escalating their level of force. The force continuum instructs officers to respond with a level of force that is appropriate to the situation at hand, acknowledging that deadly force is the last resort and should be used only when a suspect poses a serious threat to the officer or another individual.

Looking at NYPD's guidelines today, officers are provided with clear examples of circumstances in which they should not use deadly force. Specifically, NYPD officers should not use deadly physical force or discharge their firearms (1) against another person unless they have probable cause to believe that they must protect themselves or another person from imminent death or serious physical injury; (2) when doing so will unnecessarily endanger innocent persons; (3) in defense of property; (4) to subdue a fleeing felon who presents no threat of imminent death or serious physical injury to themselves or another person present; (5) to warn the suspects; (6) to summon assistance except in emergency situations when someone's personal safety is endangered and unless no other reasonable means is available; (7) at or from a moving vehicle unless deadly physical force is being used against the police officer or another person present, by means other than a moving vehicle; and (8) at a dog or other animal except to protect themselves or another person from physical injury and there is no other reasonable means to eliminate the threat. Officers are also not allowed to, under any circumstances, cock a firearm. Firearms must be fired double action at all times.

Despite much more restrictive policies governing the use of deadly force being employed by the majority of police departments, high-profile cases involving police killing of citizens have drawn substantial public attention and even created community outcries and crises. Many citizens believe that police officers are allowed too much discretion in applying deadly force, and that these cases should be carefully monitored through civilian review process. Many cities have established civilian review boards or agencies to receive, investigate, and/or review citizen complaints against police misconduct. According to the American Civil Liberties Union (ACLU), by the end of 1991, more than 60 percent of the country's largest cities had some form of civilian review system. While the degree of citizen involvement in the review process varies from jurisdiction to jurisdiction, the final decision making in terms of the disposition of the complaints lies solely in the hands of the police chiefs.

Some jurisdictions also give the governance of use of deadly force directly to city councils. In January 2009, for example, the New York City Council passed a legislation that requires the NYPD to beef up their annual report to the council by detailing (1) the circumstances surrounding incidents where officers fire their weapons; (2) a precinct-by-precinct and borough-by-borough breakdown of shooting incidents; (3) the reason for the firearm discharge (i.e., accidental, adversarial, etc.); and (4) the race, gender, and age of any individual engaged in adversarial conflict with an officer or third party that results in a firearms discharge. The report is hoped to allow for better oversight of NYPD's use of deadly force.

Frequency of Deadly Force

A fundamental question about police use of deadly force is how often deadly force is employed by police officers around the country. Unfortunately, there is no quick answer to this question. Several factors contribute to the absence of such information. The first and perhaps biggest hurdle impeding the understanding of the true scope of the issue is a lack of reliable, national data from any federal agency. While the Supplementary Homicide Reports compiled by the Federal Bureau of Investigation (FBI) as part of the Uniformed Crime Reports (UCR) include information on deaths at the hands of police officers, the accuracy of the data is questionable. Another source of data is the annual figures for "death by legal intervention of the police" reported by the National Center for Health Statistics (NCHS) of the U.S. Heath Service. The dataset, however, significantly underestimates the deaths caused by police shootings.

A second and related factor is that police departments vary in their recording and reporting practices of use of deadly force. For example, some departments do not count incidents where officers shoot but miss the suspects as use of deadly force cases. Similarly, some departments include both justified and unjustified use of deadly force in their recording, while others distinguish the former from the latter. Police agencies also depart from one another in recording police shootings involving multiple shots and officers. Finally, given that jurisdictions differ significantly in crime rates and other social–contextual characteristics, simply reporting the frequency of use of deadly force may blur the true factors that cause the variation in use.

Studies Show Use of Deadly Force Is Rare

With these confounding issues in mind, previous studies have consistently shown that police use of force in general and use of deadly force in particular is rare. For example, data from the Police-Public Contact Survey (PPCS) collected by the Bureau of Justice Statistics (BJS) indicated that, of the 43.5 million persons who had face-to-face contact with the police in 2005, approximately 1.6 percent of these persons were subjected to the use of force or threat of force, a number that has remained fairly constant since 1996. The PPCS asked U.S. residents about their contact with police and what police did during those events. It thus contained survey data from sample citizens rather than official data provided by police departments.

The first substantial aggregation of state, county, and local law enforcement use of force data is the National Police Use of Force Database administered by the International Association of Chiefs of Police (IACP). The association collected data on calls for service from participating police agencies between 1991 and 2000. In 1999, the most recent year for which complete data from participating agencies was available, police used force at a rate of 3.61 times per 10,000 calls for service, which equaled a use-of-force rate of .036 percent per call. In other words, police did not use force 99.96 percent of the time. Both BJS and IACP data represent general information on police use of force data and do not contain specific information on deadly force.

Given that the above numbers include various forms of force used by the police, it safe to presume that police use deadly force at an even lower rate. For example, NYPD officers reported the use of a firearm in only five incidents among a total of 1,762 occasions in which physical force was employed to subdue a subject. In other words, only four percent of use-of-physical-force cases involved use of deadly force. In New Jersey, police agencies in the entire state responded to 8.5 million calls in 1991, and officers fired their weapons on only 167 occasions, resulting in a rate of 0.0196 percent. In addition to the ratio of use of weapons to calls for service, police use of deadly force is also reported through other measures. Due to variation in methodology (e.g., data collection, measures, sample jurisdictions, and time periods), the results from previous studies are not entirely comparable, and their findings should thus be interpreted with caution.

One of the measures of use of deadly force is the probability of police officers becoming involved in fatal shootings during their entire career, which has been proved to be very slim. For example, given that officers serve an average of 25–30 years before retirement, an officer employed in Jacksonville, Florida, or Portland, Oregon, would theoretically have to be on duty for 139 years or 193 years, respectively, before being involved in a fatal shooting. Another measure of deadly force is the annual estimate of justifiable fatal shootings by police. The reported number varies from 250–300 to over 1,000. One study reported that nationwide, police officers attempted to fatally shoot approximately 3,600 people per year. Of these, 600 suspects were fatally wounded, 1,200 were injured but not killed, and 1,800 were shot at but were missed.

While the exact number of use of deadly force or fatal killings each year is not known, there is evidence to support a decline of these figures since the adoption of the defense of life standard. For example, in Memphis, Tennessee, police fatally shot a total of 34 suspected fleeing felons between 1970 and 1974, the five-year period before the Garner case, and the number fell to 19 between 1985 and 1989. In New York City, 125 police officers fired 364 shots in 2008, which was the lowest number since comparable record-keeping that began in 1971. A study of justifiable police shootings in 57 U.S. cities with populations over 250,000 reported that the number of shootings reduced from 260 in 1975, to 229 in 1983, with an average of 260 deaths per year. Another study found that in the 50 largest police departments in the United States, the number of persons shot and killed decreased about 30 percent between 1970 and 1984. National estimates showed that 559 citizens were killed by the police in 1978, and the figure declined to 300 in 1987.

Determinants of Deadly Force: Four Perspectives

Four theoretical perspectives have been formulated to explain police coercive behavior and use of deadly force.

Situational Explanations

Situational explanations, which are the most common factors selected by researchers to assess police coercive behavior, posit that police use of force is affected by situational characteristics of police-citizen interactions. A number of variables were considered under this line of inquiry, including citizen characteristics and attitudes, victim-suspect relationship, victim preferences, weapon presence, and evidence strength. Research on the impact of citizens' race, gender, wealth, and age on use of force has generated inconsistent findings. Some researchers, for example, have found that officers were more likely to arrest or use improper force against African American suspects when controlling for other variables, whereas other studies have reported that race was a not a significant predictor of police arrest decisions and use of force. Similarly, some studies found that males were more likely to be arrested, while others reported no gender difference existed.

Compared to citizen demographic characteristics, citizen demeanor during police-citizen encounters was found to exert a more consistent and stronger impact on police coercive behavior, with disrespectful or irrational citizens being more likely to be arrested and to be targets of force. Other studies suggested that police were more inclined to make an arrest if the evidence of the offense was stronger and a weapon was presented during the conflict. It is important to note that the majority of past studies used the simple dichotomy of force and no force, while use of deadly force has rarely been independently measured in multivariate analyses. Bivariate analyses on deadly force have indicated that racial minorities, poor citizens, and males were much more likely to be the subjects of police deadly force than their counterparts.

Officer Behavior

Officer behavior explanations assert that officers' individual backgrounds and occupational outlooks, such as personal characteristics (race, gender, education, and experience); work assignments; and attitudes, perceptions, and personality influence their coercive behavior during police-citizen encounters. Previous studies of the effect of officers' characteristics on police coercive behavior have generated mixed results. For example, some found that black and white officers, as well as male and female officers, differed in their coercive behavior toward citizens, but others found that they acted similarly. One study found that better-educated officers tended to use deadly force less often than their less-educated counterparts.

Organizational Explanations

Organizational explanations state that variation in departmental characteristics tend to influence officers' use of force. Some researchers focus on the effect of formal organizational features, such as rules and regulations, standard operating procedures, and incentives and disincentives, while others stress the influence of the informal agency structure, such as police culture, informal networks, and cliques. Empirical studies found that departments with higher levels of bureaucratization and more aggressive policies were associated with higher rates of force. A recent study of Philadelphia police showed that internal working environment (e.g., the abolition of the restrictive shooting policy and organizational subculture) outweighed external discretion control policies (e.g., state statues and legislative interventions) and neighborhood factors (e.g., population and crime rates) in shaping police shooting behavior.

It's the Neighborhood

Neighborhood explanations assert that police use of force can be explained in terms of demographic and institutional characteristics of communities. Previous research showed that police officers were more likely to issue citations, make arrests, and engage in coercive and abusive behavior in minority and racially mixed neighborhoods. Many fatal shootings by police have occurred in black communities. Research also found that poor neighborhoods were more likely to be subjected to control or coercive activities. Similarly, neighborhoods with high crime rates were also more likely to be subjects of coercive police response.

Pro: Arguments Supporting the Use of Deadly Force

The use of deadly force remains a controversial issue in society. Several main arguments provide support for the use of deadly force by police. First, deadly force represents one of the most important symbolic elements of the state's sovereign power over its members. Although the use of such extraordinary authority has to be constrained in a democratic society, the state's general authority to exercise the power through designated agents is necessary and nonnegotiable. In some extreme cases, such as war against hostile countries, the survival of the state may depend upon the ability of its armed forces to effectively use deadly force to defeat enemies. While the police are not the only institutions endowed with the power by the state, they are perhaps the most visible agents who are most likely to engage in the use deadly force within the nation's domestic territory.

Second, deadly force is an essential feature of the police profession. While the police rarely apply deadly force in their daily work, they are vigorously trained to handle and constantly reminded about the potential risk and unpredictability associated with their working environment that requires them to exercise deadly force. Use-of-deadly-force situations often involve split-second decisions that require officers to make swift calls based on their training and judgment. The urgent nature of the circumstance, the potential harm to the subject, and the psychological impact on the officer are all signals of the problematic and memorable nature of police use of deadly force. As the most visible and immediate social-control agents in society, the police have no choice but to undertake this unpleasant part of their control responsibility. The police may be viewed as a tainted profession, but a society may not survive without the exercise of coercion by this group of officials. The power and necessity to use deadly force justifies the existence of the police forces.

Deadly force, if used properly, can protect the lives and property of both officers and citizens. Use of deadly force should be viewed and employed as the last resort to prevent damage or further damage caused by the perpetrators. While the use of deadly force may lead to the death of the suspect, it is justified by the positive ends, which are the stopping of a potential threat and violence inflicted by the suspects, and the saving of innocent citizens' lives.

Con: Arguments Against the Use of Deadly Force

The loss of a human being's life cannot be reversed, regardless of the cause triggering the use of deadly force. In many violent confrontations, lethal force has been justified; but in other incidents, it has not. The deaths caused by unjustified force not only signal the limitations of police training and professional judgment, but also bring tragedy to friends and relatives of the deceased.

Deadly force is not evenly distributed across social groups. It has an uneven, adverse effect on socially disadvantaged groups. Poor people and racial minorities, especially those who live in neighborhoods with low socioeconomic status, high crime rates, and mediocre/negative police–community relations, are much more vulnerable than those who live in affluent and predominately white neighborhoods. Police display different mentalities and behaviors when they patrol the streets of poor, minority neighborhoods;

they anticipate a greater possibility of experiencing violent confrontations, and use a correspondingly higher level of coercion within these neighborhoods. Citizen resistance to police authority is also conceptualized differently by police across various social groups. Uncooperative and hostile attitudes and behavior displayed by young, minority persons are perceived by the police as greater threats to police authority and safety, and thus are subjected to higher levels of control. The use of force, including deadly force, to control threatening members of socially disadvantaged groups is heavily embedded in a police occupational culture that emphasizes authority and control when engaging with citizens.

Deadly force, either justified or unjustified, has tremendous negative effect on police–community relations. For example, data from the Police–Public Contact Survey showed that of those who had force used against them in 2005, 83 percent felt that the force was excessive. Police use of force remains problematic, since perceptions of appropriate levels of force for a particular situation are highly subjective. Such a perceptual gap between officers and citizens tends to shape police–community relations by weakening the political support and cooperation citizens render to police and their willingness to participate in police and community anticrime programs and efforts.

See Also: 2. Arrest Practices; 9. Police Brutality; 14. Riot and
    Demonstration Responses; 18. Vigilantes.

Further Readings

Alpert, Geoffrey P. "The Force Factor: Measuring and Assessing Police Use of Force and Suspect Resistance." In *Use of Force by Police: Overview of National and Local Data*. Washington, DC: National Institute of Justice, 1999.

Alpert, Geoffrey, and Roger Dunham. *The Force Factor: Measuring Police Use of Force Relative to Suspect Resistance*. Washington, DC: Police Executive Research Forum, 1997.

Bayley, David, and James Garofalo. "The Management of Violence by Police Patrol Officers." *Criminology*, v.27 (1989).

Bazley, Thomas, Thomas Mieczkowski, and Kim Michelle Lersch. "Early Intervention Program Criteria: Evaluating Officer Use of Force." *Justice Quarterly*, v.26 (2009).

Brandl, Steven, Meghan Stroshine, and James Frank. "Who Are the Complaint-Prone Officers? An Examination of the Relationship Between Police Officers' Attributes, Arrest Activity, Assignment, and Citizens' Complaints about Excessive Force." *Journal of Criminal Justice*, v.29 (2001).

Christopher, Warren. *Report of the Independent Commission on the Los Angeles Police Department*. Los Angeles: Independent Commission on the Los Angeles Police Department, 1991.

Desmedt, John. "Use of Force Paradigm for Law Enforcement." *Journal of Criminal Justice*, v.12 (1984).

Dunham, Roger, and Geoffrey P. Alpert. *Critical Issues in Policing*. Prospect Heights, IL: Waveland Press, 1997.

Friedrich, Robert. "Police Use of Force: Individuals, Situations, and Organizations." *Annals of the American Academy of Political and Social Science*, v.452 (1980).

Fyfe, James. "Blind Justice: Police Shootings in Memphis." *Journal of Criminal Law and Criminology*, v.73 (1982).

Fyfe, James. "Race and Extreme Police-Citizen Violence." In *Race, Crime, and Criminal Justice*, edited by R. L. McNeely and Carl E. Pope. Thousand Oaks, CA: Sage, 1981.

Gallo, Frank, Charles Collyer, and Patracia Gallagher. "Prevalence of Force by Police in Rhode Island Jurisdictions: Implications for Use-of-Force Training and Reporting." *Criminal Justice Review*, v.33 (2008).

Garner, Joel, Christopher Maxwell, and Cedrick Heraux. "Characteristics Associated With the Prevalence and Severity of Force Used by the Police." *Justice Quarterly*, v.19 (2002).

Geller, William, and Kevin Karales. "Shootings of and by Chicago Police: Uncommon Crises. Part I: Shootings by Chicago Police." *Journal of Criminal Law and Criminology*, v.72 (1981).

Hoffman, Peter, and Edward Hickey. "Use of Force by Female Police Officers." *Journal of Criminal Justice*, v.33 (2005).

Kania, Richard, and Wade Mackey. "Police Violence as a Function of Community Characteristics." *Criminology*, v.15 (1977).

McLaughlin, Vance. *Police and the Use of Force: The Savannah Study*. Westport, CT: Praeger, 1992.

Meyer, Marshall. "Police Shootings of Minorities: The Case of Los Angeles." *Annals of the American Academy of Political and Social Science*, v.452 (1980).

Pate, Anthony, and Lorie Fridell. *Police Use of Force: Official Reports, Citizen Complaints, and Legal Consequences.* Washington, DC: Police Foundation, 1993.

Reiss, Albert, Jr. "Police Brutality—Answers to Key Questions." *Transaction*, v.5 (1968).

Schuck, Amie. "The Masking of Racial and Ethnic Disparity in Police Use of Physical Force: The Effects of Gender and Custody Status." *Journal of Criminal Justice*, v.32 (2003).

Smith, Douglas. "The Neighborhood Context of Police Behavior." In *Communities and Crime*, edited by Albert J. Reiss Jr. and Michael Tonry. Chicago: University of Chicago Press, 1986.

Smith, Douglas. "The Organizational Context of Legal Control." *Criminology*, v.22 (1984).

Terrill, William. "Police Use of Force: A Transactional Approach." *Justice Quarterly*, v.22 (2005).

Terrill, William, Fredrik Leinfelt, and Dae-Hoon Kwak. "Examining Police Use of Force: A Small Agency Perspective." *Policing: An International Journal of Police Strategies and Management*, v.31 (2008).

Terrill, William, and John McCluskey. "Citizen Complaints and Problem Officers: Examining Officer Behavior." *Journal of Criminal Justice*, v.30 (2002).

Terrill, William, and Michael Reisig. "Neighborhood Context and Police Use of Force." *Journal of Research in Crime and Delinquency*, v.40 (2003).

Toch, Hans. "The Violence-Prone Police Officer." In *Police Violence: Understanding and Controlling Police Abuse of Force*, edited by William A. Geller and Hans Toch. New Haven, CT: Yale University Press, 1996.

Toch, Hans. *Violent Men.* Cambridge, MA: Schenkmen, 1980.

Walker, Samuel, Geoffrey Alpert, and Dennis Kenney. "Early Warning Systems for Police: Concept, History, and Issues." *Police Quarterly*, v.3 (2000).

Westley, William. "Violence and the Police." *American Journal of Sociology*, v.59 (1953).

White, Michael. "Examining the Impact of External Influences on Police Use of Deadly Force Over Time." *Evaluation Review*, v.27 (2003).

Worden, Robert. "Situational and Attitudinal Explanations of Police Behavior: Theoretical Reappraisal and Empirical Assessment." *Law and Society Review*, v.23 (1989).

16

Vehicle Searches

Michael C. Gizzi
Illinois State University

V ehicle searches are an essential part of law enforcement efforts to combat crime, particularly the War on Drugs. In the United States, people are often defined by their vehicles, as well as their ability to be mobile. The automobile provides citizens with a freedom that was not possible in previous eras. Yet that freedom also serves to assist those individuals inclined to commit crimes. The automobile is probably the most important tool that individuals use for the trafficking of illicit drugs. As a result, the ability to search vehicles suspected of engaging in criminal behavior is equally important for law enforcement officers. The search of a vehicle creates a conflict between citizens and police, defined by an individual's constitutional right to be free from unreasonable searches and seizures under the Fourth Amendment, and the police need to search for evidence of criminal behavior. Thus, any time a vehicle on the road is stopped by a police officer, there are Fourth Amendment issues that define the scope and nature of the police–citizen contact.

The U.S. Constitution provides the context in which vehicles may be searched, and considers the types of searches that are possible under the Fourth Amendment. Particular attention is provided to what police may and may not do when stopping a vehicle, and the types of searches they can utilize. Police use different types of searches, including the vehicle exception, plain view, dog sniffs, inventory searches, consent searches, and searches incident to arrest. While all of these types of searches are important, none has been more important in fighting the War on Drugs than the use of a vehicle search incident to a legal arrest. The widespread police use of search incident to arrest—established in 1981 when the Supreme Court decided *New York v. Belton*—has been called into question with the 2009 decision in *Arizona v. Gant*. There have been changes in the law regarding vehicle searches since the *Gant* decision, with both positive and negative results.

History of Vehicle Searches

The Fourth Amendment of the U.S. Constitution says that "The right of the people to be secure in the persons, houses, papers, and effects, against unreasonable searches and seizures, shall not be violated, and no Warrants shall issue, but upon probable cause, supported by Oath or affirmation, and particularly describing the place to be searched, and the persons or things to be seized." The Fourth Amendment does not prohibit all searches; it prohibits unreasonable searches, and it requires that before a search can be conducted, a warrant based on probable cause is necessary. Both searches and seizures are deprivations of liberty. A search of a person or their effects is an invasion of their privacy.

Prior to 1967, the Supreme Court defined searches through the trespass doctrine, which held that for government action to be a search, it had to invade a "constitutionally protected area," namely persons, houses, papers, and effects. In the *Katz v. United States* decision in 1967, the Supreme Court overruled the trespass doctrine, and Justice Potter Stewart argued that the Fourth Amendment protected people, not things. While *Katz* did not establish a general right to privacy, the decision established a standard that is used today to determine whether a government intrusion is a search. Justice Stewart argued "what a person knowingly exposes to the public, even in his own home or office, is not a subject of Fourth Amendment protection. But what he seeks to preserve as private, even in an area accessible to the public, may be constitutionally protected. In the concurrence that the case is remembered for, Justice John Marshall Harlan II argued that a search is defined by a two-pronged test. A person must "exhibit an actual (subjective) expectation of privacy, and second, that expectation be one that society is prepared to recognize as 'reasonable.'"

Not only did *Katz* establish a rule for deciding whether particular government action was a search, it also set a standard that has been persistent throughout Fourth Amendment case law in 40-plus years since the case was decided. The ruling in *Katz* reiterated the basic rule that "searches conducted outside the judicial process, without prior approval by judge or magistrate, are *per se* unreasonable under the Fourth Amendment—subject to only a few specifically established and well-delineated exceptions." Vehicle searches are among those exceptions. Long before the *Katz* decision articulated the notion of an expectation of privacy, court decisions had held that there was a reduced expectation of privacy in a vehicle.

Searches of vehicles without a warrant have a long history in the United States. As law professor Joel Samaha points out, the very Congress that wrote the Fourth Amendment established an exception that permitted law enforcement officers to search any ship or vessel without a warrant if they had reason to suspect the presence of stolen goods. This exception, first held to ships, was expanded in 1815 to include vehicles (such as a horse and carriage). By the early 20th century, Congress enabled government officers to seize automobiles suspected of transporting alcohol into Indian Territory. In 1925, the Supreme Court established what today is called the Automobile Exception.

Federal officers enforcing the National Prohibition Act had searched and seized 68 quarts of liquor from a vehicle. The act permitted warrantless searches of any person in the act of transporting intoxicating liquors in any wagon, buggy, automobile, water, or aircraft. Writing for the Supreme Court, Chief Justice William Howard Taft held in *Carroll v. United States* that in interpreting the Fourth Amendment, there is a difference between "a search of a store, dwelling house, or other structure ... and the search of a ship, motor boat, wagon, or automobile for contraband goods." In the case of vehicles, it is not practicable to have law enforcement agents secure a warrant "because the vehicle can be quickly moved out of the locality or jurisdiction in which the warrant must be sought." In allowing warrantless searches, Taft limited them to those instances where government officials have probable cause to believe that the vehicles are carrying contraband or illegal merchandise. The *Carroll* decision is based on the concept that in a vehicle there is a reduced expectation of privacy, due primarily to its mobility. And as a result, the Court established an important precedent permitting warrantless searches of vehicles. When probable cause of the presence of illegal contraband or evidence of a crime is present, police have the ability to do a warrantless search of a vehicle.

Search Tools Available to the Police

In addition to the automobile exception, police have several tools available that enable them to search vehicles, most often tied to the use of a traffic stop. After stopping a vehicle, an officer approaches the driver, and asks for license, registration, and proof of insurance. If there are passengers, the officer can ask them for identification as well. The officer can ask the driver (and passengers) to step out of the vehicle while the stop is being conducted. In speaking with the driver, the officer has the ability to scan the interior of the vehicle, and can uses his senses—what is called plain view—to visually search the vehicle. If the stop occurs at night, the officer can use a flashlight to scan the interior of the vehicle. If he observes the presence of contraband, or smells drugs or alcohol, the officer's observations can provide either the probable cause to make an arrest, or at least reasonable suspicion of a crime.

If the officer believes the occupants of the vehicle are dangerous, he can remove them from the vehicle and do a pat-down or frisk to search for weapons. If there is reasonable suspicion that the occupants are armed, the officer can conduct what is called a *protective sweep* or *vehicle frisk* of the passenger compartment to do a quick search for weapons. The scope of the protective sweep is limited to examining the items in the car when it is reasonable to believe a weapon could be found.

The use of specially trained narcotics dogs to search the exterior of a vehicle is permitted at any time. In 2005, the Supreme Court ruled in *Illinois v. Caballes* that officers can have a K-9 unit sniff a vehicle during a routine traffic stop, without having established reasonable suspicion. If the dog "alerts" to drugs, it becomes the means to establish probable cause for the presence of narcotics, which then makes a trunk search permissible even though the trunk has generally been viewed as immune from vehicle searches absent a warrant. While some states require reasonable suspicion to use a dog sniff, the Supreme Court has held that a dog search absent suspicion is permissible under the Fourth Amendment. The court's argument is that because the dog only "alerts" on illegal contraband that no person has an expectation of privacy in possessing, the dog sniff is not considered a search under the Fourth Amendment.

When a vehicle is impounded by police, an administrative search of the vehicle is conducted to inventory the contents, including a list of personal property, and any containers within, including purses, backpacks, or clothing. In 1976, the Supreme Court held in *South Dakota v. Opperman* that in conducting inventory searches, police have considerable discretion, but they are not to use an inventory search as a ruse to conduct a search that would otherwise not be permissible. However, as long as the department has established routine written procedures for the use of inventory searches, they are permissible.

The 1987 case *Colorado v. Bertine* reaffirmed the permissibility of conducting inventory searches and held that they do not require probable cause or warrants to conduct, because the purpose of the search is not related to a criminal investigation. Instead, the goal of an inventory search is to protect the owner's property while it is in police possession; protect law enforcement against potential lawsuits for the loss, theft, or destruction of property; and to protect law enforcement against any hidden dangers (like weapons or explosives) that might be in the vehicle. Yet, if in the process of conducting an inventory of the vehicle, the officer happens to uncover probable cause of a crime (such as illegal contraband or drugs), that evidence is admissible in court.

Incident to Arrest

While the automobile exception and other search tools are extremely important for vehicle searches, in the past 40 years, the development of the ability to search a vehicle "incident to arrest" has probably been the most significant development in the evolution of vehicle searches. At the time of an arrest, the police can conduct a search of the arrested person "incident to arrest" without a warrant. In the 1969 case *Chimel v. California,* the Court ruled that in arresting an individual, an officer could search the arrested person as well as the area within his immediate control. Sometimes called the *reaching distance* or *grabbable area rule,* the ruling in *Chimel* carved out a physical area adjacent to the arrestee that could be searched. In 1973, the Court decided *United States v. Robinson,* which solidified the legal standing of search incident to arrest. Justice William Rehnquist argued that a search incident to arrest was justified to ensure officer safety and to preserve evidence. Together, *Chimel* and *Robinson* provide an important foundation for vehicle searches, in that when an arrest occurs in a vehicle, the officer is given the ability to conduct a search of the arrestee's reaching distance.

Chimel's reaching-distance rule left some uncertainty with how much of a passenger compartment could be searched, given the subjectivity of the rule, and the fact that no two person's "reaching distance" were exactly the same. The Supreme Court examined this issue in 1981, when it established a new bright-line rule in *New York v. Belton,* holding that incident to a legal arrest, officers could conduct a complete search of the passenger compartment of a vehicle, including containers both opened and closed. In *Belton,* the Court argued that the *Chimel* rule had proved difficult to administer, and so the Court established a rule that permitted vehicle searches of the passenger compartment for any arrest. While the automobile exception permitted searches of the entire vehicle where probable cause existed that contraband was present, the *Belton* rule permitted searches of the passenger compartment any time an officer made an arrest, even when illegal contraband was not suspected at the time of the arrest.

The *Belton* rule proved to be one of the most important tools available to police in conducting the war on the drugs. Since *Belton* permitted a search for any arrest—and did not tie the search to the *Robinson* rationale of officer safety or the preservation of evidence—police could arrest someone for driving without proof of insurance, and then proceed to search the entire passenger compartment of their vehicle. Over time, courts ruled that in vehicles with a hatchback or an open trunk (like in a SUV or a station wagon), the search could include the open cargo areas. Only locked trunks were not subject to search. Other cases extended the ability to search a passenger compartment. In 2001, the decision in *Atwater v. City of Lago Vista* held that an officer could place an individual under arrest for virtually any offense, even one that precluded a jail sentence if convicted. In 2004, the Court ruled in *Thornton v. United States* that a vehicle search was permissible even if the arrest did not occur at the vehicle, as long as the arrestee was the "recent occupant" of the vehicle.

Arizona v. Gant

Much of this has come into question with the 2009 decision in *Arizona v. Gant*, where the Supreme Court made a major modification to *Belton's* bright-line rule. Under *Gant*, the police may search the passenger compartment of a vehicle incident to a recent occupant's arrest only if it is reasonable to believe that the arrestee might access the vehicle at the time of the search or if the vehicle contains further evidence of the crime prompting the arrest. The Court reaffirmed *Chimel*, holding that if the arrestee is still in the vehicle, the search is only valid "for the area from within which [an arrestee] might gain possession of a weapon or destructible evidence." This does not pertain once the arrestee is outside of the vehicle and in custody. Once the arrestee is not able to gain access to the vehicle, there is no justification for the search. The end result of the *Gant* decision was to significantly undermine the contemporary search incident-to-arrest rationale.

Belton still applies if the arrest is for an offense to which it is reasonable to conclude that the passenger compartment might contain further evidence of the crime. If the arrest is made over a drug offense, a full vehicle search incident to arrest would be allowed, but if the arrest was for driving without proof of insurance, the search would be impermissible. In the latter example, the most that could occur is that the search might "undo" the crime, as the officer could find proof of insurance. The arrestee would still be subject to a search of his or her person incident to arrest; and if that search uncovered evidence of drugs, that would provide the necessary justification for the full vehicle search.

Vehicle Searches and the War on Drugs

For more than 30 years, the federal government has encouraged state and local law enforcement to aggressively utilize the traffic code as a means of drug interdiction. In 1984, the Drug Enforcement Agency began Operation Pipeline, a drug interdiction program for state and local highway officers intended to train them in development of drug courier profiles and the laws surrounding traffic stops and drug prosecutions. Although the profile itself has changed over the years, officers have been trained to identify likely drug "mules" or couriers. Much of the War on Drugs has been fought on the nation's highways. Over 27,000 officers in 48 states have been trained through Operation Pipeline.

The success of programs like Operation Pipeline come from the ease by which it is possible for law enforcement to use the traffic code as the basis for an investigatory stop to seek out more serious crime. When the Supreme Court decided *Terry v. Ohio* in 1968, it established the modern law of "stop and frisk." In doing so, the Court defined the parameters for police–citizen encounters. *Terry* gave police authority to temporarily detain an individual with less than probable cause. To stop an individual, the officer must demonstrate articulable facts that establish a reasonable basis for his or her suspicion. These facts do not have to rise to the level of probable cause, but merely suspicion of wrongdoing. *Terry* made it possible to develop profiles of likely drug traffickers going through the nation's airports, train stations, and bus depots, as it enabled officers to initiate a nonconsensual contact with a suspect who met the profile of a drug dealer.

While a Terry stop was very effective in seeking out likely hijackers or drug dealers in bus or train stations, such a stop is more difficult when done in the context of automobiles on the nation's highways. It is much easier to establish reasonable suspicion for a suspected drug trafficker getting off a train than it is to observe individuals in a moving vehicle. Using a drug profile alone, it is difficult to generate enough suspicion to pull over a vehicle.

Officers had a much easier option for accomplishing the same goal. Rather than making an investigatory Terry stop based on reasonable suspicion, a vehicle could be stopped for violating virtually any minor traffic infraction. Whether they were speeding, weaving in traffic, driving with a broken tail-light, or had dirt on a license plate, almost any driver could be pulled over by an officer who was determined to find probable cause for a traffic stop. This is appealing because once the traffic violation has been witnessed, the officer has probable cause to stop the vehicle and either issue a summons or even arrest the driver for the violation. At any point in time, a driver could be pulled over for violating one of 100 minor infractions under the traffic code. As a result, officers conducting drug interdiction often will use the pretext of a traffic stop to conduct a criminal investigation.

Whren v. United States

The use of pretextual traffic stops was given the approval of the Supreme Court in the 1996 case *Whren v. United States*. Undercover police officers in the District of Columbia used the pretext of a traffic violation—driving at "an unreasonable speed"—to stop a vehicle. The stop resulted in an arrest for cocaine possession based on the officer's plain view of drugs. The defense sought to have the traffic stop ruled an unreasonable seizure, because "it had not been justified by probable cause to believe, or even reasonable suspicion that petitioners were engaged in illegal drug dealing activity." Writing for the court, Justice Antonin Scalia argued that the decision to stop an automobile is reasonable whenever the police have probable cause to believe a traffic violation has occurred.

Whren provided law enforcement with a definitive statement that the traffic code could be used as the pretext for criminal investigations, as long as the officer had probable cause for the traffic violation. In permitting pretextual stops, the Supreme Court ultimately gave sanction to the use of traffic stops as a means to conduct criminal investigations, using the search tools described above.

While *Whren* unleashed an ongoing flurry of controversy over the concern about racial profiling underlying the case, the Court refused to address the issue, claiming that the constitutional challenge was based on the Fourth Amendment, not the Fourteenth Amendment. Scalia rejected the defense argument that the use of "ulterior motives" would invalidate an otherwise legal traffic stop. While he acknowledged that the Constitution prohibits "selective enforcement of the law based on factors such as race," he continued that "the constitutional basis for objecting to intentionally discriminatory application of laws is the Equal Protection Clause, not the Fourth

Amendment." In essence, the Court declared that when a motorist's defense is based on the issue of selective enforcement, the proper basis for their argument should be the Fourteenth Amendment Equal Protection Clause.

Pro: Arguments in Favor of *Gant*'s Search Limits

The *Gant* decision places significant limits on the ability to conduct vehicle searches incident to arrest. *Gant* limits officers from searching a vehicle incident to arrest to those cases where the defendant is unsecured, or to those cases where it is likely the officer will find further evidence of the crime that sparked the arrest. In the former instance, where the arrestee is unsecured, the scope of the search is defined by *Chimel*'s "reaching-distance" rule, and thus the search would not include the entire passenger compartment. Moreover, since it is standard operating procedure to handcuff and remove an arrestee from a vehicle, the *Chimel* search probably would not occur. Instead, the arrestee would be removed from the vehicle and his or her person would be searched before being placed in the patrol car. If the original arrest is for a crime where it is reasonable to believe that further evidence could be found—perhaps in a case where a traffic stop led to plain view of drug paraphernalia by the officer—then *Gant* permits the officer to conduct the *Belton* search of the vehicle incident to arrest.

The limitation of the ability to search a vehicle's passenger compartment incident to arrest is a positive development in Fourth Amendment law, because it eliminates the entitlement that police officers had as a result of the *Belton* decision. The bright-line rule in *Belton* allowed officers to search the passenger compartment of a vehicle in any arrest. *Belton* created a disconnect between the rationale underlying search incident to arrest. When a minor traffic offense is used as the basis for an arrest, there is usually no reason to conduct a vehicle search.

The facts in *Arizona v. Gant* illustrate this nicely. After receiving an anonymous tip that a particular residence in Tuscson, Arizona, was involved in the drug trade, police went to the residence and knocked on the door. They spoke to Rodney Gant, who answered the door and identified himself, but claimed that he was not a resident of the house. The officers withdrew, ran a background check on Gant, and discovered that he had a suspended driver's license. They returned to the residence and found two other people, who were arrested. Gant was not there, but came back to the residence driving a car while the officers were present. Having observed Gant driving and knowing that he had a suspended driver's license, the officers placed him under arrest for driving on a suspended license, handcuffed him, and placed him in the back of a police cruiser. Only then did the officer proceed to search Mr. Gant's car, finding both a gun and cocaine. Since Gant was handcuffed and sitting in the back seat of a patrol car, there was no officer safety rationale to justify searching his vehicle. Moreover, he was arrested for driving under a suspended license. Thus, there was no preservation of evidence rationale either.

The decision in *Gant* is a victory for individual rights and due process. For more than 30 years, citizens have been stopped by police based on little more than a hunch of criminal activity. They are arrested for minor violations and then have their vehicles searched as a result. Disproportionately, the individuals stopped in this manner are members of racial or ethnic minorities. A volume of literature on racial profiling demonstrates that African Americans and Hispanics are far more likely to be stopped by police officers than white drivers. While *Gant* will not eliminate pretextual traffic stops or the use of racial profiling, it will limit the ability of police to use minor arrests as the rationale for vehicle searches. In doing so, *Gant* has the potential to restore some of the balance in the Fourth Amendment on the side of due process. The desire for effective crime control and the need to win the War on Drugs has shifted the balance away from individual rights. While Justice John Paul Stevens's majority opinion in *Gant* did not focus on Mr. Gant's rights, the end result of the decision is to rein police in and force them to find other methods to conduct searches and criminal investigations.

Con: Arguments Against *Gant*'s Search Limits

The decision in *Arizona v. Gant* reworks the law of search incident to arrest, and has created a general sense of uncertainty for law enforcement since the decision was handed down. For close to 30 years, police officers relied on the bright-line rule in *New York v. Belton,* which the Supreme Court established partly out of a desire to create easily administrated rules. The *Belton* court acknowledged that it was important that police be given clear rules to use when making decisions in field situations. The reaching-distance test is inherently ambiguous, as it is entirely dependent on the arm length of the suspect. The bright-rule from *Belton,* however, was easy to implement, and served law enforcement well. It was an indispensable tool as police tried to keep the upper hand in what Chief Justice Rehnquist once called a "veritable national crisis" in the illicit drug trade. By limiting the ability to search vehicles incident to arrest to only those cases where the arrest is for an offense where it is reasonable to expect to find further evidence of the crime, the Court gives the upper hand to criminals, and makes the nation less safe.

Ultimately, while the *Gant* decision will create confusion among law enforcement, officers will find other ways to achieve the same end. Although the number of cases in which vehicle searches incident to arrest occur will likely decline, police will have other strategies available to them. In the months following the *Gant* decision, the Federal Bureau of Investigation published recommendations for officers. One of the tactics they encouraged was to make greater use of consent searches. If the officer asks the driver for consent to search the vehicle, and consent is given, then the Fourth Amendment no longer applies. If consent to search is given voluntarily and not under coercion, then the search will be permissible. For example, while an officer could not make a *quid pro quo* to a suspect where he threatens to place the driver under arrest (rather than issuing a citation) if he does not consent to a search, the reality is that police officers are highly trained and quite capable of getting people to consent to searches.

The second strategy that officers could use is to impound vehicles in cases where the arrest does not permit a vehicle search. If they impound a vehicle, then the police can do an inventory of the vehicle—and can thus search it. All that a department needs is a written policy describing normal operating procedures for inventory searches. With that in place, it is unlikely that the courts would invalidate properly executed administrative searches. The use of inventory searches does entail the risk that a defense attorney could make the case that the sudden use of impoundment, when there has been no history of using them before *Gant*, is a violation of the spirit of the decision, but that is why the federal government has encouraged departments to make sure clear policies are in place.

Conclusion

Vehicle searches are an essential tool in the arsenal of law enforcement in their efforts to combat crime. The automobile has become a defining feature of American life in the past 75 years; yet, the courts have devalued the privacy interests of citizens while in their vehicles. At the same time, the mobility that automobiles provide citizens also provides criminals with a much easier task in transporting contraband. It is out of that mobility that the courts established the automobile exception to the Fourth Amendment. Over time, the courts have augmented that with several tools that enable police to search vehicles suspected of engaging in criminal behavior.

The search of a vehicle incident to legal arrest—the primary tool used in vehicle searches—has created turmoil and uncertainty since the 2009 Supreme Court decision in *Arizona v. Gant*. This case places significant limits on the ability of the police to legally search the passenger compartment of a vehicle when making an arrest, with the primary implication that it will limit law enforcement's ability to effectively wage the War on Drugs. Yet, it is unclear how much of a change will be generated by *Gant*, as police develop new strategies to accomplish the same goals and make better use of their remaining tools.

See Also: 2. Arrest Practices; 8. Plain View Doctrine; 13. Profiling; 19. Warrants.

Further Readings

Arizona v. Gant, 556 U.S. __; 129 S.Ct. 1710 (2009).

Carroll v. United States, 267 U.S. 132 (1925).

Chimel v. California, 395 U.S. 752 (1969).

Drug Enforcement Agency. Operations Pipeline and Convoy. http://www.usdoj.gov/dea/programs/pipecon.htm (Accessed February 16, 2009).

Gumbhir, Vikas K. *But is it Racial Profiling? Policing, Pretext Stops, and the Color of Suspicion*. New York: LFB Scholarly Publishing, 2007.

Harris, David A. *Profiles in Injustice: Why Racial Profiling Can't Work*. New York: New Press, 2001.

Heumann, Milton, and Lance Cassak. *Good Cop, Bad Cop: Racial Profiling and Competing Views of Justice in America*. New York: Peter Lang, 2003.

Illinois v. Caballes, 543 U.S. 405 (2005).

New York v. Belton, 453 U.S. 454 (1981).

Samaha, Joel. *Criminal Procedure*. Belmont, CA: Wadsworth, 2008.

Schott, R. "The Supreme Court Reexamines Search Incident to Lawful Arrest." *FBI Law Enforcement Bulletin*, v.78/7 (July 2009).

Solari, J. "The United States Supreme Court's Ruling in *Arizona v. Gant*: Implications for Law Enforcement Officers." *The Federal Law Enforcement Informer* (May 2009).

Terry v. Ohio, 392 U.S. 1 (1968).

Thorton v. United States, 541 U.S. 615 (2004).

United States v. Robinson, 414 U.S. 218 (1973).

Whren v. United States, 517 U.S. 806 (1996).

17

Vehicular Police Pursuits

Matthew Pate
SUNY University at Albany

The conditions under which police officers decide to engage and sustain the vehicular pursuit of fleeing suspects have evolved markedly over the last 50 years. This evolution has taken place across three primary dimensions: court decisions, agency policy, and officer training. These conditions of police pursuits are located in each of these evolutionary dimensions within the recent history of American policing.

Police pursuits are a frequent topic in popular media. They are often subject to dramatic coverage by trailing helicopters and news reporters supplying a turn-by-turn narrative as the chase unfolds. This sensationalism has given rise to a serious reconsideration of the terms under which police agencies will initiate and continue the pursuit of a fleeing suspect. This is due in large part to a web of inherent dangers and civil liabilities arising from pursuits gone awry.

As such, many modern pursuit policies were developed in response to the injury or death of officers, suspects, and civilians; the damage or destruction of public and private property; and the balance of interests between apprehension of a fleeing suspect and its potential costs. Accordingly, administrators must consider many factors when developing an agency pursuit policy. Fortunately, modern policymakers have the benefit of several decades of police scholarship, legal precedent, and public response to inform their decisions.

Brief History of Police Pursuits

As Geoffrey Alpert and Thomas Madden document, vehicular police pursuits have increased both in number and frequency since the 1960s. In their work on the topic, Alpert and Madden describe the dominant mentality of police pursuits in the 1960s as one of apprehension at all costs. By the 1970s, concerns started to shift toward the latent costs of this single-minded approach. Informed by the rising number accidents, injuries, and deaths incurred as a result of ill-fated pursuits, police administrators began to include defensive driving as a required part of the officer training curriculum. By the 1980s, the governing sentiment had migrated from one dominated by narrow law enforcement priorities to one couched in bystander safety and accident reduction. Accordingly, administrators in this era began to focus on the development of pursuit policy, officer training, and accountability measures. By the 1990s, a much fuller development of modern pursuit policy and administrative thinking on the topic became evident.

During the 1990s, police administrators began to address growing pursuit-related concerns by balancing law enforcement goals with those of public safety. Notable strategies to mitigate risk, injury, and damage included items listed above, but with particular emphasis on officer decision-making skills, more effective supervision, and stronger agency policy development. As administrative thinking about pursuit policy has matured, some agencies have adopted a no-pursuit policy, which prohibits officers from engaging in a vehicular chase of fleeing suspects. There are many reasonable arguments supporting both pursuit and no-pursuit policies.

Legal Challenges to Pursuits

One of the clearest measures of public interest has been defined in civil court cases regarding officer negligence. As far back as the 1930s, law enforcement agencies have dealt with the civil liability that may arise from injurious or destructive pursuits. The expansive body of legal precedent continues to inform agency policy today. As many scholars have noted, a well-crafted, closely followed agency policy can provide an effective shield against many negligence claims. By examining a few particularly significant cases, it is evident just how important the threat of civil liability can be for law enforcement agencies trying to develop a pursuit policy.

Before discussing the individual cases, it is helpful to understand a few basic legal concepts important to the ensuing court decisions. Among the most important of these concepts is the doctrine of vicarious liability, sometimes also termed *imputed liability*. This legal doctrine imposes responsibility upon one person for the failure of another, with whom the first person has a special relationship (i.e., a police officer and their supervisors or agency administrators) to exercise such care as a reasonably prudent person would use under a given circumstance. This doctrine assigns liability for an injury to a person who did not cause the injury, but who has a particular legal relationship to the person who did act negligently.

A closely related theory of liability that is premised on imputed negligence is the doctrine of *respondeat superior* ("let the master answer"), which is based on an employer–employee relationship. This doctrine holds the employer responsible for a lack of care (negligence) on the part of an employee in relation to those to whom the employer owes a duty of care. For respondeat superior to apply, the employee's negligence must occur within the scope of his or her employment.

The employer is held legally responsible for employee negligence because the employee is regarded as an "agent" of the employer. This is to say, the employee is acting at the behest and under the guidance or approval of the employer. If a negligent act is committed by an employee acting within the general scope of their employment, the employer may be held liable for damages. This emanates from the idea that the employer may have failed to train or adequately supervise the employee, or simply failed to foresee the potential for said negligence to occur. As is common in such matters, the scope of civil liability for agencies and other governmental bodies has legally evolved over several decades.

Significant Cases Shaping Emergency Vehicle Operation

City of Lansing v. Hathaway (1937) is one of the earliest cases to address the issue of emergency vehicle operation and public safety. In this case, the city of Lansing, Michigan, sought to recover repair expenses for a fire truck and compensation for injured firefighters that resulted from a collision between a city fire truck and an automobile driven by the defendant, Hathaway. Hathaway drove through an intersection with the green light in his favor when he was struck by the fire truck. The court held Hathaway was not negligent due to the fact that he acted as any citizen would in that situation. Additionally, the court ruled that the city had both a duty to respond in a reasonable regard and was responsible for the safety of the public while operating an emergency vehicle. While this case has been superseded in many respects, the court specifically identified public safety as a governing concern for public employees. This theme has been revisited in many similar cases.

Another landmark case related to police pursuits is *Draper v. City of Los Angeles* (1949). This case is notable because it is one of the first instances in which the plaintiff's vehicle was struck not by the police, but by the individual taking flight from the police. In this case, the fleeing suspect, Howard Pratt, had stolen a car and was in flight from the police when he ran through an intersection, striking a vehicle operated by Draper. In his complaint, Draper alleged that the police had failed to drive with proper regard for the safety of others. Draper further claimed that the police had essentially forced Pratt through the intersection.

The officers involved made the counterargument that they were at least 275 feet behind Pratt when he drove through the stop sign and struck Draper. They argued further that they had slowed sufficiently to safely stop at the intersection and go around another vehicle.

Owing Duty and Safe Operation

The court held that the officers were not required to warn the public of Pratt's driving and as such, the officers did not owe any duty to Draper other than to operate their vehicle with due regard. Accordingly, Pratt was found to have been the sole cause of the accident. The concept of "owing duty" emerged in subsequent court cases as a powerful determinant of liability for police, and is perhaps the most significant aspect of the Draper decision in the evolution of pursuit policy. Two prime examples of this are also found in the cases of *Dent v. City of Dallas* (1986) and *Marion v. Flint* (1976).

In *Dent v. City of Dallas*, the court ruled that a finding of negligence cannot be made unless there is a "duty owed to the injured person." As such, in instances where no duty is owed to an individual, neither the officer (nor agency) can be found liable. In this regard, *Dent* is a direct extension of the finding made in *Draper*. Likewise, *Marion v. Flint* has much in common with *Draper* in that the complainant, Marion, was also struck by a suspect's vehicle as he fled from police.

What makes *Marion* notable on a general level is the court's dependence upon Michigan statute, which outlines special standards applicable to operators of emergency vehicles. The central tenet of the statutory requirement is built on the concept of "safe operation" of the vehicle as opposed to any possible endangerment of the public. While this may seem a semantic point, it sets up an emphasis on proper, or safe, operation of emergency vehicles. This in turn establishes the basis for an era marked by increased driver training for police officers.

The issue of officer training was deemed critical again 13 years later as the U.S. Supreme Court issued a ruling in *City of Canton v. Harris* (1989). In this case, the Court held that failing to train police officers may be the basis for managerial liability under Title 42, U.S. Code Section 1983. In other words, police supervisors and administrators could potentially be held liable for a line officer's negligence should it be proven that they failed to properly and adequately provide relevant officer training.

Beyond matters of proper training, the plaintiff in *Marion v. Flint* also claimed the officers were negligent because they were not acting under their statutory duty. The court based its decision on this dimension of the complaint on a precedent found in *Mckay v. Hargis* (1958). The decision in *Mckay* is important because the judge invoked a "reasonable man" standard for determining whether the officers in question acted within the scope of their official duties.

Officers are not inherently given blanket protection by statute when pursuits occur, as these cases might suggest. An example may be found in *Fiser v. City of Ann Arbor* (1981). In this case, the officer was found to have shown disregard for traffic and other environmental conditions. The court found the officer did not exhibit "due care" for the safety of the public. In reaching their decision, the court relied upon a standard set in *Gibson v. City of Pasadena* (1978). In *Gibson*, officers pursued a violator at speeds exceeding 100 miles per hour through 25 intersections, 12 of which had traffic signals. In this case, the officers' actions were found to be negligent.

In *County of Sacramento v. Lewis* (1998), the Supreme Court deliberated an incident in which a speeding motorcyclist crashed his vehicle and was subsequently run over and killed by a police cruiser while in flight from police. The plaintiff argued that the officer violated pursuit policy and the motorcyclist's Fourteenth Amendment due-process guarantees. The Court sided with the police, holding the motorcyclist's due-process claim was not valid because "only a purpose to cause harm unrelated to the legitimate object of arrest" would be sufficient to hold the officer's conduct in violation of the plaintiff's rights, and that none had been demonstrated in this case.

In the case of *Scott v. Harris* (2007), an officer rammed the rear of the suspect's vehicle, causing it to crash. As a result of injures sustained in the crash, the suspect was paralyzed. He subsequently filed suit on Fourth Amendment grounds, in which he claimed the officer's ramming his vehicle constituted an excessive use of force, and as such, was an unlawful seizure. The Supreme Court found in favor of the officer, ruling the risk to pedestrians and other motorists posed by the suspect's driving was sufficient to justify the officer's actions. The Court also rejected the idea that police should adopt a blanket policy of nonpursuit. In this, the Court noted a suspect's incentive to flee any time police attempted a traffic stop should this be implemented. The effect of *Scott* has been wide-reaching. The Court's decision effectively ended excessive-force complaints based in the Fourth Amendment.

Conditions Acceptable for Pursuit

For policymakers, these cases provide several instructive criteria. Factors such as officers' speed and view of traffic, roadway and weather conditions, and the degree of exigency are each considered as the courts determine the reasonableness of officer actions. Again, once the court determines the officer's reasonableness, evidence must show a duty to the injured party for negligence to exist.

In addition to what one might normally construe as a pursuit, the courts have issued numerous decisions circumscribing the permissible conditions under which police may terminate the flight of a fleeing suspect. In the U.S. Supreme Court case *Brower v. Inyo County* (1989), the primary point of debate revolved around the police use of roadblocks. In this case, the plaintiff, Brower, fled from police in a stolen car. To stop Brower, police set up a roadblock positioned behind a blind curve. On the other side of the curve, police faced headlights in the direction of Brower's travel. Blinded by the headlights, Brower died as a result of crashing into the roadblock. The courts ruled this roadblock to be a Fourth Amendment seizure due to the fact that Brower had no way to escape it.

In its finding, the Court referred to precedence set in *Tennessee v. Garner* (1985). *Garner* itself represents a landmark Supreme Court decision that wholly changed the extent to which officers could reasonably use force against a fleeing suspect. Subsequent to *Garner*, police are explicitly required to balance whether the totality of the circumstances justified seizure at any cost. In the *Garner* decision, the Court ruled that deadly force could be used against a fleeing suspect only if the suspect presented an immediate and serious threat. As the suspect in *Garner* appeared unarmed, the police use of deadly force to affect "seizure" was held to be excessive. In this light, Brower's theft of an automobile and subsequent flight were not, therefore, sufficiently threatening to meet this standard.

Related to the use of roadblocks, the police practice of ramming a fleeing suspect's vehicle has come under close court scrutiny. As with Brower, ramming has been held to be a Fourth Amendment seizure, and may only be used in the event of a life-threatening felony.

As these cases demonstrate, policymakers must be cognizant of the dangers to both the public and the fleeing suspect when deciding upon an acceptable level of interdiction. The level of permissible force must be strongly conditioned upon the seriousness of the suspect's offense and the totality of the circumstances in which the flight takes place.

Pursuit Scholarship

The evolution of police pursuit policy has been facilitated through several decades of academic research. One of the primary ways in which discussion has been aided is through an examination of relevant pursuit-related statistics. According to John Hill's 2002 report published in the *FBI Bulletin*, both the number of pursuits and pursuit-related injuries and deaths have increased over time. Estimates indicate an annual national pursuit-related death toll somewhere between 300 and 500 persons. For the period 1994–98, an average of one law enforcement officer was killed every 11 weeks in a pursuit, and one percent of all U.S. law enforcement officers who died in the line of duty were killed in vehicle pursuits. Unrelated bystanders account for 42 percent of the persons killed or injured in police pursuits. Nationally, approximately one percent of high-speed pursuits result in a fatality.

At the extremes, some sources suggest that as many as 40 percent of all police pursuits end in a crash, 20 percent in personal injury, and one percent in death. Similar studies show that less than 17 percent of pursuits are initiated for a known felony. By extension, these researchers conclude the vast majority of police pursuits are initiated for traffic violations or misdemeanors.

Pursuit Management Task Force Study

In a large study of law enforcement agencies in the western United States, the Pursuit Management Task Force, funded by the National Institute of Justice Office of Science and Technology, issued an important set of pursuit-related findings in 1998. The first of these findings has implications for the use of vehicle stopping technologies such as spike strips or electronic engine-interruption devices.

Their 1998 report concluded that over 50 percent of all pursuit collisions occurred during the first two minutes of a pursuit. Likewise, the authors found that more than 70 percent of all collisions happen by the fifth minute, and 83 percent take place before the sixth minute of a pursuit. The authors conclude these findings demonstrate a strong need to rapidly deploy pursuit termination technologies. They find that "large, complex, or stationary devices" are of little value unless preemptively deployed. Given the time frame in which pursuits typically unfold, devices that require elaborate staging appear to have very limited practical use.

Corollary to this, because most collisions take place within a few minutes of pursuit initiation, the use of police vehicles as "deployment platforms" for more transportable technologies is strongly supported. In a review of common technologies, spiked strips have been found to be the most prevalent and effective technology in use.

Among the other informative statistics arising from this study are the following observations: 99 percent of responding agencies allowed their officers to pursue, and 97 percent had written pursuit policies; 85 percent of these pursuit policies required a supervisor's approval/input; and 41 percent permitted the use of tire deflation devices. Half of the agencies allowed officers to use one of the following to stop vehicles: ramming, boxing-in, or channeling techniques. Three percent of agencies allowed for the use of Pursuit Intervention Technique (PIT) maneuvers. Twenty-five percent of surveyed agencies were aware of pursuit technologies, but chose not to use them. Reasons for this decision ranged from cost concerns, to availability and liability issues, to a lack of knowledge on the effectiveness of such technologies.

The Pursuit Management Task Force report is also noteworthy because it shows public support for reasonable police pursuits. This finding is somewhat limited, however, as the study authors note a general lack of public knowledge about relevant technologies and police practices. Even so, the report suggests the public appears willing to permit police pursuit within certain tolerances.

The report also finds that line officers tend to strongly support the use of pursuits. This support was couched in the perceived need for a strong supervisory climate. Line officers also preferred the use of termination technologies such as those described above. This suggests officers have a growing awareness of potential liabilities, and as a result, have learned to lean on both supervisory instruction and more nuanced methods of apprehension.

International Association of Chiefs of Police Report

Cynthia Lum and George Faschner authored a 2008 report for the International Association of Chiefs of Police (IACP) in which they review the bulk of extant pursuit-related scholarship. In this project, they summarize several dominant themes present in the literature. The first of these regards what they term *evidence-based practices*. In other words, the authors state that police policy and practices can and should be couched in empirically derived research products.

Lum and Faschner note that early pursuit studies suffered from methodological flaws, but that sufficient time has elapsed for a more reliable and valid body of scholarship to evolve. Moreover, they encourage practitioners to use and adopt the fruits of this scholarship in fashioning their own evidence-based policy decisions. They state that policymakers should seek to understand and be informed by those factors that increase the likelihood of undesirable or negative outcomes arising as a consequence of officer pursuits.

The second broad point reached by Lum and Faschner admonishes policymakers about the difficulty of assessing and balancing the true costs and benefits of police pursuits. They state that these calculations imply two complex and perhaps unassailable questions. The first of these regards the accuracy of calculating the real costs and benefits of engaging in pursuits. As they conclude, the assumed benefit is the apprehension of a criminal suspect and clearance of related crimes. They point to many studies observing that a high rate of pursuits incur no injury or damage while producing arrest. They cite costs stemming from the liabilities associated with compensation for property damages, injuries, and civil process, or in terms of accident rates. Perhaps the most evocative point arising from their discussion of related costs was also made by Geoffrey Alpert and his co-authors in 1996, that pursuits gone awry may imply substantial costs for the police in terms of a loss of legitimacy if the public perceives them as being needlessly dangerous or punitive.

A third summary point contained in Lum and Fachner's study regards an interesting disparity. They find that many studies observe differences between the reasons cited for initiation of pursuits and the final charges made against apprehended suspects. They find that while many pursuits are initiated for relatively minor infractions such as traffic violations, the final charges were often different and more serious. Without issuing a conclusion as to why that might be the case, the authors suggest that this finding should be subject to more rigorous scholarly examination.

Lum and Fachner go on to state that little evidence is available to support the position that more individuals will flee if increasingly restrictive pursuit policies (no-pursuit policies) are implemented. They conclude that the seriousness of the immediate situation in which the offender makes the decision to take flight may have a more controlling force than his or her offense history or the agency's pursuit policy.

Pursuit Policy Development

Three Policy Scenarios

From the preceding discussion of police pursuit as a topic for the courts and scholars, the complexity of the issue is evident. By extension, the difficulty inherent in crafting a legally defensible and operationally sufficient pursuit policy is likewise clear. As a result, three basic policy scenarios have evolved in American policing. Alpert characterizes them in his 1987 study as: judgmental, restrictive, and discouragement.

As the name implies, a judgmental pursuit policy largely leaves the pursuit decision up to the officer. The officer is free to make determinations as to the initiation, tactics, and termination of pursuits. These policies typically include general operational guidelines for the officer. Most include some reference to the balance between apprehension goals and safety.

By contrast, restrictive policies still permit the initiation of pursuit, but place certain conditions on an officer's actions and decisions. Restrictive policies may place limits on the conditions (environmental, situational, offense seriousness, likelihood of apprehension, etc.) under which a pursuit may be initiated, sustained, or terminated. Restrictive policies may include a condition requiring the officer to receive the approval of a supervisor or other authorization prior to pursuit initiation.

The third general type of pursuit policy, discouragement, strongly limits or prohibits officers from initiating or engaging in a pursuit. Some caveats are usually present to permit pursuits in extreme cases. As Alpert notes, pursuits are least likely to occur in jurisdictions governed by a discouragement-style policy.

Regardless of the type of policy a given agency adopts, officer training is still a cornerstone of successful implementation. While training in the technical aspects of pursuit driving can be resource-intensive for agencies, it is a necessity. Likewise, officers should be well schooled in the policy requirements and operational expectations in their particular agency. As Alpert states, agency policies should involve training with respect to the extent of individual officers' abilities; the importance of the environmental and situational conditions; and factors such as the seriousness of the provoking incident, the likelihood of suspect apprehension, and the probability of suspect termination of the pursuit. Ideally, a combination of well-crafted policy and detailed training will establish clear expectations for the officer while providing him with an array of appropriate responses for whatever situations may arise. In so doing, the agency will help shield itself and its officers from possible civil liability claims, and at the same time increase safety.

In stark contrast, agencies without written pursuit policies or those with inadequate policies position themselves for increased public ire and greater liability claims. While agency administrators certainly need to depend on the discretion and judgment of their officers, failing to provide an adequate rubric for decision making portends trouble. Echoing frequently held sentiments, Marjie Britz and Dennis Payne argue in their 1994 study that agencies without written policies invite lawsuits, adverse media coverage, and negative public opinion. As they point out, the media rarely gives the same coverage to successfully concluded, uneventful pursuits as they do those with spectacular or tragic ends. This imbalance can leave the public with the misinformed impression that most police pursuits end with dramatic, damaging, or injurious finishes.

Public Relations and Communication

Corollary to well-crafted policy and extensive training, agencies should also develop a supervisory culture vested in strong communications. The supervisory chain must be such that clear expectations are communicated throughout the organization. In his 1983 article on police pursuits, Erik Beckman places the onus on agency supervisors to monitor and quickly correct any deviances from written policy. In his view, retraining and the proper documentation thereof are critical parts of the process, if the agency and officer are to be protected from liability claims. Several other scholars reach similar conclusions on the importance of consistent training and communication of performance expectations.

Police officers are sworn to protect and serve the public. They must endeavor to meet these obligations without needlessly endangering the public. Part of this balanced task will inevitably require the occasional pursuit of fleeing suspects. In the course of said pursuits, the public may be exposed to increased risk. As such, policymakers have their own difficult obligation to reconcile court decisions, evidence-based practices, and public sentiment with the operational dictates of stopping offenders in flight.

To best meet the rightful safety expectations of the public, the requirements of the Constitution, and agency law enforcement goals, policymakers must draft guidelines that provide both clear instruction and accountability measures. Line officers must be given extensive training such that agency and supervisory expectations are widely understood. Those officers who fail to meet the standards should be retrained and disciplined to the extent required to achieve conformity and uniform practices.

Pro: Arguments in Support of Vehicular Police Pursuits

Geoffrey Alpert, Professor in the Department of Criminology and Criminal Justice at the University of South Carolina, has for the past 20 years concentrated his research and training on the evaluation of high-risk police activities, including the use of force, deadly force, pursuit driving, racial profiling and accountability systems. He argues that an officer's ability to give vehicular pursuit is a vital part of the deterrence equation. If a suspect knows that they will not be pursued by an officer under any circumstances, there is little to stop the suspect's flight. Furthermore, supporters of pursuit-capable policies argue chaos likely would ensue if police were restricted from pursuing suspects. Supporters of this perspective argue that a variety of law enforcement goals would be unattainable without some ability to give chase in a police vehicle.

Con: Arguments Opposing Vehicular Police Pursuit

Opponents of vehicular police pursuit argue that the practice presents an unacceptable risk to the public. They counter that the potential peril to innocent bystanders simply exceeds the value of any particular law enforcement apprehension objectives. Almost paradoxically, Louis Barth, in an article in *The Police Chief* (1981), contends that the greater the speed of the offender, the greater the danger to the public; therefore, the greater the need for apprehension. As such, many agencies have chosen a middle-ground policy that allows for pursuit, but subject to numerous terms and restrictions.

In making the case against police pursuits, Donald Van Blaricom, a former Bellevue, Washington, police chief who wrote a precedent-setting policy restricting pursuits, attempts to dispel some of the prevalent myths used to defend the practice. Van Blaricom observes that many officers believe that suspects must have committed more serious acts that will be discovered subsequent to apprehension—otherwise, they would not have fled. Likewise, he asserts that officers defend the use of pursuits with the assumption that a no-pursuit policy will inevitably lead to a free-for-all in which every suspect will flee. To support his position against pursuits, Van Blaricom cites research documenting no measurable increase in suspect flight after adoption of no-pursuit policies.

Few would argue the propriety of officers performing their duties with access to reasonable resources. That said, a balancing act between all elements of public safety, law enforcement goals, and risk mitigation has evolved. In this difficult process, policymakers must be open-minded, but informed by the larger realm of public and departmental best interests.

See Also: 2. Arrest Practices; 16. Vehicle Searches.

Further Readings

Alpert, G. P. "Police Pursuit: Policies and Training." *National Institute of Justice Research in Brief* (May 1997).

Alpert, G. P., D. J. Kenney, R. G. Dunham, W. Smith, and M. Cosgrove. *Police Pursuit and the Use of Force.* Unpublished final report. Washington, DC: National Institute of Justice, 1996.

Barth, Louis H. "Police Pursuits: A Panoply of Problems." *The Police Chief* (February 1981).

Beckman, E. "High Speed Chases: In Pursuit of a Balanced Policy." *The Police Chief* (January 1983).

Britz, M., and D. Payne. "Policy Implications for Law Enforcement Pursuit Driving." *American Journal of Police*, v.13/1 (1994).

Brower v. Inyo County, 489 U.S. 593 (1989).

City of Lansing v. Hathaway, 280 Mich 87; 273 NW 403. (1937).

Dent v. City of Dallas, 729 SW 2nd 114 (Tex. App., Dallas 1986).

Draper v. City of Los Angeles, 91 Cal. App. 2d 315, 205 P.2d (1949).

Fiser v. City of Ann Arbor, 417 Mich. 461, 339 N.W.2d (1983).

Gibson v. City of Pasadena, 83 Cal.App.3d 651 (1978).

Hill, J. "High-Speed Police Pursuits: Dangers, Dynamics, and Risk Reduction." *FBI Law Enforcement Bulletin*, v.71 (July 2002).

Lum, C., and G. Fachner. *Police Pursuits in an Age of Innovation and Reform. The IACP Police Pursuit Database.* Alexandria, VA: International Associations of Chiefs of Police, 2008.

Marion v. Flint, 248 NW 2d 580 (1976).

Mckay v. Hargis, 88 NW 2d 456 (1958).

Pursuit Management Task Force. *U.S. Department of Justice Office of Justice Programs National Institute of Justice.* (August 1998). http://www.ncjrs.org/pdffiles/fs000225.pdf (Accessed October 2010).

Sacramento v. Lewis, 523 U.S. 833 (1998).

Scott v. Harris, 550 U.S. 372 (2007).

Tennessee v. Garner, 471 U.S. 1 (1985).

Van Blaricom, D. P. "Control of Police Vehicular Pursuit." *Law Enforcement Executive Forum* (2003).

18

Vigilantes

Frederick Hawley
Western Carolina University

The presence of vigilantes and the institution of vigilantism has existed in the United States from colonial times. Vigilantism, or popularly phrased as "taking the law into one's own hands," is the practice of resorting to alternative methods of social control in lieu of those afforded by the state. A vigilante is a member of a movement or organization dedicated to using these methods, usually in the hope of establishing stability in a milieu that he or she regards as chaotic or lawless. Specifically, vigilantes create temporary or alternative criminal justice arrangements to replace the ineffective, unavailable, or unsatisfactory status quo afforded by the state.

Although police agencies generally state that they are opposed to vigilante-type organizations due to their potential for unorganized violence, they are more likely concerned about the implied critique that the very existence of such groups suggests. By going outside the law, the vigilante points to and erodes the already fragile authority of criminal justice agencies and the state, and thereby subverts the legitimacy of the political order. It is therefore seemingly paradoxical to note that most vigilantism in American history has conservative roots, and supports and reifies existing local social and economic arrangements. Historically, vigilantes have often been businessmen, large ranchers, and representative of rising young local elites. In general, in the context of the American narrative, they are not outsiders.

Vigilante Beginnings

Vigilantism has many historical and contemporary manifestations. Vigilante movements usually emerge in a frontier or quasi-anarchic context where the authority of the state is weakened due to geographical distance or socio-cultural breakdown, such as during or following a revolution or war. The case of the California gold rush in the 1840s would be an example of the former, and lynching in the post–Civil War south an example of the latter. Sometimes, political differences or feuds among local rural elites erupted into vigilante and counter-vigilante groups, such as occurred in rural South Carolina in the 1770s and in Texas in the 1800s. Methods of punishment by vigilantes have included tarring and feathering, running culprits out of town "on a rail," and other forms of public humiliation. Occasionally, on the frontier and in the south, hanging was utilized, though it was not as commonly used as whipping or other methods of exposing the victim to ridicule. But urban areas other than the wild west sometimes had outbreaks of vigilantism. Quarreling political factions erupted into insurrectionary violence in the 1850s in New Orleans, as groups self-identifying as vigilantes took control of the city in a short-lived coup.

Modern Vigilante Groups

More recently, unofficial criminal justice groups such as the Guardian Angels, who patrol high crime urban neighborhoods (without official sanction) in order to deter crime, are criticized as vigilantes. In the recent past, an individual protecting himself from possible victimization in public transportation was labeled "the subway vigilante," and those using computers to publicly expose corrupt officials in China are called "Internet vigilantes." Other forms of computer-based vigilantism involve luring potential sex offenders to rendezvous with underage pseudo-victims. Thus, the meaning of the term *vigilante* in contemporary, popular usage has evolved to refer to people who use violence, or the threat of violence; or other nonstate-sanctioned, nontraditional, private means to deal with what they view as problematic behavior or injustice. While in the past, the term implied at least an appearance of a quasi-judicial component—such as a kangaroo court—in current parlance, it refers less to a court-like procedure and rather more to the popular enforcement aspect. In this light, the Internet is a type of frontier that, in the absence of significant state regulation, encourages a vigilante mentality to some degree.

Vigilante Precursors: Kin-Based Order and Early Justice

People living in folk societies prior to the advent of court systems did not practice vigilante justice, as neither organized society nor a court system existed then. Vigilantism, no matter how loosely the term is used today by the media, is always an alternative to the justice procedures and structures of an existing state, no matter how rudimentary that state and its manifestations might be. So, prior to the existence of organized government and justice institutions in a particular society, peasants in that society practiced folk law and a primitive system based on orally transmitted, rudimentary mores and kinship-based concepts of order. Under the *wergild* system used in Germanic Europe, every life and body part was afforded a certain value. Even an accidental killing would cost one clan a certain amount of value (*gild* = money) that they would have to pay to the clan of the victim. In the absence of a state and formal institutions, this form of restitution was considered basically fair by members of these Germanic tribes. If one tribe or clan did not pay *wergild* when it was merited, the society might dissolve into feuding factions.

In Europe in the Middle Ages, peasants living in tiny principalities, under shaky control of a minor baron or under the aegis of a religious authority, might have never had any real state under which to experience law and order, and continued using kin-based systems until the state imposed control. Taking the law as they knew it into their own hands was their only real recourse. In theory, their taxes to a local lord or to the religious authorities was to provide them some modicum of protection under feudal order, but that was often unsatisfactory, almost always arbitrary, and grossly biased against their class interests.

Under English common law, the practice of observing and responding to the hue and cry (*hutesium et clamor*), which is often mischaracterized as vigilantism, was actually an obligation imposed by the state to pursue and capture accused felons. For example, upon hearing the noise bruited about from hamlet to hamlet, villagers were expected to drop everything they were doing, pick up any primitive weapons at their disposal, and bring the malefactor to a local noble or court. Resistance by the accused could bring death at the hands of the supposedly enraged peasantry, but this was frowned upon by royal courts. It has been suggested that sympathetic villagers might have been less than diligent in their pursuit of the accused. However, hundreds could be assessed a fine for the crime of an individual criminal, whether fugitive or in custody. Likewise, in the early cities of the

1300s, citizens were held responsible for rudimentary criminal justice: A night watch had to be carried out, and the city gates and marketplace had to be guarded and protected. Citizen responsibility for these duties was not vigilantism, as it was enjoined by the authority of the state. Similarly, constables were appointed by the state to head settlements and aid sheriffs and justices of the peace.

British institutions were sorely tried by a period of seemingly radical vigilantism that broke out during the late 1600s and 1700s. Ironically, the outbreaks of collective and individual violence were instantly inspired by an overly vigorous enforcement of harsh laws (rather than too lax, as is usually the case in conditions that underlay vigilantism) pertaining to hunting. Feudal rights and privileges were abrogated, and common lands were seized by rich landowners. Peasantry and minor gentry, now essentially barred from hunting, had crops threatened by the burgeoning herds of deer on formerly common lands—preemptively seized by nobles and representatives of the king—held near royal hunting preserves. Groups of angry villagers and peasants attacked the preserves, slaughtered hundreds of the king's deer, and cut down fruit trees. In some outbreaks, fisheries and crops were damaged and royal servants and tax officials were attacked. Many poachers blackened their faces (and were thereafter known as *Blacks*) as camouflage and disguise when perpetrating various acts of vandalism against royal properties and interests, and the property of unsympathetic gentry and nobility. In the 1720s, several gamekeepers were killed by poachers, and at least 16 poachers were hanged in response. Numerous poachers died in prison, and others were transported to the colonies in America.

A more broad-based revolutionary movement was feared; this led to the passage of the infamous Black Act, which created more than 50 new capital offenses in British law and substantially increased penalties for almost any crime committed against royal hunting, farming, husbandry, and fishing prerogatives. The strong attachment to gun ownership and hunting in the United States, in part, may be a result of this forced removal of peasantry from traditional homes and pastimes. Many of the settlers of colonial America were of British peasant stock and strongly resented the gross assertion of royal power that legislation such as the Black Act represented. Although the activities of the Blacks were seemingly an example of radical antiestablishment violence, the vigilante peasantry were trying to return to the status quo, and were actually a conservative force in this assertion of power of property over people.

The event surrounding the passage of the Black Act notwithstanding, the limited system of justice carried out by local strongmen or royalist appointees endured well into the 1700s in England, when a wave of crime was sparked by the first stirrings of the Industrial Revolution. In response to that period of dramatic social dislocation and disorder, two revolutions in law enforcement occurred in England with the establishment of London's Bow Street Court in the mid-1700s, and later the beginnings of the first modern police organization in 1829. Folk justice and conventional manifestations of vigilantism ceased having much relevance at that time in British society.

Historical Vigilantism in the United States

Prior to the 1770s, and well afterward in rural areas, folk customs primarily derived from Europe such as *charivari* (rough music) were popular in enforcing customs that were outside the province of formal law and order. Local men, often masked, would congregate outside the home of local offenders of morality and make noise by singing obscene ditties and banging pots and pans. The offenders, often incongruously married couples or outsiders who crossed local mores, were suitably chastised. This public shaming was likely intended more as a general deterrent than to punish a troublesome individual. Sometimes, however, government officials—such as tax officials or revenuers—received rougher treatment, such as tarring and feathering, or having to "ride a rail." This particularly painful form of folk justice, which later became popular in the Civil War military courts, involved forcing the malefactor to straddle a suspended rail while his feet were weighted with bricks, or sometimes heavy rifled muskets. Often, the offender was carried about while thus suspended and cruelly jostled. Tarring and feathering was popular in the American revolutionary period, and was also the particular favorite of anti-abolition mobs on both sides in the period immediately preceding the Civil War. This took the form of the offender being stripped to the waist, coated with hot pitch, and then dusted with feathers. Though painful, the point of this exercise was not to kill, but to debase the offending individual publicly; this spectacle seldom led to fatalities.

Violence erupted throughout the colonies when the nascent states declared their independence. While factional violence raged throughout the south, South Carolina was the site of particularly violent vigilante movements. The British government authority was weak and did not extend to the outer reaches of the colonies, and settlers were victimized by outlaw bands and partisans. Some farmers and merchants formed groups known as

Regulators, who took on military trappings and drove out various bands of outlaws and partisans while often fighting among themselves. Well before the actual outbreak of hostilities in the American Revolution, as early as 1771, South Carolina Regulators came into active conflict with British forces. In Virginia, similar groups delivered troublemakers and British loyalists to Judge Lynch's Court (supposedly an actual historical figure), where they received summary judgment, usually public humiliation such as tarring and feathering; less often, the sentence was hanging. The equation of lynching with hanging in the popular mind came about well after the revolutionary period. In the late 1700s, as the authority of the American state became ascendant in the eastern part of the country and state courts became operational and relevant, these movements faded from the scene, a pattern often repeated throughout the national narrative.

Vigilantes in the 1800s

Although state courts existed, communications were very slow in the 1800s. In times of perceived emergency, such as an anticipated organized slave revolt, dozens of vigilance committees and committees of investigation came into existence. This happened in 1835 in Mississippi, when solid citizens and plantation owners created patrols and rounded up suspects in order to deal with threatened slave revolts, outlaws, and crooked gamblers. Events at Beattie's Bluff excited property owners in nearby counties, and several slaves, after a brief extralegal trial process, were hung out of hand. A white New Englander was tried by a committee and hung after publicly admitting his complicity. This seemed to calm the anxious whites of the area and supposedly prevented wholesale lynching.

That same year, considerable hysteria was generated by "land pirates," who, from 1880 until 1885, operated on the Natchez Trace, a treacherous trade and postal route leading from Natchez, Mississippi, to Nashville, Tennessee. Many crimes in that area, both real and imaginary, were attributed to bands of land pirates, particularly John A. Murrell, supposedly one of the cruelest and most bloodthirsty. He formed a clan and built a conspiracy to steal and recruit slaves along the Natchez Trace and lead them in revolt, pillaging and looting the populace, which generated great fear among citizens. Vigilance committees were created, lynching occurred, and anyone who could not account for any unusual behavior or presence in the area was at risk until the hysteria played out. More vigilante action followed as professional gamblers were lynched in Vicksburg and expelled from Natchez in that same year. Eventually, Murrell's plan was thwarted and he was sentenced at trial, and the days of the land pirates ended.

Other outbreaks of vigilantism occurred throughout the slavery period in the region until the Civil War. After the war, vigilantes, operating under the color of various white supremacy groups, including the Ku Klux Klan and Redshirts, tried to restore a form of the old order by intimidating former slaves and radical members of the carpetbaggers (slang for the newly formed Republican Party). Occasionally, they also harassed criminals and those whose morals were suspect. They were very successful at destabilizing the federal regime and stymieing reform desired by Washington. Due to these factors and northern weariness with the entire enterprise, the Reconstruction experiment was abandoned after the election of 1877. Vigilante violence, intended to enforce white supremacy—often carried out with the connivance of local authorities—continued into the 1960s, though much reduced. When vigilantes were brought into federal and local courts to answer for their crimes, juries chosen from local panels were more responsive to white supremacist regional mores than the letter of the law, and seldom convicted accused offenders. In recent years, prosecutors in several southern states have reopened cases and successfully prosecuted KKK-type vigilantes.

California, however, was the scene of the most celebrated vigilante episode in American history. In rural areas, which had very recently shifted from the weak control of the Mexican state to the equally inefficient control of the United States, obtaining justice was problematic. Kangaroo courts and lynching laws were common, as no real alternative was apparent. While crime was dealt with harshly and in an extrajudicial fashion in the gold fields to the east and northeast, San Francisco—with weak courts and governmental institutions—was forced to deal with a serious crime problem. The gold rush in 1848 attracted fortune-seekers and criminals from throughout the United States as well as all settled continents. An Australian gang of Irish origin—the Sydney Ducks—was particularly troublesome in this regard. However, many formerly respectable villagers and townsmen from the east turned to crime out of impoverishment, drunkenness, and sheer desperation. Isolation from civilizing influences and institutions was destabilizing to many who had gone west. Many brought weapons and violent habits with them. Southerners were mentioned in this regard in letters home from the gold fields.

The result was a city in chaos, according to the contemporary partisan press and self-glorifying histories written by Californians. Mercantile interests were particularly upset at the tolerance of violence, vice, and gross intoxication that followed in the wake of prospectors who had struck it rich. Street violence and corruption were rife. In 1851, the San Francisco Committee of Vigilance was constituted, set up patrols, and held court sessions. Most "convicted" malefactors were publicly whipped, but a few Ducks were transported to Australia. When the committee was reorganized in 1856 with many prominent citizens as members, it added political corruption—in particular, the Democratic Party's political machine—to its list of concerns. During its three months of existence, the 1856 committee controlled the press and was backed by armed militia, developing into a political force that actively and sometimes violently opposed the Democratic Party and its elected officeholders, which controlled the politics of the city. When the committee ended, political power was transferred to the People's Party. By 1867, this party had become absorbed into the Republican Party. It is difficult to assess how much of the vigilantism of 1856 was based on legitimate reaction to crime, and how much was simply partisan violence.

Justice, Southern Style

In the 1850s, New Orleans politics were exotic and complicated. Political elites were particularly concerned with wresting power from the working class and the corrupt, anti–Catholic American (Know Nothing) political party that had, paradoxically, flourished in predominantly Catholic New Orleans. To this end, the Democratic "vigilante" movement staged an abortive coup in 1859, in which U.S. officer (and future Confederate General) P.G.T. Beauregard played a prominent role. U.S. senator and Democratic political kingpin, John Slidell, was also implicated in this clumsy attempt to return power to former Whigs and local merchant elites. Government buildings were seized by the vigilance committee, but the conspiracy soon fell apart and the vigilantes retreated into the swamps. After the war, several vigilante-type coups occurred in the Crescent City that rose to insurrectionary levels. Large numbers of Reconstruction-regime police were needed to quell the violence and restore the federally supported local government. Later in 1891, a celebrated vigilante lynching of 11 alleged Mafiosi gained international attention and caused a rift between Italy and the U.S. government.

Texas had at least two periods of regulator-type vigilantism. In the 1830s and 1840s, the frontier area between Texas and Louisiana was extremely crime-ridden and volatile. As this area was the border first between Spain and the United States, then Mexico and the United States, criminals fleeing these jurisdictions flocked to this lawless zone; it became known as the

Sabine [River] Strip and retains a troubled reputation to this day. Vigilantes known as "regulators" used heavy-handed attempts to clear out rustlers and escaped slaves. Their tactics were so problematic that "moderators" arose as a countermeasure. The regulator/moderator conflict was only successfully repressed when the Republic of Texas (then an independent state) sent in militia.

In addition, following the chaos and dislocation of the Civil War, vigilante movements arose in the state to control cattle rustlers and outlaws in general. Summary justice in the form of hangings was doled out to all those caught with altered brands or stolen cattle or merchandise. Local sheriffs, some of whom were thought to be in cahoots with outlaws, could not or would not protect accused criminals who were sometimes killed in their cells by outraged vigilantes. Ultimately, Texas Rangers were called in and were finally able to bring a halt to the violence and attendant family feuds. A further complicating factor was the evident bad blood between ex-Confederates (who were often involved in vigilante violence) and the targets of their ire, often freed slaves, Republicans, or unemployed cowboys who had turned to outlawry. Family feuds also added more violence to the mix. Shootouts and ambushes in public venues continued until the early 1900s, though true vigilantism had ceased by the 1890s. This period gave rise to both a myth approving vigilante action, and ironically, to the myth of the effectiveness and toughness of the Texas Rangers.

Contemporary Vigilante Movements and Impulses

One of the most visible and important vigilante-type group emerged out of the urban crime crisis of the late 1970s. The Guardian Angels were founded by Curtis Sliwa in New York City in 1979. This group of red-beret-wearing young people began patrolling city streets attempting to deter crime, and were frequently featured in television documentaries and talk shows. As they do not have any judicial pretensions and enjoy limited support from local elites, they are not a real vigilante group, though are continually labeled as such by media. Nonetheless, their vigilante-type tendencies and the conceptual critique that they present of the perceived inefficiency and ineffectiveness of the criminal justice system is apparent. They were, and remain, unpopular with police and urban authorities, who view them as instigators and poseurs with the potential to create friction. Some in government and media view them as little more than a gang. Although they have chapters in various locales in the United States and Canada, they remain a marginal and fugitive group and have faded from the media spotlight since the 1980s.

In the 1980s in New York City, crime had become so pervasive that individuals became frustrated and began to try to protect themselves through more aggressive measures. Though not properly vigilantes, they were labeled as such by the media. Such was the case of Bernard Goetz in 1984. Goetz, a mild-mannered, self-employed technician, feeling menaced on the subway by four African American youths, shot them at close range. The "subway vigilante," as dubbed by the media, was eventually convicted of a weapons possession charge and received a light sentence. One of his victims was eventually awarded a large cash settlement in a subsequent civil case. Goetz, who was exercising a type of preemptive self-defense—although excessive—cannot properly be labeled a vigilante due to his lack of involvement in organized group action or a quasi-judicial function. However, he was clearly acting in an area where the state had been perceived as having failed in its duties to protect its citizens. For some New Yorkers, he was seen as a hero, an everyman who fought back against thuggery and urban chaos. But to others, he was seen as an out-of-control vigilante—a manifestation of systemic dysfunction, popular malaise, and perverse celebrity.

More recently, the case of the Minuteman Project is apposite. Highly disturbed by the large numbers of immigrants crossing the border from Mexico, and the apparent permeability of that border, this group of vigilantes has established patrols along the Texas/Mexico frontier. The name of the group implies a link with forefathers from a heroic age, and these activists see themselves in a similar patriotic light. In 2005, they were involved in a disturbance in California, and Minutemen speakers were shouted down by protestors at Columbia University in 2006. They have been instrumental in forcing the Mexican government to stop furnishing border-crossing migrants with maps for fear that the vigilantes would use them to plan ambushes. Some conservatives have voiced support for this organization, but some American liberals and Mexican leaders have expressed their dislike for vigilante actions of this type. More recently, former members have complained about an influx of extremists into the group.

Internet and Cyber Vigilantes

The advent of computer-based crime and deviance has left law enforcement lagging behind criminal and deviant elements. Because of the prevalence of sexual exploitation of minors by predators and other forms of computer-facilitated deviance, individuals and groups have targeted persons and corporations for boycotts and various forms of action to demonstrate their disapprobation or simply to harass and punish the malefactor.

Media and Entrapment Controversies

Media have propelled the activities of Perverted Justice, a California-based nonprofit organization, into prominence. These activists pose in online chat rooms as lonely children, engaging in sexual dialogues with adults who believe they are soliciting minors. If the individual gives the decoy their name and other information, a rendezvous is set up, often at the purported residence of the minor—where unbeknownst to the eager would-be predator, law enforcement agents and sometime the cameras of NBC's *To Catch a Predator* may lie in wait. After desultory conversation with the minor, he or she makes an excuse to leave the room momentarily, and the would-be offender is confronted by a television personality who asks pointed questions. Upon his exit, the perpetrator is confronted by police officers and the attendant humiliations of apprehension, arrest, and booking, all with cameras rolling.

This practice has excited some controversy over claims that it is perilously close to entrapment. Additionally, some members of the group have allegedly harassed those they believe to be predators online and have contacted the purported offender's family, employers, and neighbors. They have also reportedly posted photos of the homes, addresses, and photographs of alleged sexual predators. Groups such as this also post a list of corporations that engage in activities that might put children at risk from sexual predation. Unlike many vigilante-type organizations, Perverted Justice receives considerable support from various law enforcement agencies, politicians, media personalities, and child safety activists. Critics include Websites, organizations, and individuals concerned about Perverted Justice's errors, lack of accountability, and the issue of entrapment.

Other individuals and groups have targeted criminals and those implicated in controversial legal cases for informal investigations. The residences of known sex offenders have been subjected to picketing, modern-day *charivaris*, and Internet harassment by outraged citizenry. Vigilantes have taken their accusations online, and have roundly criticized the criminal justice system. Others have retaliated against Nigerian scam artists and other fraudulent email scams and Websites through various tricks and subterfuges. Such "scam-baiters" attempt to leverage the scammer's own game by entrapping the scammer or luring him into dangerous or foolish situations, or posting emails and photos of the scammer.

Internet-oriented activists have also focused attention and ridicule on those they wish to shame into making public apologies, or those they wish to see caught or punished. One individual who made defamatory remarks about various groups on a reality television show was swamped with angry emails from enraged viewers and had to resign from several community boards due to the reaction. In at least one case, an Internet service host who had hosted scams and malware sites was driven off the Web by concerted efforts of Internet activists. The host simply moved to other service providers. Two boys who tormented a cat and posted the film of the incident on the Internet were tracked down by Internet detectives, and caught and punished by authorities. A South Korean woman who refused to clean up her dog's feces on the subway was targeted with a storm of Internet vilification. Eventually, the harassment led her to resign from her university and make a public apology, in which she threatened to commit suicide. A small candy company that refused to allow a child to use the bathroom was similarly targeted for a massive Internet campaign. The manager's home was featured on Google Earth, as was his contact information. The president of the company was driven to make a public apology for the incident.

China has furnished a receptive forum for Internet vigilantism. After a husband posted information about his wife's affair, her lover was harassed by thousands of outraged citizens. Teams of citizens (who met online) actively harassed him to the point where his family had to barricade themselves in their residence to escape the public reaction. Other cases have surfaced involving Internet denunciations of official nonresponse to the Sichuan earthquake and to general nonfeasance and misfeasance by public officials.

The Internet is a frontier where rules and laws are nebulous, and enforcement is sorely lacking. Like citizens of early America, where the institutions of the new nation had not caught up to territorial realities, Internet citizens are frustrated into taking on the task of enforcement themselves.

Vigilantes in Popular Media

The theme of vengeance and the individual who achieves private justice outside the system goes back to the most ancient of Greek dramas. Aeschylus's *Oresteia*, dating from 458 B.C.E., is a trilogy of plays dealing with private vengeance. Other Greek playwrights dealt with the theme extensively, as did Shakespeare more recently. Hamlet, for example, finds vengeance and justice in the eponymous play, but meets a bad end himself.

Western Films and the Golden Age of Television

Classic American cinema dealt with private vengeance extensively, and contemporary cinema continues to feature this as a prominent motif. Many westerns of the 1950s and 1960s featured the theme of inadequate law and order on the frontier and the struggle of individuals to achieve private justice. *The Ox-Bow Incident,* filmed in 1943, is a classic of the western vigilante genre. Featuring posters replete with noose-carrying rowdy cowboys, the picture is grim and features characters representing different points of view about justice and vengeance in general. With a predictable denouement, it serves as an indictment of "taking the law into one's own hands." In *High Noon* (1952), the sheriff is saved by the intervention of his bride at the last minute when other civilians prove too cowardly to support their local lawman. Public justice was not equal to the task, but private intervention saved the day. Again, an unlikely civilian, a lawyer, saves the day, as well as civilization on the frontier in *The Man Who Shot Liberty Valence* (1962). A federal marshal was mistakenly hanged by a lynch mob In *Hang 'Em High* (1968). Ironically, amid much meandering philosophical discourse about the death penalty from the celebrated Hanging Judge Parker, he tracks down the members of the lynch mob, one at a time, and achieves private justice. John Wayne in *The Searchers* (1956) plays a Civil War veteran who tracks down the Indians who kidnapped his sister, kills many, and retrieves her in the postwar trans-Mississippi West.

One program that explicitly dealt with historical vigilantes can be found from the golden age of television westerns—the late 1950s and early 1960s. *The Californians* (1957), set in 1850s San Francisco, featured a newspaper editor and dealt with the vigilante movement as a continuing plot motif. However, many other westerns regularly dealt with private vengeance. *Have Gun Will Travel* (1957) was essentially a detective program set in the wild west. But Paladin, the main character, was an agent of private vengeance, as the word *paladin* denotes a champion or knight errant. This "knight without armor in a savage land" (as the theme song intoned), represented private individuals up against cattle barons, local bullies, and damsels in distress.

Many detective shows had private vengeance as themes of the program or within individual episodes. During the English spy craze of the early 1960s, *The Avengers* (1961)—though not a true vigilante series—concerned a highly unconventional British spy agency that avenged great wrongs and dealt with bizarre crimes and super-criminals with high style.

Vigilantes in Contemporary Entertainment

More modern offerings include the classic *Death Wish* film series (1974–94). Charles Bronson plays an everyman whose family is victimized by horrendous crimes. He embarks on a mission of street-level vengeance and achieves some justice. Clint Eastwood also pursues the role of vigilante, though as a cop acting as judge, jury, and executioner, in *Dirty Harry* (1971). This film and others in the series are often considered vigilante films. *Magnum Force* (1973), in which Eastwood's Dirty Harry pursues vigilante cops and a renegade judge, examines themes of justice and vengeance from a particularly ironic point of view. Ultimately, Harry takes the vigilantes down. In *The Equalizer* (1985), British actor Edward Woodard plays a private detective revenge artist who takes on cases that the police can not handle. Bruce Willis in the *Die Hard* series (1988–2007) is also a cop, albeit on vacation in a different jurisdiction, when he pursues terrorists. Eastwood has continued to pursue roles of private justice through the decades; in 2008, his retired, blue-collar character saves a community and a young immigrant at great personal sacrifice in *Gran Torino*. And *The Forgotten* (2009) has a team of predictably quirky nonpolice individuals investigating closed cases.

Female vigilantes include Ashley Judd, who in *Double Jeopardy* (1999) is framed by her husband and unjustly imprisoned, then escapes and eventually exacts revenge. Likewise, Jody Foster in *The Brave One* (2007) is a female fury. *Avenging Angel* (1985) is about a reformed prostitute who avenges her police officer benefactor.

In cinema and television, the detective, cop, or cowboy hero is usually justified in his use of violence, but mob violence is roundly condemned. Thus, the system is reinforced by a prosocial subtext, but private justice has primacy of place in the American television and cinematic narrative.

Pro: Support for Vigilantism

Vigilantism does not lend itself to arguments in its favor. However, under frontier conditions (such as prevailed in the new nation in the 1700s and 1800s), and in the absence of a clear system of law and justice, individuals were forced to take private justice where they could find it. In the present day, this may be applicable to Internet vigilantism as well. There is no legal support for vigilantism, but the concept does enjoy credibility in drama, popular cinema, and television, as well as among some political extremists of both the right and the left. Despite official disapproval, vigilantism is a prevalent motif in the American consciousness.

Con: Opposition to Vigilantism

Seeking of vengeance frequently leads to gross abuses (such as lynching), weakening of the power of incipient or extant states, feuding, and general cynicism about the criminal justice system. It is also illegal in many cases. Also, from a Christian theological perspective, vigilantism is suspect, in that man usurps the divine prerogative of retribution.

See Also: 3. Bounty Hunters and Rewards; 9. Police Brutality; 10. Police Corruption and Code of Silence.

Further Readings

Ayers, Edward L. *Vengeance and Justice: Crime and Punishment in the 19th Century American South*. New York: Oxford, 1984.

Brown, Richard M. *Strain of Violence: Historical Studies of American Violence and Vigilantism*. New York: Oxford, 1975.

Courtwright, David T. *Violent Land: Single Men and Social Disorder from the Frontier to the Inner City*. Cambridge: Harvard University Press, 1998.

Cutrer, Thomas W. "Southwestern Violence." In *Encyclopedia of Southern Culture*, edited by C. R Wilson and W. Ferris. Chapel Hill: UNC Press, 1989.

Lane, Roger. *Murder in America: A History*. Columbus: Ohio State University Press, 1997.

Neely, Richard. *Take Back Your Neighborhood*. New York: Donald I. Fine, 1990.

Richards, Leonard. *The California Gold Rush and the Coming of the Civil War*. New York: Knopf, 2007.

Thompson, E. P. *Whigs and Hunters: The Origins of the Black Act*. New York: Pantheon, 1975.

Wyatt-Brown, Bertram. *Southern Honor*. New York: Oxford University Press, 1982.

19

Warrants

Shamir Ratansi
Central Connecticut State University

Warrants are a controversial topic that affects both law enforcement and citizens alike. Under the Fourth Amendment to the U.S. Constitution, citizens are protected from unreasonable searches and seizures to both persons and property. Similarly, law enforcement officials must also comply with the requirements set forth in the Fourth Amendment to ensure a valid arrest or search and seizure. The issues surrounding warrants are complex, and even experienced officers can sometimes get confused in terms of the rationale behind some of the restrictions. For example, the simple stopping and questioning of a person could constitute the seizure of their person and could be considered a violation of their constitutional rights. Moreover, not all arrests and searches require a warrant; only incidents that the courts consider unreasonable or without probable cause are prohibited by the amendment.

The definition of *search* refers to the intrusion by an agent of the state into an area that a person reasonably believes is protected or private. For example, a person's home would be considered an area that is private. There are also parameters set limiting the extent of searches by law enforcement officials. Searches generally are limited to any goods associated with crimes, instruments of the crimes, weapons, persons thought to be involved in criminal acts, forensic evidence, and contraband. The definition for a *seizure*, according to the court ruling in *U.S. v. Jacobsen* (1984), is generally a meaningful interference of property through a legal process.

A search warrant is an order signed by a judge that legally entitles police officers to arrest or search for specific objects or materials at a definite location at a specified time. Police officers must attain a warrant by first presenting an affidavit to a judge or magistrate. An affidavit is a written statement provided by an officer that states that there is probable cause to believe that criminal activity or evidence of a crime is at a specific location. Establishing probable cause has to be more than simple suspicion; it has to be based on supporting facts and circumstances that reasonably justify that an offense has been committed or where items can be found. The officer then presents the affidavit to the judge or magistrate and swears under oath that the statement is truthful. If the judge or magistrate is convinced of probable cause, then a warrant is issued. The warrant contains the reason for requesting the arrest or search, the names of the persons presenting the affidavits, what specifically is being searched for, and the signature of the judge.

The term *arrest* is also included under the seizure clause of the Fourth Amendment. To arrest a person is to restrain them from their own will and hold them under the law. Generally, an arrest is deemed reasonable if the officer views the commission of the offense or has probable cause that the defendant committed it. Usually, if the officer does not view the offense, he or she must rely on their experience, training, and skills to justify an arrest warrant. An arrest warrant is issued in cases where evidence is gathered and presented to a magistrate by an officer to determine whether the criterion of reasonableness has been met to apprehend the suspect. A warrant may also be issued for a suspect in a private residence when there is no reason for an immediate arrest or when the entry into the home is for a minor offense. The restrictions on the arrest of a person are fairly clear compared to the restrictions associated with the search of a person or property and the seizure of property.

Once a search warrant is granted, the police may only search the place noted on the warrant and usually only seize the property described. Warrants are very specific; for example, an officer may not search the house if the warrant is only for the garage. Additionally, if the warrant is for a specific person, then the officer may only search that person, even if another person is present. Upon completion of the warrant, the officers must produce a return of the warrant, which is an itemized inventory of all items or property seized by the officers.

The Supreme Court has ruled on numerous cases in the interpretation of the Fourth Amendment and has set standards for concepts such as "probable cause" and "reasonable suspicion." Based on these Court decisions, many situations exist in which warrantless arrests or searches are permissible. The language and criteria for these warrantless searches can at times be confusing and detailed. Therefore, an understanding of when, how, and why warrants are applicable is crucial for all law enforcement officers.

All police officers are affected by the Fourth Amendment, and warrants are extremely important in that searches and seizures are pivotal in the removal of weapons and drugs from the street, building of criminal cases, and possible prevention of crime. Additionally, the requirement of warrants for searches and seizures has both supporters and opponents. Those in favor generally point toward the protection of constitutional rights and limitations to law enforcement powers. Those opposed usually focus on the exclusion of evidence on technicalities, when that evidence is crucial to the pursuit of truth finding in the criminal justice system. As the world becomes more complex, technology and innovation are creating new questions regarding the constitutionality of searches and seizures by law enforcement.

The History of Warrants

The genesis of American search and seizure laws stems from England. Orders known as Writs of Assistance entitled the king's soldiers to search homes and businesses without court-ordered warrants. These writs were introduced in England around 1662; by 1669, by an act of Parliament, they were extended to be applicable in the colonies. The English government had a long history of abusing power both in England and the colonies. Therefore, the new settlers were eager to gain independence from this oppressive, distant government. In an effort to secure a person's right to privacy, the founding fathers included the following in the Fourth Amendment to the U.S. Constitution:

> The right of the people to be secure in their persons, houses, papers, and effects, against unreasonable searches and seizures, shall not be violated, and no warrants shall issue, but upon probable cause, supported by oath or affirmation, and particularly describing the place to be searched, and the persons or things to be seized.

The Fourth Amendment does not specifically require a warrant for a search and seizure, but rather states that it must be done so in a reasonable fashion with probable cause. The Supreme Court has steadfastly established that searches and seizures without a warrant are unreasonable and, therefore, unconstitutional. However, the court has also recognized that many exceptions exist in terms of arrests or searches and seizures that do not require a warrant, yet are considered reasonable and constitutional.

The Legality of Warrants

There have been several landmark Supreme Court decisions regarding warrants and the Fourth Amendment. The laws pertaining to an arrest and a search are two separate and distinctive entities in regard to law enforcement procedures. The rules for arrests are relatively straightforward compared to the rules for searches and seizures. Therefore, the majority of court cases revolve around the validity of searches and seizures. To properly understand the importance of search warrants within the criminal justice system, an examination of the exclusionary rule is necessary.

In *Mapp v. Ohio* (1961), the Court set a precedent on how officers could conduct a search and seizure. The case involved the actions of a number of officers looking for a bombing suspect who arrived at Dolree Mapp's home. Mrs. Mapp shared the home with her daughter and refused to let officers in without a search warrant. A few hours later, with additional officers, the police forcefully entered the home and after a search found obscene pictures of Mapp's daughter in a trunk. The Supreme Court overturned Mapp's conviction for possession of obscene material and imposed the exclusionary rule. The court ruled that the search was unreasonable and without probable cause, and the evidence used by the prosecution was therefore inadmissible. Under the rule, any evidence obtained as a result of a violation of a person's constitutional rights may not be used in a court of law to prosecute that person.

However, over time, the Court has also established several good-faith exceptions to the exclusionary rule. For example, evidence obtained by the police is still admissible if the error on the warrant was committed by someone else, such as the magistrate or a court employee. Also, cases in which the police make a mistake in gathering evidence may still end up being admissible as long as the error was honest and reasonable. The police may even defend a search if they believe that the person who gave them access was in fact the person who had the authority to do so. The case of *United States v. Leon* (1984) established the good faith exception to the exclusionary rule. In 1981, Burbank, California, police began surveillance of suspected drug dealer's homes, followed leads based on the vehicles seen at those homes, and received information from an informant. Based on this activity, detectives obtained a search warrant from a judge. Later, the search warrant was found to be invalid because the police lacked probable cause for the issuance of a warrant. However, the evidence seized in the search was still upheld, because the police were relying on the validity of the warrant.

The Supreme Court has also been very specific in terms of procedures for law enforcement officers on serving warrants. Police officers are usually required to announce their intentions and status before entering a premise. In *Wilson v. Arkansas* (1995), the Supreme Court required officers to "knock and announce" to meet the reasonableness requirements of the Fourth Amendment. The decision was meant to protect the citizen's right to privacy as well as a measure to reduce the risk of potential violence or destruction of private property. However, the rule does not apply in cases where there is a possibility of harm to officers or others, an escaped arrestee, or the chance of destruction of evidence.

Additionally, if a suspect does not allow entry, then the officer may forcibly enter the premise. In *United States v. Banks* (2003), the Court deemed that 15–20 seconds was an adequate amount of time to wait before forced entry was acceptable as a means to execute a search warrant. The opening of a closed, unlocked door or window is also considered forced entry. Search warrants can also be served at night, and in some cases, as a special "no-knock" warrant. For example, some types of criminal activity only occur after hours, and serving a warrant in the daytime would be futile. A no-knock search warrant with prior judicial authorization is also granted when the suspect is known to have a history of noncompliance or when the announced entry would result in easy destruction of evidence.

When a Warrant Is Not Necessary

The majority of searches occur without a warrant. There are numerous situations, as established by the courts, where a search warrant is not necessary. These exceptions include, but are not limited to: searches incident to arrest, consent, stop and frisk, plain view, emergency, and vehicle searches.

A warrant for a search is not necessary when a person is lawfully arrested; however, the officers only have a limited area in which to conduct the search. For example, in *Chimel v. California* (1969), officers went to Ted Chimel's house to serve a warrant for his arrest for burglarizing a coin store. After giving Chimel the warrant, the officers told him they wanted to search the house. The officers searched for over an hour, even getting Chimel's wife to help. Numerous stolen coins were found, but they could not be used as evidence based on the decision of the Court that the coins had been unconstitutionally seized. In the *Chimel* case, the Supreme Court stated that the area of search on the arrested person is limited to their immediate control, wingspan, or arm's reach. If the officers wished to search the house, a search warrant was necessary. A search after an arrest is justified even without probable cause to ensure officer safety, the prevention of escape, or the concealment or destruction of evidence.

One of most common exceptions are warrantless searches with consent. The Court has set specific guidelines in terms of how consent is given and who can give consent. In *State v. Barlow Jr.* (1974), the Court decided that warrantless searches were acceptable when consent was given, exigent circumstances existed, or when no right to privacy existed and that the consent was free and voluntary. Moreover, in *Monroe v. Pape* (1961), the Court also recommended that consent be asked at an appropriate time (daytime) and could be withdrawn by the citizen at any time, requiring officers to end the search. Officers, however, cannot make a search if probable cause is not established, even if consent is given (*Florida v. Royer*, 1983). The Court has still not resolved the validity of consent given by a citizen based on the threat of a warrant by an officer without an actual warrant.

Officers are also allowed to stop and frisk a suspect without a warrant if they are reasonably concerned about their safety or the public's safety. For example, in 1963, Detective McFadden was patrolling in plain clothes when he noticed two men repeatedly taking turns looking into a business window. When the two men met up with a third man, Detective McFadden approached the three males and proceeded to pat them down, revealing pistols on two of the men. In the subsequent case, *Terry v. Ohio* (1968), the Court found that the stop was a constitutional frisk based on the officers training, experience, and belief that the men were about to commit a crime and were armed. As a result, officers are allowed to stop and question persons if the officers believe they have committed or are about to commit a crime. Additionally, the item being felt in the pat-down must be identified immediately, and officers must have reasonable suspicion; thus, random stopping and questioning of citizens is not acceptable.

The Plain View Doctrine

Under the plain view doctrine, officers may also seize items that are within sight during a legal procedure. For example, in *Coolidge v. New Hampshire* (1971), the Court found that the defendant's Fourth Amendment rights had not been violated as a result of the seizure of two cars in plain view during his arrest. However, in order for the plain view doctrine to be applied, several conditions must be met first. The officer has to be legally present at the location of the search, and the items seized must have been found inadvertently. The officer must also immediately recognize that the seizure is evidence.

Other court rulings have deemed that officers responding to an emergency at a person's house are allowed to seize any evidence in plain view (*Mincey v. Arizona*, 1978). In a similar case in 1984, officers entered a Mr. Hicks's apartment looking for a shooter after a bullet was fired into the apartment below. The officers' entry into the apartment was considered legal, as it qualified as an emergency. During the search, the officers found a number of firearms and also noticed some expensive stereo equipment that appeared to be out of place in the dire apartment. The officers moved the stereo equipment to get the serial numbers from the back of the units, and a check later at the station revealed that the equipment had been stolen in an armed robbery. Mr. Hicks was later found and charged with numerous offenses. In *Arizona v. Hicks* (1987), the Court ruled that the officers conducting the search had done so illegally. The moving of the stereo equipment was considered an additional search, one that was not related to the original purpose of the entry.

A search warrant is also not necessary in exigent circumstances such as emergencies or extenuating circumstances in which the officer is justified in intruding on a person's privacy. In this case, the law enforcement objective overrides a citizen's rights, but in so doing, the officer must establish probable cause and be able to defend that no time was available to secure a warrant. The officer must demonstrate that there was the potential for danger to life, escape, or destruction of evidence. The original exigent circumstances were addressed in *Warden v. Hayden* (1967).

Warrant Requirement Exemption for Vehicles

The rules for what is reasonable for acquiring a search warrant are quite different for automobiles, and the courts have created exemptions based on the issue of mobility. The precedent for warrantless searches of vehicles was set some 85 years ago in *Carroll v. United States* (1925). During the Prohibition Era, two undercover officers were planning on buying some bootleg liquor from George Carroll and John Kiro. Unfortunately, the deal fell through and the bootleggers backed out of the deal. Two months later, the agents recognized Carroll's car and pulled him over. The subsequent search of the vehicle resulted in the seizure of 68 bottles of liquor. Carroll's appeal to the Supreme Court resulted in a decision that established that the right to search an automobile does not depend on the right to arrest the driver or occupant. The officer must have probable cause for believing the automobile's contents violated the law and that the conveyance would be gone before a search warrant could be obtained.

The police also have a right to search a vehicle incidental to an arrest. *New York v. Belton* (1981) reaffirmed that officers may search a vehicle's interior and all its contents after an arrest has been made. Vehicles that are used in the commission of a felony may also be searched without a warrant. In *Thornton v. United States* (2004), the Court also allowed police to search a car after the arrestee has gotten out of the car and walked away. In *Florida v. Jimeno* (1991), the Court entitled officers to search and open containers in the vehicle. Moreover, officers who enter a vehicle to search for identification numbers and come across a gun protruding from under the seat are allowed to seize it under the plain view doctrine (*New York v. Class*, 1986).

The automobile exception also applies to passengers; in 1999, the Supreme Court ruled in *Wyoming v. Houghton* that officers may also check a passenger's belongings in the car if they feel that the object of the search may be concealed within. Additionally, in *Maryland v. Pringle* (2003), officers stopped a car with three passengers for speeding. A legal search of the car revealed over $700 in cash in the glove compartment and drugs behind the passenger seat. Pringle, the passenger in the front seat, was arrested and convicted of drug possession. The Court ruled that the officer acted reasonably and had probable cause given the circumstances. This ruling only authorizes officers to arrest passengers if probable cause exists that a crime has been committed in the car.

Checkpoints are another exception to the warrant rule, and are considered legally valid only if they target all vehicles passing through the point and the intrusion for the driver is minimal and reasonable. The stops are reasonable based on the expectation that public roads are not highly private, and due to the heavy regulation imposed on automobiles. If suspicion of violation of a law is detected, then further inquiries such as sobriety tests are permissible. Random stops of vehicles without probable cause are not permissible.

In *United States v. Drayton* (2002), the Court also allowed officers to question and request consent for a search for bus passengers. Warrantless searches are also acceptable for public school teachers and administrators who are allowed to search students if they reasonably believe school rules or the laws have been violated. The list of areas and conditions where searches are permissible without warrants has also increased since September 11, 2001, to insure security at airports and other susceptible public venues. Additionally, technology used by citizens (computers, mobile devices, emails, etc.), coupled with advances in detection methods used by officers, has raised new concerns in terms of the protections guaranteed under the Fourth Amendment.

Pro: Arguments in Favor of Warrants

Proponents of warrants state that they are a means of protecting Americans' Fourth Amendment rights, based on the criteria for probable cause and reasonable suspicion that must be established before law enforcement can proceed. Warrants are therefore beneficial in that they require the approval of a magistrate placed between citizens and the police. This lets an objective mind decide when a person should be arrested or a home should be searched in order to enforce the law. The requirement of the sworn affidavit from an officer also forces him to go the extra distance in establishing good reasons to engage in an arrest or search.

Warrants also prevent unconstitutional searches and deter officer misconduct. In an effort to maintain cases and prevent crime, officers may be more diligent in how they carry out their law enforcement activities. An officer would not want evidence excluded or to face civil liability for his actions. Warrants help law enforcement officers avoid expensive mistakes. Additionally, warrants may go beyond reducing harms to a person's constitutional rights and dignity; they may even prevent property damage, physical injury, or death.

For officers, the benefits of attaining a warrant revolve around issues of liability. In an arrest or search and seizure with a warrant, the affidavit for probable cause has been reviewed and approved by an impartial magistrate. Therefore, subsequent actions related to the case by law enforcement are presumed valid. Consequently, if the defendant wishes to contest the validity of the warrant, the task is considerably more difficult when questioning the reasoning of the magistrate.

Having a warrant is also a strong defense in a civil case if a defendant seeks damages for alleged violations of his or her constitutional rights. In most cases, the officer will not be held liable even if an error was found; and under judicial immunity, the magistrate cannot be held civilly liable for damages, even if they are responsible for the error. The only case in which the issuance of a warrant may be used as a valid defense against the state is if there are obvious mistakes on the warrant that the officer should have noticed, such as a missing signature.

Warrants also add to the professional image of the police officer. Officers have to be well versed on the stringent requirements involved with warrants, as well as current on Supreme Court decisions. Given the importance of valid arrests and searches, officers have to undergo increased training and challenging ethical scenarios involving citizens' Fourth Amendment rights. All of this can result in better treatment of citizens and a possible reduction in officer misconduct. The process involved in getting a warrant, including the approval of the magistrate, also adds an element of integrity to the judicial system. The message sent by requiring warrants for certain arrests and searches and seizures is that no one is above the law.

Con: Arguments Against Requiring a Warrant

Opponents of warrants argue that they are not really a means of protecting Fourth Amendment rights, but rather a biased technique used to make citizens feel protected. For example, terms such as *probable cause* and *reasonable suspicion* have not been clearly defined by the Supreme Court, and are overly subjective concepts. The criteria for meeting the requirements for an issuance of a warrant are also very low. In most cases, sufficient criteria for degree of certainty in terms of probable cause and reasonable suspicion is generally anything above 50 percent. Critics also assert that magistrates are not impartial and are simply "rubber stamps" who cannot be trusted. It has been argued that as a member of the central government, a magistrate should not be the sole decision maker on the issuance of a warrant; juries composed of members from the community should help make the decision. Finally, the standard for probable cause for an officer is likely very different than the standard held by citizens.

Critics also point out that the Court has consistently decreased the scope under which a warrant is necessary for searches, thus substantially limiting its need by officers. For example, giving officers the right to search passengers' belongings as granted in *Wyoming v. Houghton* (1999) may result in an abuse of power. Moreover, requiring warrants and the threat of the exclusionary rule may not deter officer misconduct. The court has made several provisions for officers based on their honesty and reasonability.

Impropriaties to warrants may not even come into question as the major-ity of police cases are not affected if the arrest does not end in a court pros-ecution. In fact, most searches do not result in prosecution, and cases are generally resolved through plea bargaining. Therefore, searches and seizures may not be about prosecution, but rather about the confiscation of goods. For example, contraband is not returned to the suspect, even if the search and seizure was unconstitutional, and officers may not face any discipline or penalty for their actions. Many searches are made for purely preventative reasons.

For officers making a search without a warrant, there can be many possible negative consequences in terms of evidence. A defendant can chal-lenge the determination of probable cause for the search, and the court has to review it. If probable cause is not established, any evidence seized cannot be admitted in court, thus potentially weakening the prosecution's case. Opponents of warrants contend that the exclusionary rule and its high standards assist in letting criminals go free on technicalities. More-over, the rules for searches and seizures are confusing, and officers should not be expected to know all of the legal nuances. Warrants are limiting the ability for officers to effectively carry out their roles as agents of law enforcement.

There can also be severe consequences for the officer if the arrest or search and seizure are determined to be unconstitutional. The officer could be sued in a civil case for damages or even prosecuted criminally. Critics also contend that the likelihood of perjury by an officer is increased as they try to justify the arrest or search and seizure to meet the requirements of warrants. Additionally, if challenged, not many would side against the testimony of an officer compared to the testimony of an unsavory criminal. Some opponents to warrants also believe that reviews of the search or arrest by officers done after the fact would be more accurate. The magistrate could review the facts and decide whether to suppress the evidence or admit it. Pre-screening for a warrant is difficult, burdensome, and highly subjective for both the officer and magistrate. Post reviews would be clearer and less subjective, and may also deter bad officer conduct.

More importantly, changes in American culture after September 11, 2001, have resulted in an expansion of government powers and less em-phasis on warrants by citizens. Critics contend that Americans have given less precedence to individual freedom in exchange for collective security. The Patriot Act, for example, repealed a number of restrictions giving greater search and seizure powers to law enforcement officials. The government can now conduct more warrantless searches without notification, confiscate property from suspected terrorists, and monitor citizens without judicial review. The Supreme Court has also been more flexible in terms of the Fourth Amendment siding with law enforcement in the name of national security. The sources for information that can be searched have also expanded to include financial, medical, library, and travel records. Opponents to warrants also contend that as technology moves forward, law enforcement's use of devices such as global positioning systems on cars or thermal imaging cameras on homes to gain evidence for search or arrest warrants are blurring the lines of privacy guaranteed to citizens. Additionally, reliance on computers, emails, and cell phones has changed the format in which personal information is stored, raising questions on rights to privacy and accessibility.

See Also: 8. Plain View Doctrine; 13. Profiling; 16. Vehicle Searches.

Further Readings

Alschuler, Albert W. "Studying the Exclusionary Rule: An Empirical Classic." *The University of Chicago Law Review*, v.75/4 (2008).

Arizona v. Hicks, 480 U.S. 443 (1987).

Bloss, William P. "Warrantless Search in the Law Enforcement Workplace: Court Interpretation of Employer Practices and Employee Privacy Rights under the Ortega Doctrine." *Police Quarterly*, v.1/51 (1998).

Carroll v. United States, 267 U.S. 132 (1925).

Chimel v. California, 395 U.S. 752 (1969).

Comparato, Scott A., and Scott D. McClurg. "A Neo-Institutional Explanation of State Supreme Court Responses in Search and Seizure Cases." *American Politics Research*, v.35/5 (2007).

Coolidge v. New Hampshire, 403 U.S. 443 (1971).

Florida v. Jimeno, 499 U.S. 934 (1991).

Florida v. Royer, 460 U.S. 491 (1983).

Junker, John M. "The Structure of the Fourth Amendment: The Scope of the Protection." *The Journal of Criminal Law and Criminology*, v.79/4 (1989).

Kerr, Orin S. "Searches and Seizures in a Digital World." *Harvard Law Review*, v.119/2 (2005).

Longyear, Michael. "To Attach or Not to Attach: The Continued Confusion Regarding Search Warrants and the Incorporation of Supporting Documents." *Fordham Law Review*, v.76 (2007).

Machado Zotti, Priscilla H. *Injustice for All: Mapp v. Ohio and the Fourth Amendment*. New York: Peter Lang, 2005.

Mapp v. Ohio, 3657 U.S. 643 (1961).

Maryland v. Pringle, 540 U.S. 366 (2003).

Mincey v. Arizona, 403 U.S. 443 (1978).

Monroe v. Pape, 365 U.S. 167 (1961).

New York v. Belton, 453 U.S. 454 (1981).

New York v. Class, 475 U.S. 106 (1986).

Skogan, Wesley G., and Tracey L. Meares. "Lawful Policing." *Annals of the American Academy of Political and Social Science*, v.593 (2004).

State v. Barlow, Jr., 320 A.2d 895 (Me, 1974).

Stuntz, William J. "Warrants and Fourth Amendment Remedies." *Virginia Law Review*, v.77/5 (1991).

Terry v. Ohio, 392 U.S. 1 (1968).

Thornton v. United States, 541 U.S. 615 (2004).

United States v. Banks, 540 U.S. 31 (2003).

United States v. Drayton, 536 U.S. 194 (2002).

United States v. Jacobsen, 466 U.S. 109 (1984).

United States v. Leon, 468 U.S. 897 (1984).

Vaughn, Michael S., and Rolando V. del Carmen. "The Fourth Amendment as a Tool of Actuarial Justice: The 'Special Needs' Exception to the Warrant and Probable Cause Requirements." *Crime and Delinquency*, v.43/1 (1997).

Warden v. Hayden, 387 U.S. 294 (1967).

Wetterer, Charles M. *The Fourth Amendment: Search and Seizure*. Springfield, NJ: Enslow, 1998.

White, Welsh S., and Robert S. Greenspan. "Standing to Object to Search and Seizure." *University of Pennsylvania Law Review*, v.118/3 (1970).

Wilson v. Arkansas, 514 U.S. 927 (1995).

Woody, Robert H. *Search and Seizure: The Fourth Amendment for Law Enforcement Officers*. Springfield, IL: Charles C Thomas, 2006.

Wyoming v. Houghton, 526 U.S. 295 (1999).

York, James. A. "Search and Seizure: Law Enforcement Officers' Ability to Conduct Investigative Traffic Stops Based on an Anonymous Tip Alleging Dangerous Driving When Officers Do Not Personally Observe Any Traffic Violations." *University of Maryland Law Review*, v.34 (2003).

20

Zero-Tolerance Policing

Elizabeth E. Martinez
University of Notre Dame

Zero-tolerance policing (ZTP) is a controversial policing style that has taken several forms over time and has been implemented in a variety of institutional settings. There are disagreements regarding the historical origin and the theoretical basis for ZTP. It is related to other similar policies designated by other terms, such as *broken windows, hot spots, order-maintenance policing,* and *quality of life policing.* A more descriptive, or neutral, term for these types of strict enforcement in the criminal justice system is *intensive enforcement.*

Although early instances of ZTP can be found in the areas of domestic violence and neighborhood improvement, many agree that the policing style and terminology of ZTP has an origin in the federal policies launched during the 1980s in the War on Drugs lead by the Reagan administration, and as is more commonly cited, with strategic innovations in the policing of the subways and streets of New York City during the 1990s. With these historical points in mind, police authorities and consultants, including moral entrepreneurs who were engaged in the War on Drugs and the ZTP initiatives in New York, have contributed to the diffusion of intensive-enforcement policies across the United States and to other countries, especially the United Kingdom, most often under the rubric of zero tolerance.

Even though proponents of zero-tolerance approaches tend to attach ZTP to criminological theories of rational choice and social disorganization, there is debate regarding the rational basis of ZTP. Another critique of zero tolerance is that it is often a political slogan, rather than a concrete policy.

Scholars also question the purpose and outcomes of ZTP. Zero tolerance policies have been implemented in a number of institutional settings, not only in the police departments of large cities, but also in neighborhoods, schools, prisons, and the military, with varying degrees of success and/or public disapproval. Despite critiques, intensive enforcement polices continue to be used by police agencies and other authorities. This is true even where community policing initiatives are also implemented.

Definition and Varieties

Often discussed in contrast with community policing, zero-tolerance policing is defined as a policy of strict enforcement of law, without regard to the particularities of a case or the nature of the offense. Thus, ZTP is a strict-enforcement policy starting with interrogation and arrest, followed by decisions to prosecute, through the meting out of often-severe punishments— even, or especially when, the offense is considered a petty offense. Some of the petty offenses that have come under ZTP programs include graffiti or jumping turnstiles in a subway to evade the fare.

While community-policing initiatives emphasize citizen involvement and police accountability, ZTP accentuates the government's exercise of authority and its monopoly over the legitimate control of antisocial behavior. Community-policing initiatives, which were funded by the Community Oriented Policing Services (COPS) program at the federal level in the United States, started to fall into a quiet decline following the emergence of ZTP, and accelerated after the September 11, 2001, terrorist attacks. According to some observers, the various forms of ZTP or intensive-enforcement policies contribute to the problem of mass incarceration in the United States.

Zero tolerance can be pursued at the points of fieldwork, arrest, prosecution, convictions, and sentencing. For instance, instead of allowing for the traditional use of discretion by police officers in decisions to arrest, as discussed in work on police discretion by Michael and Don Gottfredson and by Wayne LaFave, jurisdictions engaging a zero-tolerance policy require—or claim to require—the absolute enforcement of all laws, including mandatory arrest. In the area of domestic violence, for instance, ZTP is used to require police officers to arrest the violent spouse, usually the husband or male partner, after any phone call to the police alleging spousal abuse and visit of the police to the scene.

ZTP also can mean punishing all offenses under sentencing guidelines that discount or disregard mitigating factors. Similar policies in the realm of sentencing include "three strikes" laws requiring life sentences for a third felony conviction, and other forms of mandatory punishment that turn on a mechanized understanding of the offender's criminal history, rather than providing for judicial discretion or a nuanced review of the facts of a case. Although the federal sentencing guidelines are not considered a form of ZTP, they are another type of uniform enforcement.

Origin and History

Broken Windows and Hot Spots

In the literature on ZTP, there are several competing stories regarding its origin. According to Laura McNeal and Christopher Dunbar in their article *In the Eyes of the Beholder: Urban Student Perceptions of Zero Tolerance Policy* in a 2010 issue of *Urban Education*, the origin of the policy can be found in the Gun Free Schools Act of 1994, but here the authors are discussing zero-tolerance policies with regard to school violence, not the more general policy orientation. According to other sources, the origin of ZTP can be found in the Safe and Clean Neighborhoods Act of 1973 in New Jersey, a law that was later the subject of a now-famous article by James Wilson and George Kelling titled *Broken Windows*, and published in the *Atlantic Monthly* in 1982. In the article, Wilson and Kelling say that police agencies need to protect communities from not only violent strangers, but also the disorderly people who congregate on the street, including panhandlers, drunks, addicts, rowdy teenagers, prostitutes, loiterers, and the mentally disturbed.

The central claim of the article takes the form of a slippery slope argument, a type of argument commonly made but subject to an inherent, logical fallacy in that it proves only the assumption being made: If broken windows are not fixed, then vandals will break more windows; and if more windows are broken, someone is going to move into the building, become a squatter, and light the building on fire. Likewise, if litter is not picked up off the street, then more litter will accumulate, and eventually someone will leave a bag of trash. These visible signs of disorder and chaos will eventually lead to a generalized or normative view that no one cares about the neighborhood, as well as the belief that committing crime in the area is acceptable—not only crimes of public disorder, but also violent crimes and more egregious property crimes. Thus, the broken windows theory assumes that zero tolerance of public disorder can lead to a reduction in crime rates, including homicide rates. For these reasons, the theory is closely associated with ZTP as a law enforcement policy.

The term *hot spots* is also related to ZTP because it refers to areas of high crime linked to social disorganization. According to some research findings, it is not effective to spread the police evenly throughout a city; instead, it is more effective to concentrate police efforts in the hot spots. According to research by university criminologists John Eck and Edward Maguire and others, increasing the number of police or using community-policing programs are generally not effective in reducing crime.

Other related terms are *quality of life* and *order maintenance,* which some authorities centrally involved in ZTP would prefer to use because they are more accurate and less politically charged.

Origins in the War on Drugs

The consensus regarding the origin of ZTP is that it germinated during the so-called War on Drugs, with federal, low-tolerance and intensive-enforcement policy initiated by the Reagan administration in the 1980s, which featured the 1986 Anti-Drug Abuse Act and created a cabinet-level drug czar. During the War on Drugs, First Lady Nancy Reagan told students to "just say no to drugs." During the implementation of this policy, U.S. Customs Commissioner William Von Raab decided to use the term *zero tolerance*, altering slightly the term *zero defect*, which was previously used by Nixon White House chief of staff Bob Haldeman. The report of the Reagan administration's White House Conference for a Drug-Free America stated that there should be "zero tolerance" for illegal drugs in the United States.

Continuing their exhaustive outline of the history of the term, Newburn and Jones explain that the term *zero tolerance* has been deployed regularly by politicians and the media and used in connection with a number of different policy initiatives, including campaigns regarding domestic violence against women in Canada and the United Kingdom in the early 1990s, but it is most closely associated with the policing strategies adopted by the New York Police Department in the 1990s under the direction of police chief William Bratton and New York Mayor Rudolph Giuliani, who was elected in 1993. Bratton had served as the chief of transit authority in New York and used intensive enforcement policies to reduce subway crimes and fare evasion.

Bratton later attempted to distance himself from the term *zero tolerance*, preferring instead the expressions *order-maintenance* and *quality of life*. He acknowledges that phrases such as zero tolerance send a powerful message and so catch on quickly, but also says the phrase can be misleading when it comes to understanding the complexity of metropolitan policing, which will never fully eradicate public disorder and street crime. For these reasons, Bratton states that "zero tolerance is neither a phrase that I use nor one that captures the meaning of what happened in New York City, either in the subways or on the streets."

Intensive enforcement polices, even when implemented under terminology that is less politically charged than zero tolerance, continue to be used by many police agencies and other authorities. This is true even where community-policing initiatives, which seem to be contradictory in purpose, are also in place. In her study of international policing trends and the perceptions of police authorities, Cynthia Lum also finds that the widespread use of technology has largely superseded the hands-on approach that was central to community-policing styles, as local law enforcement officials are increasingly removed from direct contact with the public.

Theoretical Grounding

The debate circling the rational basis of ZTP is grounded in the fact that under zero tolerance, the punishment often does not fit to the crime. Opponents of ZTP take the position that it removes the discretion and decision making from police officers, judges, and others in ways that can become irrational. Minor crimes are punished with certainty and severity that exceed the petty nature of the offense.

But proponents say that swift and intensive enforcement of the law is necessary in order to monitor levels of disorder and reduce overall levels of crime, including serious crime. If ZTP can be shown to reduce crime, then the policy does have a rational basis, especially because its logic takes into account the rational choices of offenders who are aware of the policy.

In addition to rational-choice theory, ZTP is associated with routine-activities theory. Under this explanation for the causes of criminal behavior, if there are opportunities for crime and a lack of guardians, crime is more likely to be committed. ZTP, however, reduces opportunities presented by such elements of disorder as broken windows and poor lighting, which in turn reduces criminal behavior in an area.

Also associated with ZTP are causal theories of crime coming under the general heading of social disorganization, including ecological theories and delinquency-areas theories about the criminogenic nature of a place.

Purpose and Outcomes

Regarding the purpose and outcomes of zero tolerance, there are a number of issues to consider when analyzing ZTP as a viable program of law enforcement. For example, the dramatic drop in crime in New York City was credited in media discourse and elsewhere to zero tolerance policies, but in the research, other causes and factors are considered more influential in the reduction of crime. Many observers point out that San Diego experienced identical drops in crime during the same time period as New York, but San Diego, under police chief Jerry Sanders, was implementing community-oriented policing, not ZTP.

Social scientific research shows mixed results regarding the link between policing disorder, such as prostitution and vandalism, and reducing serious crime. For example, crime and policing expert Wesley Skogan, of the Institute for Policy Research at Northwestern University, found in 1992 that intensive enforcement actually increased social disorder, except for one city—Newark, New Jersey—which used a program combining both ZTP and community policing efforts, such as increased foot patrol. The foot patrol program in Newark was the subject of the Safe and Clean Neighborhoods Act and the introductory passage of the *Broken Windows* article by Wilson and Kelling.

Practices and Institutional Settings

ZTP can be a policy used to clean up neighborhoods, by removing all graffiti and litter, for example. It can also be used in workplace settings to eliminate sexual harassment and bullying, and as a type of policy put into public schools. While removing guns and drugs from schools is a positive step, news stories of students being expelled under zero tolerance policies, such as for having toy guns or aspirin at school, have lead to public backlash and widespread ridicule of ZTP in public discourse.

In her work on the racial bias inherent in ZTP when implemented in schools, Augustina Reyes illuminates the problem that, 50 years after the historic *Brown v. Board of Education* decision in 1954, inequalities in public education still disproportionately affect black and Hispanic students, who are held back and often do not graduate, and also are forced from school due to unforgiving zero-tolerance discipline policies.

In the military, there is a formal policy of zero tolerance for discrimination on the basis of race or sex, but according to researchers Mary Finsod Katzenstein and Judith Reppy, the informal practices and norms of daily military life condone and promote discrimination. Further, the formal policy of "don't ask, don't tell" regarding open statements or expressions of a sexual orientation by military personnel is best understood as a form of ZTP.

Pro: Arguments in Favor of Zero-Tolerance Policing

Proponents of ZTP claim that intensive enforcement of law—as to petty crimes such as vandalism, begging, and littering—is linked to the reduction in rates of serious crime. Under this view, broken windows and graffiti are signals that the commission of serious crimes will also be tolerated as a matter of locally accepted practice. Prostitution, drug dealing on the street, loitering, and other crimes of public disorder are also considered "signal crimes." In this context, New York City Police Department (NYPD) Commissioner William Bratton made "reclaiming public spaces" a key component of his plan for change in the policing of New York City in 1994.

In the years that followed his tenure, it was widely accepted that the innovative policing program of Bratton and Mayor Rudolph Giuliani in the 1990s led to the "New York miracle" of reduced crime and city streets that were finally free of public-order crime. In studies of the relevant data by Bratton in 1997 and George Kelling and C. Coles in 1996, the use of ZTP in New York was found to have led to a dramatic drop in crime.

Another benefit of ZTP is that it prevents the use of discretion by police officers regarding whether to arrest the violent spouse, usually the husband or male partner, in cases of domestic abuse. Proponents of ZTP in this institutional setting argue that this abuse of discretion, in which no arrest of the male partner was made, is based on a sexist orientation to domestic violence. Because of the increased enforcement, they say, women who were once suffering abuse without recourse are now empowered and, as a result, human lives are being saved.

Another argument in favor of ZTP is that it deters crime, such as in the case of a repeat offender who knows that he or she will face a three-strikes claim if convicted again for a felony offense. Similarly, proponents argue that ZTP policies, such as uniform sentencing guidelines, can render criminal justice outcomes less biased against offenders of color.

Con: Arguments Against Zero-Tolerance Policing

Scholars question the purpose and outcomes of ZTP, bringing into the debate a number of issues regarding whether it is a viable and legitimate program of law enforcement and crime reduction. First, the rationality of ZTP has been widely questioned, because under zero tolerance, the punishment often does not fit to the crime. Examples abound in the news about people sent to prison for life for petty offenses, such as stealing a bike.

Another critique is that ZTP is not actually a deterrent to the commission of crime, and so it is not rational on that basis. There is some evidence that shows its effectiveness, but researchers raise questions about the independence of ZTP as a causal factor in the existing studies that show a positive relationship between ZTP and rates of crime reduction. Several studies show that other factors had a stronger influence on both location-specific drops in crime rates and the overall drop in crime rates during the 1990s.

For example, despite the evidence offered by Bratton, Kelling, and Cole in support of the New York miracle, scholars assert that there was an overall crime drop in the United States during the same time period. They also argue that the New York case might be better explained by the decline in crack use during the relevant time period.

In the view of the Committee to Review Research on Police Policies and Practice, the data relied on by Bratton, Kelling, and others "do not provide a valid test of the effectiveness of generalized intensive enforcement on crime." The National Research Council clarifies the fact that ZTP was part of a larger program of new policies in the NYPD implemented under the title CompStat. The CompStat program placed authority at the precinct level and removed some of the earlier community-policing preferences that Bratton thought unduly placed the burden of problem solving and community relations on patrol officers. The overall CompStat program used by Bratton was not simply a program of intensive enforcement.

Another critique of ZTP is that it resulted in increased police brutality, including the high-profile shooting of an unarmed man, Amadou Diallo, by plainclothes NYPD officers in 1999, as well as an overall loss of quality of life that occurred in New York during the implementation of ZTP.

Zero-tolerance policy is also criticized for often being a rhetorical device or political slogan, rather than a concrete policy. Politicians are likely to invoke ZTP as a marker or symbol of their law-and-order orientation, sometimes without having a detailed program on hand regarding particular enforcement initiatives. According to researchers Tim Newburn and Trevor

Jones, the use of expressive crime-control policies, such as zero tolerance and broken windows, are problematic because politicians and policymakers may not consider the evidence for or against ZTP, but instead are apt to rely on such powerful terminology as provided by the ZTP rhetoric. Newburn and Jones caution against giving up the critique of zero-tolerance programs, saying that doing so is an important facet of public sociology.

Discriminatory Practices

From the perspective of critical criminology, there are serious questions about the implementation of zero tolerance as a method for combating visual disorder on the street, while at the same time, police agencies and policy makers ignore the ravages of white-collar crime—and ignore the structural inequalities that lead to a variety of public-order crimes, such as prostitution, vagrancy, and vandalism.

This type of critique is often accompanied by the argument that there can be no actual practice of ZTP, across all types of offenders and crimes, as a practical matter. In this view, opponents of ZTP argue that it tends to selectively target particular groups or particular offenses, to the exclusion of other groups and offenses. Thus, as implemented, ZTP is not actually a policy of zero tolerance for any and all forms of law breaking, across all types of offenders and crimes. Practically speaking, ZTP tends to target particular groups and offenses for strict enforcement, and is more often understood as a policy that targets the disadvantaged for street sweeps and mass incarceration—an exercise of intolerance that disproportionally affects marginalized populations. These biases of intensive enforcement are tied to race, class, or status.

Following this line of critique, zero-tolerance polices are often aimed at the homeless, beggars, the mentally ill, and sometimes, political protest organizations, when these groups engage in unpopular expressions in public spaces. Bratton, Wilson, and Kelling all make clear that those marginalized populations are the target of ZTP. Yet arguably similar behaviors, such as singing or fundraising on the street by other groups, are widely tolerated.

Leading scholars of poverty and urban spaces say that ZTP, along with the intensified surveillance of so-called problem neighborhoods, and police harassment of immigrants and homeless in public spaces, are outward indicators that governments are giving in to the temptation to rely on strict policing and incarceration to stem the disorders caused by mass unemployment, precarious wage labor, and a loss of social protection.

According to researcher Mark Kleinman, not every aspect of a zero-tolerance program is objectionable, in that swift and certain punishment can be an effective deterrent; however, brute-force policies do not work because they lead to mass incarceration—a social ill in and of itself. Kleinman argues that punishment policies should be swift and certain, but less severe.

See Also: 2. Arrest Practices; 9. Police Brutality; 14. Riot and Demonstration Responses.

Further Readings

Ayers, William, Bernardine Dohm, and Rick Ayers, eds. *Zero Tolerance, Resisting the Drive for Punishment in Our Schools: A Handbook for Parents, Students, Educators, and Citizens.* New York: New Press, 2001.

Bayley, David H., and Christine Nixon. *New Perspectives for Policing, 1985–2008.* A Report of the Executive Session on Policing, Kennedy School, Program in Criminal Justice Policy and Management. Washington, DC: National Institute of Justice, 2010.

Bowling, Benjamin. "Rise and Fall of New York Murder: Zero Tolerance or Crack's Decline?" *British Journal of Criminology,* v.39 (1999).

Bratton, William. "Crime Is Down in New York City: Blame the Police." In *Zero Tolerance: Policing a Free Society*, edited by Norman Dennis. London: Institute for Economic Affairs, 1997.

Eck, John E., and Edward Maguire. "Have Changes in Policing Reduced Violent Crime? An Assessment of the Evidence." In *The Crime Drop in America*, edited by Alfred Blumstein and Joel Wallman. New York: Cambridge University Press, 2000.

Innes, Martin. "An Iron Fist in an Iron Glove? The Zero Tolerance Policing Debate." *Howard Journal of Criminal Justice,* v.38 (1999).

Katzenstein, Mary Finsod, and Judith Reppy. *Beyond Zero Tolerance: Discrimination in Military Culture.* Lanham, MD: Rowman and Littlefield, 1999.

Kelling, George L., and C. Coles. *Fixing Broken Windows: Restoring Order and Reducing Crime in Our Communities.* New York: Free Press, 1996.

Kleinman, Mark A. R. *When Brute Force Fails: How to Have Less Crime and Punishment.* Princeton, NJ: Princeton University Press, 2009.

Lum, Cynthia. "Community Policing or Zero Tolerance? Preferences of Police Officers from 22 Countries in Transition." *British Journal of Criminology*, v.49 (2009).

McArdle, Andrea, and Tanya Erzen, eds. *Zero Tolerance: Quality of Life and the New Police Brutality in New York City*. New York: New York University Press, 2001.

McNeal, Laura, and Christopher Dunbar. "In the Eyes of the Beholder: Urban Student Perceptions of Zero Tolerance Policy." *Urban Education*, v.45 (2010).

National Research Council, Wesley G. Skogan, and Kathleen Frydl. *Fairness and Effectiveness in Policing: The Evidence*. Washington, DC: National Research Council, 2004.

New York City Police Department. *Police Strategy No. 5: Reclaiming the Public Spaces in New York City*. New York City Police Department, 1994.

Newburn, Tim, and Trevor Jones. "Symbolizing Crime Control: Reflections on Zero Tolerance." *Theoretical Criminology*, v.11/2 (2007).

Reyes, Augustina H. *Discipline, Achievement and Race: Is Zero Tolerance the Answer?* Lanham, MD: Rowman and Littlefield, 2006.

Vitale, Alex. *City of Disorder: How the Quality of Life Campaign Transformed New York Politics*. New York: New York University Press, 2008.

Wacquant, Loïc. *Prisons of Poverty*. Minneapolis: University of Minnesota Press, 2009.

Wilson, James Q., and George L. Kelling. "Broken Windows." *Atlantic Monthly* (March 1982).

Index

Index note: Chapter titles and their page numbers are in **boldface**.

About the General Editor

William J. Chambliss is professor of sociology at The George Washington University. He has written and edited more than 25 books and numerous articles for professional journals in sociology, criminology, and law. His work integrating the study of crime with the creation and implementation of criminal law has been a central theme in his writings and research. His articles on the historical development of vagrancy laws, the legal process as it affects different social classes and racial groups, and his attempt to introduce the study of state-organized crimes into the mainstream of social science research have punctuated his career.

He is the recipient of numerous awards and honors including a Doctorate of Laws Honoris Causa, University of Guelph, Guelph, Ontario, Canada, 1999; the 2009 Lifetime Achievement Award, Sociology of Law, American Sociological Association; the 2009 Lifetime Achievement Award, Law and Society, Society for the Study of Social Problems; the 2001 Edwin H. Sutherland Award, American Society of Criminology; the 1995 Major Achievement Award, American Society of Criminology; the 1986. Distinguished Leadership in Criminal Justice, Bruce Smith, Sr. Award, Academy of Criminal Justice Sciences; and the 1985 Lifetime Achievement Award, Criminology, American Sociological Association.

Professor Chambliss is a past president of the American Society of Criminology and past president of the Society for the Study of Social Problems. His current research covers a range of lifetime interests in international drug-control policy, class, race, gender and criminal justice and the history of piracy on the high seas.